ENGLISH
FOR EVERYONE

ENGLISH VOCABULARY BUILDER

FREE AUDIO
website and app
www.dkefe.com

Author

Thomas Booth worked for 10 years as an English-language teacher in Poland and Russia. He now lives in England, where he works as an editor and English-language materials writer, notably of course books and vocabulary textbooks.

ENGLISH
FOR EVERYONE

ENGLISH VOCABULARY BUILDER

US Editors Kayla Dugger, Jenny Siklos
Senior Editor Laura Sandford
Project Editor Thomas Booth
Senior Art Editors Amy Child, Anna Hall
Art Editors Raymond Bryant, Michelle Staples,
Jemma Westing
Illustrators Edward Byrne, Michael Parkin, Gus Scott
Project Manager Christine Stroyan
Jacket Designer Surabhi Wadhwa
Jacket Editor Claire Gell
Jacket Design Development Manager Sophia MTT
Producer, Pre-production Gillian Reid
Producers Alex Bell, Anna Vallarino
Publisher Andrew Macintyre
Art Director Karen Self
Publishing Director Jonathan Metcalf

DK India
Project Art Editor Sanjay Chauhan
Art Editor Meenal Goel
Assistant Art Editor Devika Khosla
Project Editor Nisha Shaw
Illustrator Arun Pottirayil
Jacket Designer Juhi Sheth
Managing Jackets Editor Saloni Singh
Pre-production Manager Balwant Singh
Senior DTP Designer Vishal Bhatia
Managing Art Editor Sudakshina Basu
Managing Editor Rohan Sinha

First American Edition, 2018
Published in the United States by DK Publishing,
345 Hudson Street, New York, New York 10014

18 19 20 21 22   10 9 8 7 6 5 4 3 2 1
001—305538—Jan/2018

A catalog record for this book is available from the
Library of Congress.
ISBN 978-1-4654-7440-7

DK books are available at special discounts when purchased in
bulk for sales promotions, premiums, fund-raising, or educational
use. For details, contact DK Publishing Special Markets, 345
Hudson Street, NewYork, New York 10014 or SpecialSales@dk.com.

Printed in China

A WORLD OF IDEAS:
SEE ALL THERE IS TO KNOW

www.dk.com

Contents

PEOPLE

FOOD AND DRINK

WORK

ARTS AND THE MEDIA

HEALTH

AROUND TOWN

SCIENCE AND TECHNOLOGY

How to use this book

Each unit of *English for Everyone: English Vocabulary Builder* consists of a teaching spread and a practice spread. Teaching spreads give you an illustrated vocabulary list on a particular topic. Practice spreads include a variety of exercises to reinforce what you have learned. Supporting audio for each teaching spread is available on the website and app. The best way to learn spoken vocabulary is to listen to the audio and repeat each word and phrase on the spread. If you have difficulty understanding a word or phrase, look it up in your dictionary or the word list at the back of this book.

PRACTICE SPREAD

TEACHING SPREAD

Teaching spreads

Unit number The book is divided into units. The unit number helps you keep track of your progress.

Modules Most teaching spreads are broken down into modules covering different aspects of a topic.

Module number Every module is identified with a unique number, so you can easily locate the related audio.

Write-on lines You are encouraged to write your own translations of English words to create your own reference pages.

Sample sentences Some modules show useful English phrases in the context of a sample sentence.

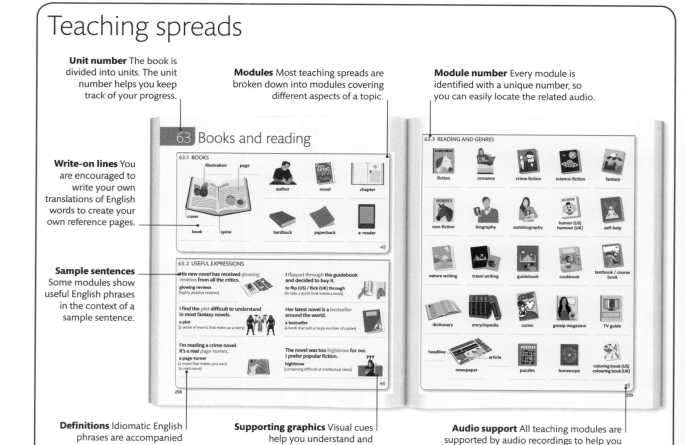

Definitions Idiomatic English phrases are accompanied by definitions.

Supporting graphics Visual cues help you understand and remember new vocabulary.

Audio support All teaching modules are supported by audio recordings to help you recognize and pronounce spoken vocabulary.

Practice exercises

Each teaching spread is followed by exercises that help to fix new words and phrases in your memory. Working through the exercises will help you to remember what you have learned and to use and recognize new English vocabulary. Answers are provided for every exercise.

Exercise number Each exercise is identified with a unique number, so you can easily locate answers.

Exercise instruction Each exercise is introduced with a brief instruction, telling you what you need to do.

Aa **37.5** LOOK AT THE PICTURE CLUES AND WRITE THE ANSWERS IN THE CORRECT PLACES ON THE GRID

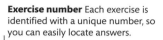

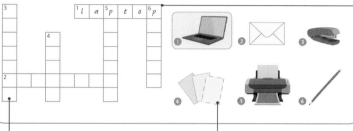

Sample answer The first question of each exercise is answered for you, to help make the task easy to understand.

Space for writing You are encouraged to write your answers in the book for future reference.

Supporting graphics Visual cues are given to help you understand the exercises.

Listening exercise This symbol indicates that you should listen to an audio track in order to answer the questions in the exercise.

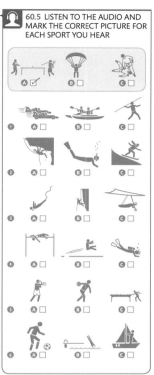

60.5 LISTEN TO THE AUDIO AND MARK THE CORRECT PICTURE FOR EACH SPORT YOU HEAR

Audio

English for Everyone: English Vocabulary Builder features extensive supporting audio resources. Every word and phrase in the teaching spreads is recorded, and you are encouraged to listen to the audio and repeat the words and phrases out loud, until you are confident you understand and can pronounce what has been said.

SUPPORTING AUDIO
This symbol indicates that audio recordings of the words and phrases in a module are available for you to listen to.

LISTENING EXERCISES
This symbol indicates that you should listen to an audio track in order to answer the questions in the exercise.

FREE AUDIO
website and app
www.dkefe.com

Answers

This book is designed to make it easy to monitor your progress. Answers are provided for every exercise, so you can see how well you have understood and remembered the vocabulary you have learned.

Answers Find the answers to every exercise printed at the back of the book.

Exercise numbers Match these numbers to the unique identifier at the top-left corner of each exercise.

01

1.3
1 India
2 Germany
3 Mongolia
4 Egypt
5 Canada
6 Thailand
7 Slovakia
8 Russia
9 Japan

1.4
1 Indonesia
2 France
3 China
4 Pakistan
5 South Korea
6 Brazil
7 Singapore
8 Argentina

1.1 COUNTRIES

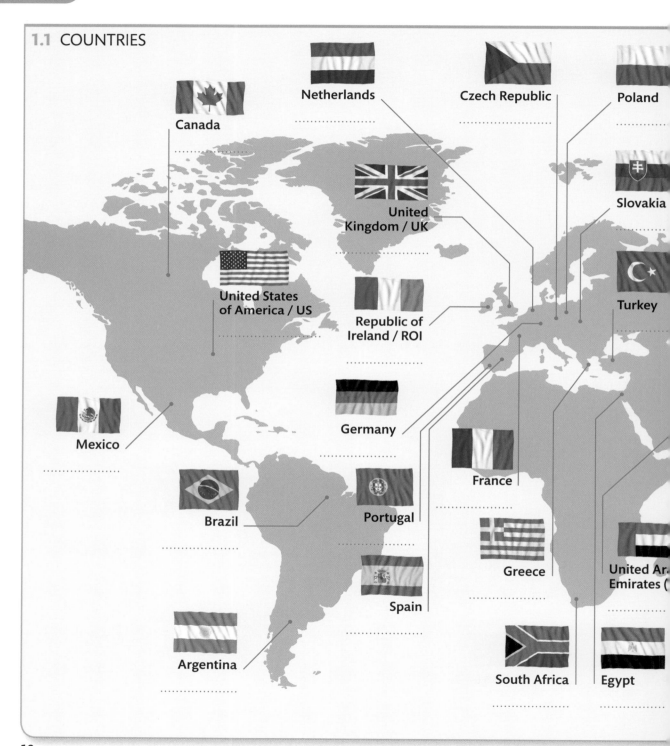

Canada

Netherlands

Czech Republic

Poland

United Kingdom / UK

Slovakia

United States of America / US

Republic of Ireland / ROI

Turkey

Germany

Mexico

France

Brazil

Portugal

Greece

United Arab Emirates (

Spain

South Africa

Egypt

Argentina

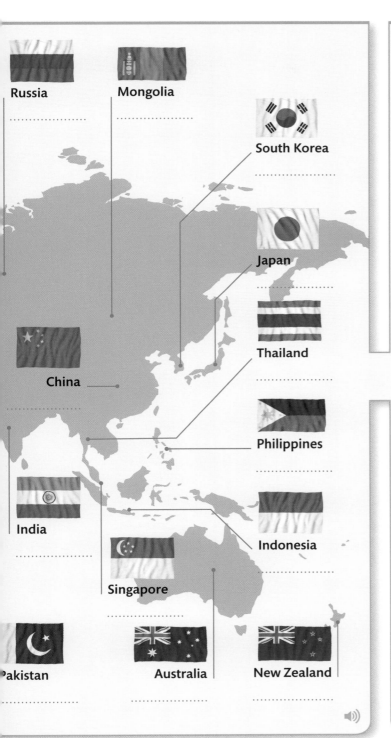

Russia

Mongolia

South Korea

Japan

Thailand

China

Philippines

India

Indonesia

Singapore

Pakistan

Australia

New Zealand

1.2 NATIONALITIES

US	⟹	American
Canada	⟹	Canadian
Mexico	⟹	Mexican
Brazil	⟹	Brazilian
Argentina	⟹	Argentinian
UK	⟹	British
France	⟹	French
Russia	⟹	Russian
Spain	⟹	Spanish
Portugal	⟹	Portuguese
Poland	⟹	Polish
Greece	⟹	Greek
Turkey	⟹	Turkish
Egypt	⟹	Egyptian
China	⟹	Chinese
Japan	⟹	Japanese
India	⟹	Indian
Pakistan	⟹	Pakistani
Mongolia	⟹	Mongolian
Australia	⟹	Australian
Germany	⟹	German

Aa 1.3 MARK THE CORRECT COUNTRY FOR EACH FLAG

South Korea ☑
China ☐
France ☐

 ❶

France ☐
India ☐
Greece ☐

 ❷

Brazil ☐
Canada ☐
Germany ☐

 ❸

Mongolia ☐
Argentina ☐
New Zealand ☐

 ❹

Pakistan ☐
Indonesia ☐
Egypt ☐

 ❺

Canada ☐
Philippines ☐
Mexico ☐

 ❻

Thailand ☐
Turkey ☐
Portugal ☐

 ❼

Indonesia ☐
India ☐
Slovakia ☐

 ❽

China ☐
Australia ☐
Russia ☐

 ❾

Poland ☐
Japan ☐
Turkey ☐

Aa 1.4 FIND EIGHT MORE COUNTRIES IN THE GRID THAT MATCH THE FLAGS

```
S G A H A I F M C S S
T A R P Q H R E V O I
M E G E M P A X D U N
P R E N T A N I I T G
M E N I C K C C B H A
E E T I A I E O D K P
C H I N A S Y T A O O
C A N A D T A L A R R
B I A B R A Z I L E E
C I N D O N E S I A C
```

 ❶

 ❷

 ❸

 ❹

 ❺

 ❻

 ❼

 ❽

1.5 LISTEN TO THE AUDIO AND MARK THE WORDS YOU HEAR

Argentina ☐ Australian ☑ Australia ☐

1. India ☐ Indian ☐ Indonesian ☐
2. Spanish ☐ Polish ☐ Turkish ☐
3. Greece ☐ Egypt ☐ Greek ☐
4. Thailand ☐ Poland ☐ Netherlands ☐
5. Chinese ☐ Japanese ☐ Portuguese ☐
6. Germany ☐ German ☐ Japan ☐
7. Mongolian ☐ Australia ☐ Mongolia ☐
8. China ☐ Chinese ☐ Canada ☐

Aa 1.6 WRITE THE WORDS FROM THE PANEL IN THE CORRECT GROUPS

COUNTRIES	NATIONALITIES
Russia	Russian

United Kingdom / UK   Japanese   Poland

~~Russia~~   Polish   Pakistan   Japan

Pakistani   British   ~~Russian~~

Aa 1.7 WRITE THE CORRECT COUNTRY UNDER EACH FLAG

South Africa

1. _____
2. _____
3. _____
4. _____
5. _____
6. _____
7. _____
8. _____
9. _____

13

02 Numbers

2.1 NUMBERS

1 one	**2** two	**3** three	**4** four	**5** five	**6** six
7 seven	**8** eight	**9** nine	**10** ten	**11** eleven	**12** twelve
13 thirteen	**14** fourteen	**15** fifteen	**16** sixteen	**17** seventeen	**18** eighteen
19 nineteen	**20** twenty	**21** twenty-one	**22** twenty-two	**30** thirty	**40** forty
50 fifty	**60** sixty	**70** seventy	**80** eighty	**90** ninety	**100** a / one hundred

2.2 ORDINAL NUMBERS

1st first	**2**nd second	**3**rd third	**4**th fourth	**5**th fifth	**6**th sixth	**7**th seventh
8th eighth	**9**th ninth	**10**th tenth	**11**th eleventh	**12**th twelfth	**20**th twentieth	**21**st twenty-first

2.3 LARGE NUMBERS

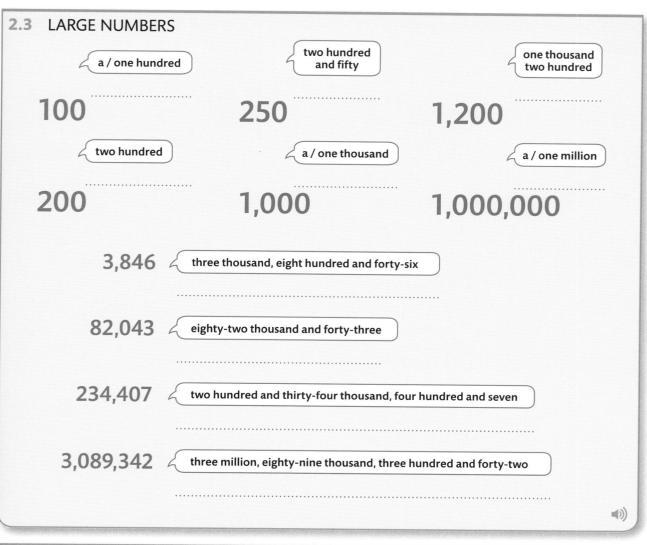

a / one hundred	
100	
two hundred and fifty	
250	
one thousand two hundred	
1,200	
two hundred	
200	
a / one thousand	
1,000	
a / one million	
1,000,000	

3,846 — **three thousand, eight hundred and forty-six**

82,043 — **eighty-two thousand and forty-three**

234,407 — **two hundred and thirty-four thousand, four hundred and seven**

3,089,342 — **three million, eighty-nine thousand, three hundred and forty-two**

2.4 FRACTIONS, DECIMALS, AND PERCENTAGES

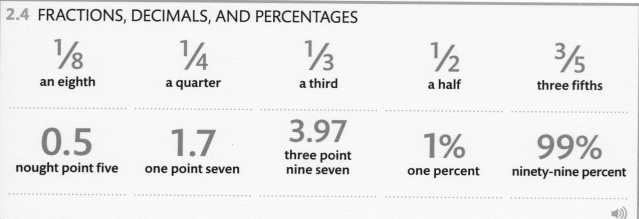

⅛	¼	⅓	½	⅗
an eighth	**a quarter**	**a third**	**a half**	**three fifths**

0.5	1.7	3.97	1%	99%
nought point five	**one point seven**	**three point nine seven**	**one percent**	**ninety-nine percent**

Aa 2.5 MATCH THE NUMBERS TO THE CORRECT WORDS

10 → ten

1. 12 — twenty

2. 20 — twelve

3. 30 — thirteen

4. 110 — thirty

5. 13 — seventeen

6. 1,100 — eight

7. 17 — one hundred and ten

8. 8 — one thousand, one hundred

Aa 2.6 REWRITE THE WORDS, CORRECTING THE SPELLINGS

14   foreteen
fourteen

1. 100   a hundrid

2. 8th   eightth

3. 1,000   a thousend

4. 40   fourty

5. 13   threeteen

6. 20th   twentyeth

7. 19   ninteen

8. 90   ninty

9. 12th   twelvth

10. 50   fivty

40	14	4
A ✓	B ☐	C ☐

1

91	19	90
A ☐	B ☐	C ☐

2

12	20	21
A ☐	B ☐	C ☐

3

1,200	120	102
A ☐	B ☐	C ☐

4

413	430	403
A ☐	B ☐	C ☐

5

300	13	30
A ☐	B ☐	C ☐

6

127	173	172
A ☐	B ☐	C ☐

2.8 WRITE THE CORRECT WORDS NEXT TO EACH NUMBER

2.5 _two point five_

1 1,200 _____

2 342 _____

3 750 _____

4 6.3 _____

5 542 _____

6 45% _____

7 3.95 _____

2.9 WRITE THE CORRECT WORDS UNDER EACH FRACTION

³⁄₅
three fifths

⅓
1 _____

½
2 _____

¼
3 _____

²⁄₃
4 _____

Time expressions

3.1 THE CALENDAR

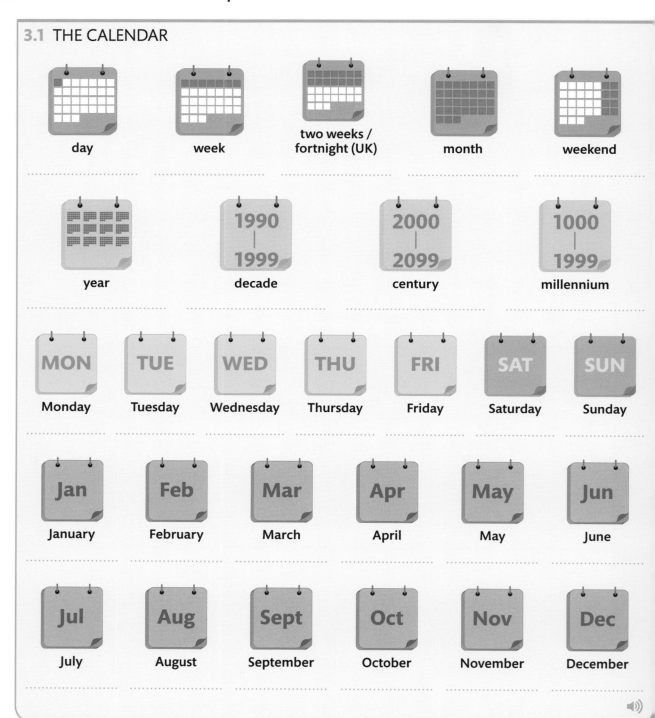

day

week

two weeks /
fortnight (UK)

month

weekend

year

decade

century

millennium

MON — Monday

TUE — Tuesday

WED — Wednesday

THU — Thursday

FRI — Friday

SAT — Saturday

SUN — Sunday

Jan — January

Feb — February

Mar — March

Apr — April

May — May

Jun — June

Jul — July

Aug — August

Sept — September

Oct — October

Nov — November

Dec — December

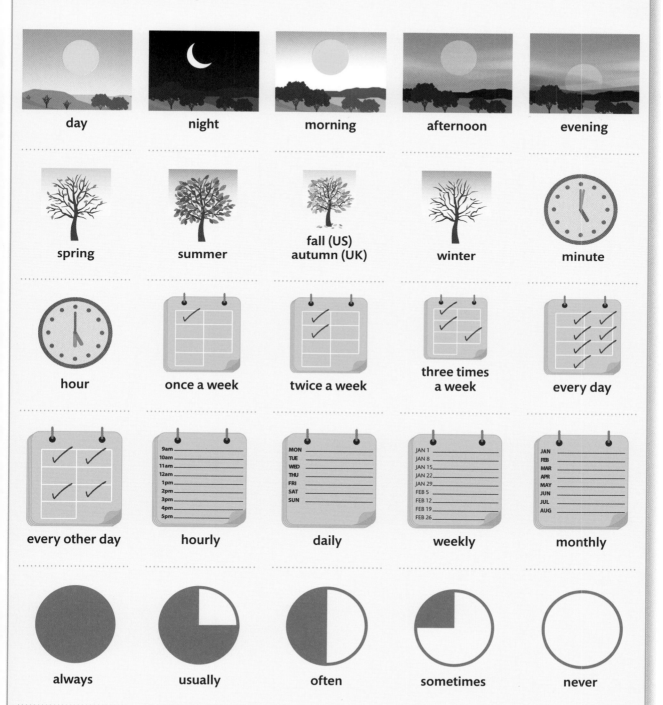

day

night

morning

afternoon

evening

spring

summer

fall (US)
autumn (UK)

winter

minute

hour

once a week

twice a week

three times
a week

every day

every other day

hourly

daily

weekly

monthly

always

usually

often

sometimes

never

Aa 3.3 COMPLETE THE WORD FOR EACH PICTURE, FILLING IN THE MISSING LETTERS

Jan J a n u a r y

1. **TUE** T _ e _ d _ y
2. **1990 - 1999** d _ _ c _ d _
3. **Nov** N _ v _ m _ _ r
4. w _ _ k
5. **Aug** A _ _ u _ t
6. y _ _ r

Aa 3.4 CIRCLE THE WORD THAT DOES NOT BELONG IN EACH LIST

Monday	(August)	Wednesday
1 October	day	week
2 evening	hour	afternoon
3 December	Friday	March
4 millennium	fall	spring
5 winter	night	morning
6 sometimes	century	always
7 summer	spring	minute
8 month	hourly	weekend
9 day	week	often

Aa 3.5 LOOK AT THE PICTURE CLUES AND WRITE THE ANSWERS IN THE CORRECT PLACES ON THE GRID

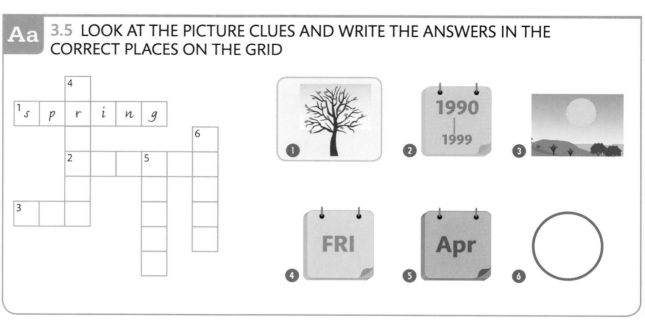

1. s p r i n g

3.6 LISTEN TO THE AUDIO AND MARK THE CORRECT PICTURE FOR EACH WORD YOU HEAR

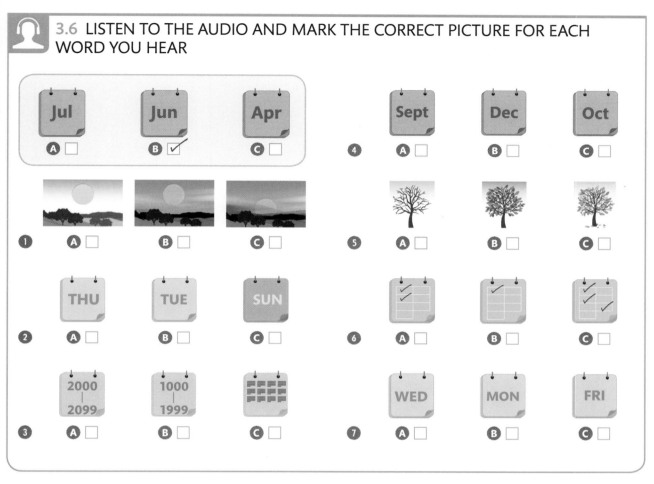

3.7 MARK THE BEGINNING AND ENDING OF EACH WORD OR EXPRESSION IN THE CHAIN OF LETTERS, THEN WRITE THE WORDS YOU FIND

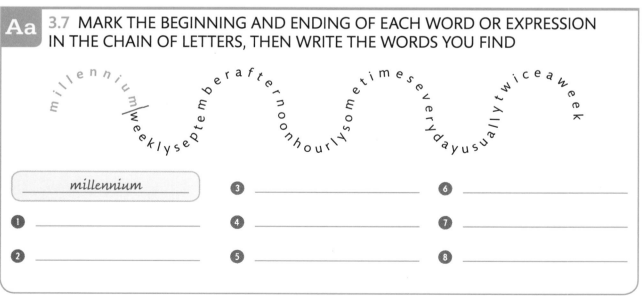

millennium

1 _____

2 _____

3 _____

4 _____

5 _____

6 _____

7 _____

8 _____

4.1 DAILY ROUTINES

alarm goes off

to wake up

to get up

to take / have a shower

to take / have a bath

to put on make-up

to shave

to wash your hair

to dry your hair

to iron a shirt

to get dressed

to brush your teeth

to wash your face

to brush your hair

to make the bed

to have / eat breakfast

to do the housework

to leave the house

to go to work

to go to school

to catch the train

to catch the bus

to drive

to arrive late

to start work

to have a break

 to have / eat lunch

 to finish work

 to leave work

 to work overtime

 to go home

 to buy groceries

 to cook dinner

 to have / eat dinner

 to clear the table

 to listen to the radio

 to watch TV

 to check your emails

 to have / drink tea or coffee

 to do / wash the dishes

 to walk the dog

 to read a newspaper

 to go out with friends

 to go to a café

 to call a friend / your family

 to do homework

 to put the children to bed

 to take out the trash (US) / rubbish (UK)

to feed the dog / cat

 to go to bed

4.2 MARK THE CORRECT PICTURE FOR EACH EXPRESSION

to get up

A ✓ B ☐ C ☐

3 to work overtime

A ☐ B ☐ C ☐

1 to put on make-up

A ☐ B ☐ C ☐

4 to buy groceries

A ☐ B ☐ C ☐

2 to get dressed

A ☐ B ☐ C ☐

5 to clear the table

A ☐ B ☐ C ☐

 ## 4.3 MATCH THE PICTURES TO THE CORRECT EXPRESSIONS

  **1**   **2** **3** **4** **5**

to go to school

to wash the dishes

to arrive late

to wash your face

to do the housework

to put the children to bed

to watch TV

1. _____

2. _____

3. _____

4. _____

5. _____

6. _____

7. _____

8. _____

9. _____

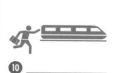

10. _____

11. _____

12. _____

13. _____

14. _____

4.5 LISTEN TO THE AUDIO, THEN NUMBER THE PICTURES IN THE ORDER YOU HEAR THEM

Ⓐ ☐

Ⓑ ☐

Ⓒ ☐

Ⓓ ☐

Ⓔ ☐

Ⓕ ☐

Ⓖ ☑

Ⓗ ☐

Ⓘ ☐

Ⓙ ☐

Ⓚ ☐

Ⓛ ☐

Describing things: facts

5.1 COLORS (US) / COLOURS (UK)

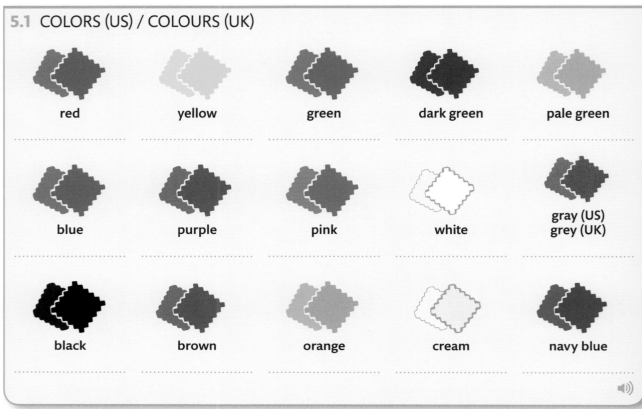

red

yellow

green

dark green

pale green

blue

purple

pink

white

gray (US)
grey (UK)

black

brown

orange

cream

navy blue

5.2 MATERIALS

plastic

wood

paper

wool

leather

metal

glass

fabric

denim

silk

5.3 ADJECTIVES

big

small / little

wide

narrow

deep

high

low

heavy

light

shallow

clean

dirty

hot

cold

long

loud

quiet

thin

thick

short

sharp

tight

loose

near

far

27

Aa 5.4 REWRITE THE WORDS, CORRECTING THE SPELLINGS

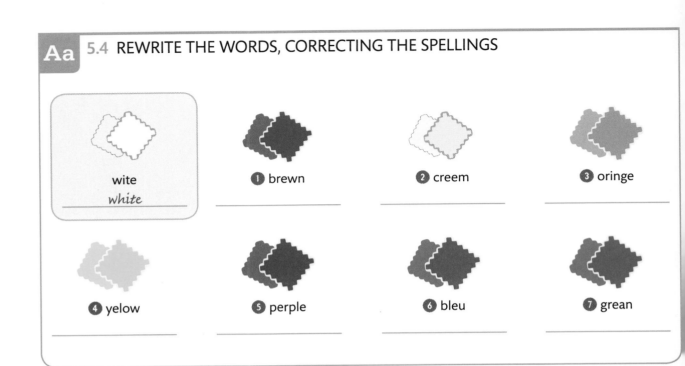

wite
white

❶ brewn

❷ creem

❸ oringe

❹ yelow

❺ perple

❻ bleu

❼ grean

Aa 5.5 MATCH THE PICTURES TO THE CORRECT WORDS

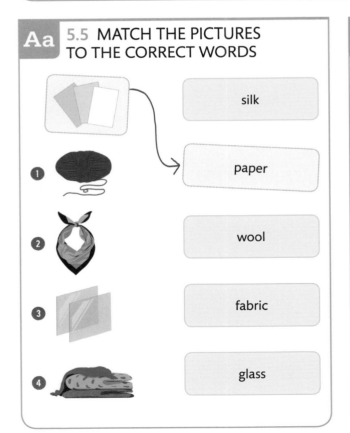

silk

paper

wool

fabric

glass

❶

❷

❸

❹

Aa 5.6 WRITE THE WORDS FROM THE PANEL NEXT TO THEIR OPPOSITES

shallow	*deep*
❶	far
❷	dirty
❸ tight	
❹	low
❺ heavy	
❻ long	

light   clean   high   near

loose   ~~deep~~   short

Aa 5.7 MARK THE CORRECT PICTURE FOR EACH WORD

narrow
A ✓ B ☐ C ☐

③ cold
A ☐ B ☐ C ☐

① wide
A ☐ B ☐ C ☐

④ heavy
A ☐ B ☐ C ☐

② loud
A ☐ B ☐ C ☐

⑤ small
A ☐ B ☐ C ☐

5.8 LISTEN TO THE AUDIO, THEN NUMBER THE PICTURES IN THE ORDER YOU HEAR THEM

A ☐ B 1 C ☐ D ☐ E ☐ F ☐ G ☐ H ☐

06 Describing things: opinions

6.1 OPINION ADJECTIVES

nice

fun

lovely

delicious

exciting

thrilling

interesting

respectable

special

graceful

pleasant

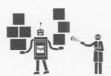
useful

important

relaxing

harmless

frightening

shocking

irritating

annoying

horrible

nasty

old-fashioned

unpleasant

disastrous

useless

stunning

magnificent

pretty

beautiful

disgusting

boring

ugly

strange / odd

confusing

tiring

6.2 GOOD

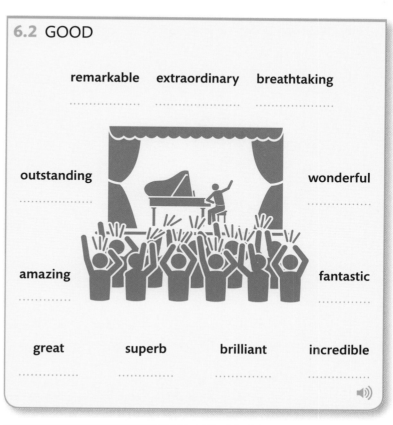

remarkable   extraordinary   breathtaking

outstanding

wonderful

amazing

fantastic

great   superb   brilliant   incredible

6.3 BAD

awful

mediocre

terrible   disappointing

Aa 6.4 FILL IN THE GAPS, PUTTING THE WORDS FROM THE PANEL INTO THE CORRECT CATEGORIES

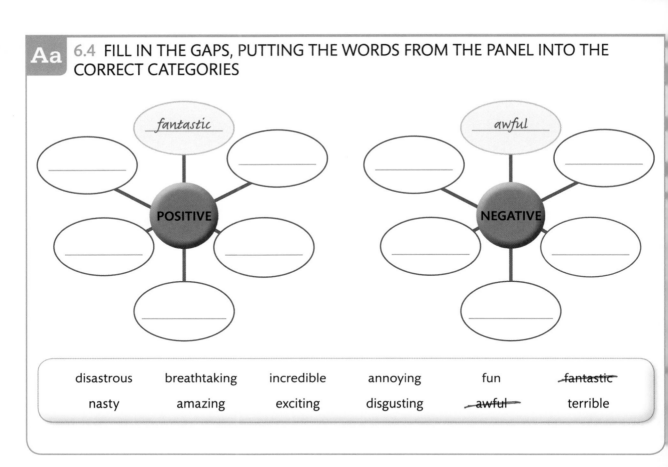

fantastic

POSITIVE

awful

NEGATIVE

disastrous	breathtaking	incredible	annoying	fun	~~fantastic~~
nasty	amazing	exciting	disgusting	~~awful~~	terrible

Aa 6.5 MARK THE BEGINNING AND ENDING OF EACH WORD IN THE CHAIN OF LETTERS, THEN WRITE THE WORDS YOU FIND

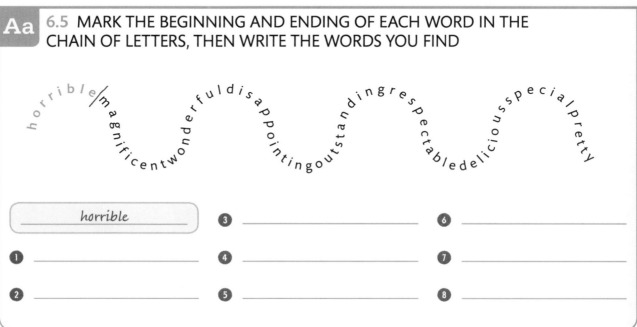

horrible/magnificentwonderfuldisappointingoutstandingrespectabledeliciousspecialpretty

horrible

1 _____

2 _____

3 _____

4 _____

5 _____

6 _____

7 _____

8 _____

32

Aa 6.6 WRITE THE CORRECT WORD UNDER EACH PICTURE

shocking

① _____

② _____

③ _____

④ _____

⑤ _____

6.7 LISTEN TO THE AUDIO AND WRITE THE WORD THAT IS SHOWN IN EACH PICTURE

confusing

① _____

② _____

③ _____

④ _____

⑤ _____

⑥ _____

Aa 6.8 FIND FIVE MORE WORDS IN THE GRID THAT MATCH THE PICTURES

```
D E L I C I O U S J A H A
S T U N N I N G V T Q P Q
A E D E M J S L D A T E M
P O T N T E R Y I P U N T
L T B E A U T I F U L K X
U S E L E S S A D E E I A
R E S P E C T A B L E L O
```

①

②

③

④

⑤

7.1 CONTACT DETAILS

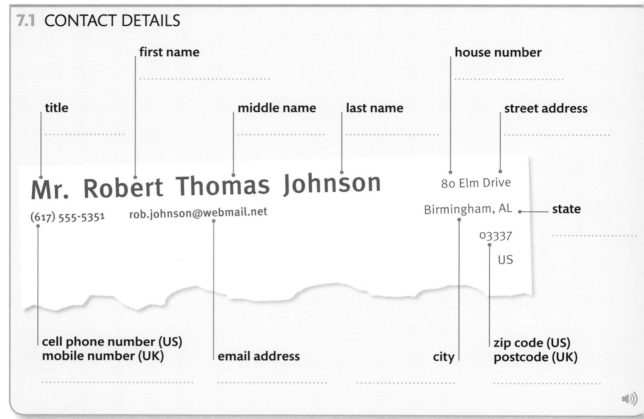

first name

house number

title

middle name   last name

street address

Mr. Robert Thomas Johnson

80 Elm Drive

(617) 555-5351   rob.johnson@webmail.net

Birmingham, AL   **state**

03337

US

cell phone number (US)
mobile number (UK)

email address

city

zip code (US)
postcode (UK)

7.2 BUSINESS CARDS

name

Daniel Thompson   **Director**   job title

23 Long Lane
Redchester
RC3 7AP
United Kingdom

BIG films

company name

☎ 019230 8934   ✉ d.thompson@bigfilms.com

website   www.bigfilms.com

business card

to introduce yourself

to exchange business cards

7.3 FORMS OF COMMUNICATION

letter

email

phone call

voicemail

text message

social networking

memo

online chat

mail (US)
post (UK)

note

7.4 SENDING EMAILS

inbox

outbox

draft

junk mail / spam

trash

attachment

subject

contact

signature

to print

to reply

to reply all

to forward

to send

to delete

Aa 7.5 LOOK AT THE PICTURE AND WRITE THE CORRECT WORD FOR EACH LABEL

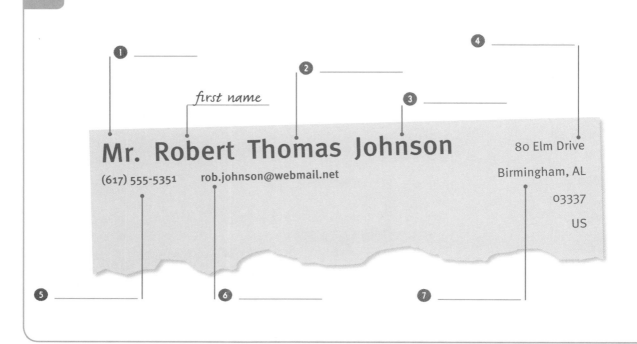

1 _____

2 _____

3 _____

4 _____

first name

Mr. Robert Thomas Johnson

80 Elm Drive

Birmingham, AL

03337

US

(617) 555-5351   rob.johnson@webmail.net

5 _____

6 _____

7 _____

Aa 7.6 LOOK AT THE PICTURE AND WRITE THE CORRECT WORD FOR EACH LABEL

1 _____

2 _____

3 _____

Daniel Thompson   **Director**

23 Long Lane
Redchester
RC3 7AP
United Kingdom

BIG films

☎ 019230 8934   ✉ d.thompson@bigfilms.com

www.bigfilms.com

website

4 _____

Aa 7.7 WRITE THE CORRECT WORD UNDER EACH PICTURE

to delete

1 _____

2 _____

3 _____

4 _____

5 _____

6 _____

7 _____

8 _____

9 _____

7.8 LISTEN TO THE AUDIO AND CIRCLE THE WORDS YOU HEAR

	(note)	memo	title
1	attachment	trash	voicemail
2	spam	to send	subject
3	inbox	email	memo
4	mail	name	outbox
5	state	signature	phone call
6	draft	contact	to send
7	note	outbox	online chat
8	to reply	memo	website
9	draft	to delete	letter
10	voicemail	to forward	phone call
11	to print	trash	title

Aa 7.9 COMPLETE THE WORD FOR EACH PICTURE, FILLING IN THE MISSING LETTERS

v o i c e m a i l

1 t e _ _ m e _ _ a g _

2 p h _ n _ _ a l _

3 n _ t _

4 l _ t _ e _

5 _ m _ l

6 o _ l _ n _ c _ a t

37

08 Common English idioms

8.1 COMMON ENGLISH IDIOMS

Tamsin got cold feet about giving a presentation to the sales team.

to get cold feet
[to have a sudden loss of confidence]

Susan is feeling under the weather today. I think she should go home.

to feel under the weather
[to feel unwell, sick, or ill]

Ben and Rachel are head over heels in love with each other.

head over heels
[completely and utterly in love with someone]

You're so right about Jim. He's really lazy! You've hit the nail on the head.

to hit the nail on the head
[to describe exactly what is causing a situation or problem]

Can I lend a hand carrying those papers for you?

to lend a hand
[to help someone with something]

I'm so tired today! I'm really not on the ball.

on the ball
[alert, knowledgeable, or competent]

I heard on the grapevine that Neil and Amina are getting married.

to hear something on the grapevine
[to hear information or news through gossip or rumor]

Hamid is working against the clock to finish his report this week.

against the clock
[under time pressure to get something done]

Dylan is being so naughty today! He's a pain in the neck.

a pain in the neck
[a nuisance, annoying, or difficult]

I'm looking for someone to keep an eye on my house while I'm on vacation.

to keep an eye on
[to take care of or watch carefully]

Leo has a heart of gold. He always helps his grandma with her shopping.

to have a heart of gold
[to be kind and good-natured]

I don't know who to vote for yet. I'm still **on the fence.**

to be (US) / sit (UK) on the fence
[to be unwilling to commit or make a decision]

Miriam is a teacher's pet. She always arrives early and works very hard.

a teacher's pet
[someone who seeks and gets approval from a person in a position of authority]

If you **cut corners** to finish a project on time, the quality will suffer.

to cut corners
[to do something the easiest or shortest way, at the expense of high standards]

You can't believe all her stories. **Take them with a pinch of salt.**

to take something with a pinch of salt
[to not completely believe something or someone]

I have to **face the music** and tell Julia that I broke her new vase.

to face the music
[to confront the consequences of your actions]

I didn't mean to offend Luisa, but I think her reaction was **over the top.**

over the top
[an overreaction or a lack of restraint]

You two really **let your hair down** at Sunita's party last night.

to let your hair down
[to let yourself go or relax]

I haven't really won the lottery. I was just **pulling your leg.**

to pull someone's leg
[to tease or fool someone]

I'm planning a surprise party for Joe. Don't **let the cat out of the bag.**

to let the cat out of the bag
[to tell a secret to someone who shouldn't know about it]

Aa 8.2 MARK THE SENTENCES THAT ARE CORRECT

Can I lend an arm carrying those papers for you? ☐
Can I lend a hand carrying those papers for you? ☑

① Tamsin got cold legs about giving a presentation to the sales team. ☐
Tamsin got cold feet about giving a presentation to the sales team. ☐

② I'm so tired today! I'm really not on the ball. ☐
I'm so tired today! I'm really not off the ball. ☐

③ Susan is feeling under the weather today. I think she should go home. ☐
Susan is feeling out of the weather today. I think she should go home. ☐

④ I have to take the music and tell Julia that I broke her new vase. ☐
I have to face the music and tell Julia that I broke her new vase. ☐

Aa 8.3 MATCH THE PICTURES TO THE CORRECT SENTENCES

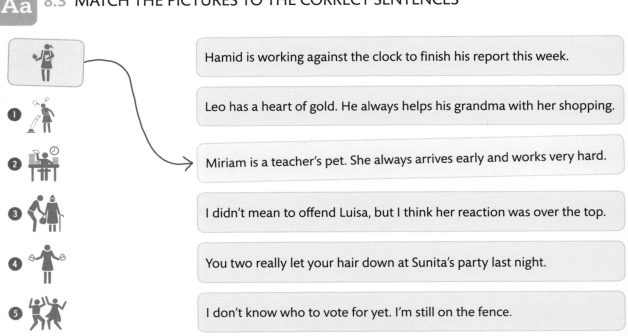

Hamid is working against the clock to finish his report this week.

Leo has a heart of gold. He always helps his grandma with her shopping.

Miriam is a teacher's pet. She always arrives early and works very hard.

I didn't mean to offend Luisa, but I think her reaction was over the top.

You two really let your hair down at Sunita's party last night.

I don't know who to vote for yet. I'm still on the fence.

Aa 8.4 FILL IN THE GAPS, PUTTING THE WORDS IN THE CORRECT ORDER

| grapevine | the | that | on |

I heard ___on___ ___the___ ___grapevine___ ___that___ Neil and Amina are getting married.

| the | hit | the | on | You've | nail |

① You're so right about Jim. He's really lazy! _____ _____ _____ _____ _____ _____ head.

| of | cat | the | let | out |

② I'm planning a surprise party for Joe. Don't _____ _____ _____ _____ _____ the bag.

| pinch | them | of | with | Take | a |

③ You can't believe all her stories. _____ _____ _____ _____ _____ _____ salt.

| corners | cut | to | you |

④ If _____ _____ _____ _____ finish a project on time, the quality will suffer.

8.5 LISTEN TO THE AUDIO, THEN NUMBER THE SENTENCES IN THE ORDER YOU HEAR THEM

Ⓐ I haven't really won the lottery. I was just pulling your leg. ☐

Ⓑ Ben and Rachel are head over heels in love with each other. ☐ 1

Ⓒ I'm looking for someone to keep an eye on my house while I'm on vacation. ☐

Ⓓ Dylan is being so naughty today! He's a pain in the neck. ☐

Ⓔ I have to face the music and tell Julia that I broke her new vase. ☐

Around the house

9.1 HOMES, ROOMS, AND FURNITURE

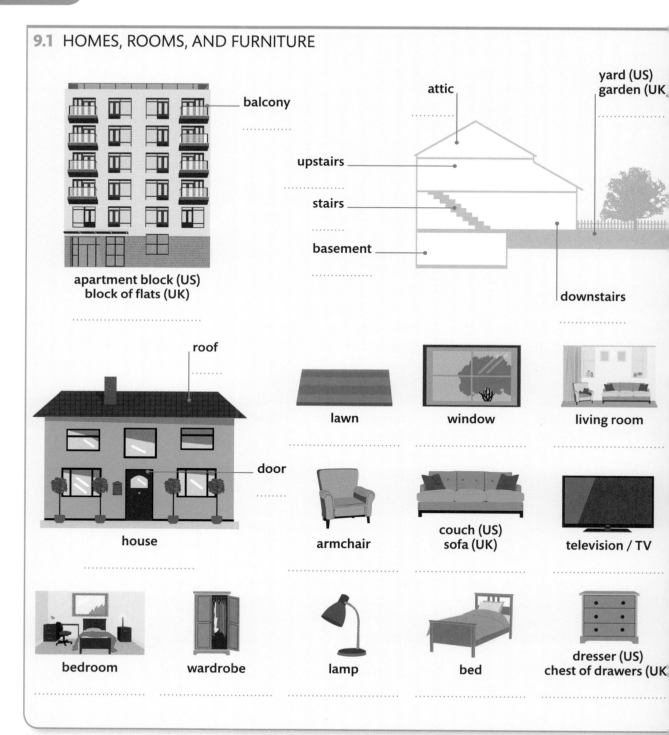

balcony

apartment block (US)
block of flats (UK)

attic

yard (US)
garden (UK)

upstairs

stairs

basement

downstairs

roof

lawn

window

living room

house

door

armchair

couch (US)
sofa (UK)

television / TV

bedroom

wardrobe

lamp

bed

dresser (US)
chest of drawers (UK)

bedside table

cushion

rug

light

dining room

table

chair

study

bookcase

desk

bathroom

shower

towel

toilet

bathtub (US)
bath (UK)

freezer

refrigerator /
fridge

kitchen

stove (US)
cooker (UK)

sink

dishwasher

cabinet (US)
cupboard (UK)

trash can (US)
bin (UK)

Aa 9.2 MATCH THE PICTURES TO THE CORRECT WORDS

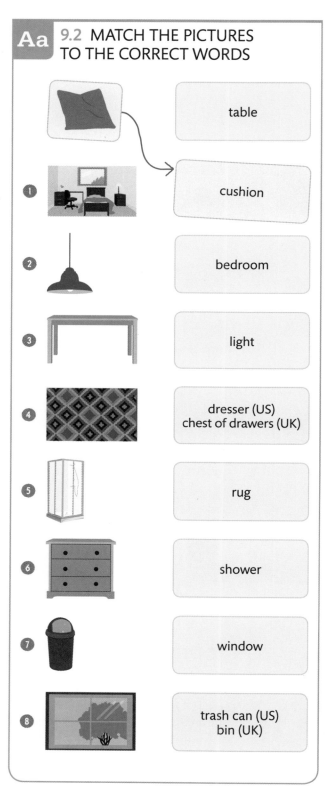

	table
1	cushion
2	bedroom
3	light
4	dresser (US) chest of drawers (UK)
5	rug
6	shower
7	window
8	trash can (US) bin (UK)

Aa 9.3 CIRCLE THE WORD THAT DOES NOT BELONG IN EACH LIST

shower	toilet	⬭stairs
1 armchair	couch	cabinet
2 light	bed	lamp
3 table	upstairs	attic
4 bookcase	roof	desk
5 lawn	yard	kitchen
6 sink	window	door
7 study	bedroom	lamp
8 towel	living room	bathtub

Aa 9.4 LOOK AT THE PICTURE AND WRITE THE CORRECT WORD FOR EACH LABEL

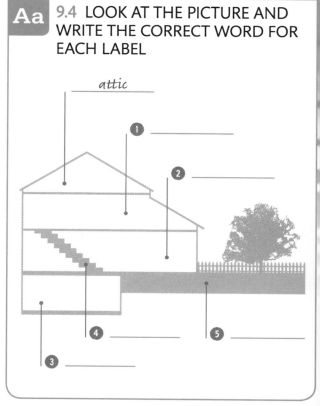

attic

1 _____

2 _____

3 _____

4 _____

5 _____

44

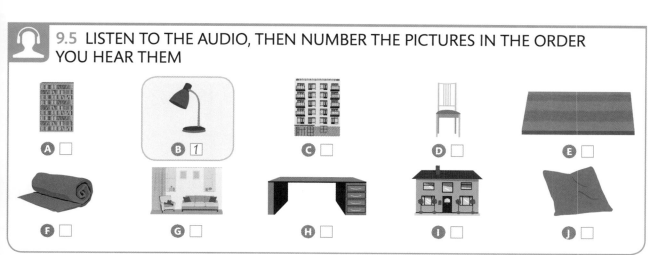

Aa 9.6 LOOK AT THE PICTURES BELOW, THEN WRITE THE NAME OF EACH OBJECT UNDER THE CORRECT ROOM

KITCHEN	BATHROOM	LIVING ROOM	BEDROOM
dishwasher			

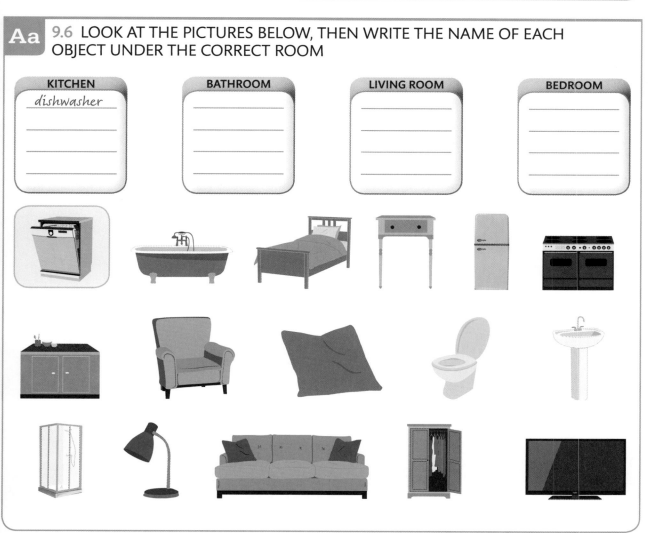

10.1 KITCHEN IMPLEMENTS

grater

peeler

whisk

cutting board (US)
chopping board (UK)

kitchen knife

scissors

can opener (US)
tin opener (UK)

bottle opener

corkscrew

wooden spoon

spatula

ladle

toaster

microwave

kettle

dinnerware (US)
crockery (UK)

plate

bowl

cup

mug

silverware (US)
cutlery (UK)

knife

fork

spoon

chopsticks

saucepan

frying pan

wok

colander

blender

rolling pin

mortar

pestle

pestle and mortar

sieve

spatula (US)
fish slice (UK)

10.2 TOILETRIES AND BATHROOM EQUIPMENT

shampoo

conditioner

moisturizer

razor

shaving foam

shower gel

deodorant

soap

toothbrush

toothpaste

mouthwash

dental floss

sponge

face wash

toilet paper

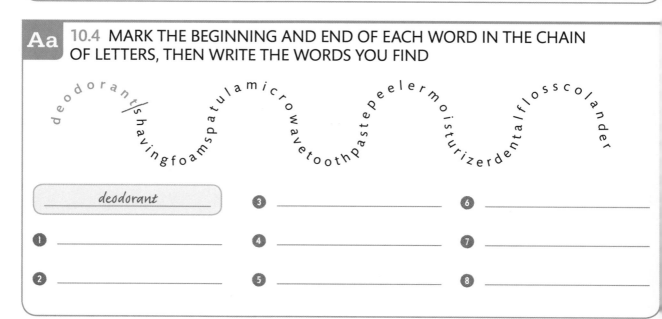

Aa 10.3 FILL IN THE GAPS, PUTTING THE WORDS FROM THE PANEL INTO THE CORRECT ROOM

whisk

mouthwash

KITCHEN

BATHROOM

| bowl | ~~mouthwash~~ | frying pan | toothbrush | knife | ~~whisk~~ |
| plate | soap | cup | shampoo | conditioner | sponge |

Aa 10.4 MARK THE BEGINNING AND END OF EACH WORD IN THE CHAIN OF LETTERS, THEN WRITE THE WORDS YOU FIND

deodorant/shavingfoamspatulamicrowavetoothpastepeelermoisturizerdentalflosscolander

deodorant

3 ____

6 ____

1 ____

4 ____

7 ____

2 ____

5 ____

8 ____

Aa 10.5 WRITE THE CORRECT WORD UNDER EACH PICTURE

kettle

1 _____

2 _____

3 _____

4 _____

5 _____

6 _____

7 _____

8 _____

9 _____

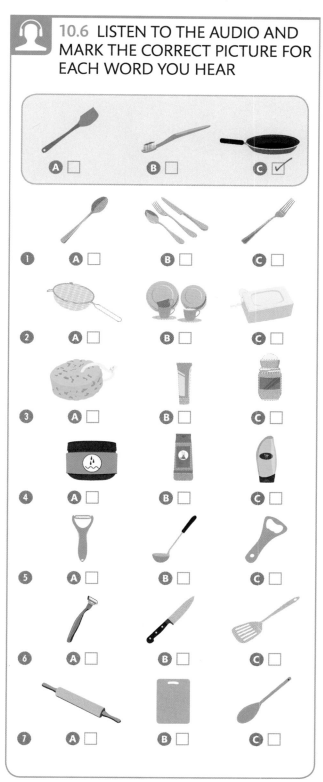

10.6 LISTEN TO THE AUDIO AND MARK THE CORRECT PICTURE FOR EACH WORD YOU HEAR

A ☐   B ☐   C ☑

1   A ☐   B ☐   C ☐

2   A ☐   B ☐   C ☐

3   A ☐   B ☐   C ☐

4   A ☐   B ☐   C ☐

5   A ☐   B ☐   C ☐

6   A ☐   B ☐   C ☐

7   A ☐   B ☐   C ☐

49

11 Chores and cleaning

11.1 HOUSEHOLD CHORES

to clean the windows

to sweep the floor

to scrub the floor

to mop the floor

to vacuum the carpet

to dust

to take out the trash (US) / rubbish (UK)

to clean up (US) to tidy (UK)

to go to the store (US) / shops (UK)

to clean the bathroom

to set the table

to clear the table

to do the dishes

to dry the dishes

to load the dishwasher

to unload the dishwasher

to do the laundry

to hang clothes

to do the ironing

to fold clothes

to make the bed

to change the sheets

to water the plants

to wash the car

to feed the pets

11.2 LAUNDRY AND CLEANING

 washing machine

 tumble dryer

 laundry basket

 laundry detergent

 clothes line (US) washing line (UK)

 drying clip (US) peg (UK)

 iron

 ironing board

 bucket

 mop

 dishwashing liquid (US) washing up liquid (UK)

 scouring pad

 sponge

 cloth

 duster

 polish

 cleaning fluid

 bleach

 vacuum cleaner

 dustpan

 brush

 broom

 recycling bin

 garbage bag (US) bin liner (UK)

 rubber gloves

Aa 11.3 FIND EIGHT MORE WORDS IN THE GRID THAT MATCH THE PICTURES

```
T D C H A B R D C S P
E U V M Q U K U V T O
K S D O M C S S D A L
F T I P T K R T I P I
U E B C X E D P B L S
B R O O M T Y A D E H
R M Z L O L A N Z R O
E E T J D B R U S H T
S C O U R I N G P A D
T C L O T H W T A C A
```

1 2 5

3 4

6 7 8

Aa 11.4 REWRITE THE WORDS OR EXPRESSIONS, CORRECTING THE SPELLINGS

to sweap the flour
to sweep the floor

 1 landry detergint
_____

 2 spong
_____

 3 recicling bin
_____

 4 to scrab the floor
_____

 5 to clare the table
_____

 6 bleech
_____

 7 to lode the dishwasher
_____

52

Aa 11.5 MATCH THE EXPRESSIONS TO THE CORRECT PICTURES

to water the plants

Ⓐ

1 to do the ironing

2 to go to the store (US) / shops (UK)

Ⓑ

3 to do the laundry

Ⓒ

4 to feed the pets

Ⓓ

5 to dry the dishes

Ⓔ

6 to dust

Ⓕ

7 to clean the bathroom

Ⓖ

8 to change the sheets

Ⓗ

11.6 LISTEN TO THE AUDIO AND WRITE THE EXPRESSION THAT IS SHOWN IN EACH PICTURE

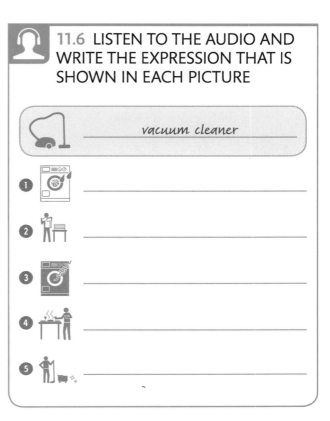

vacuum cleaner

1 _____

2 _____

3 _____

4 _____

5 _____

Aa 11.7 COMPLETE THE EXPRESSION FOR EACH PICTURE, FILLING IN THE MISSING LETTERS

i r o n i n g   b o a r d

1 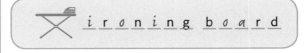 c o _ _ e _ l n _

2 r _ b _ e _ g _ o _ e s

3 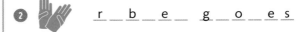 b _ c _ t

4 i _ o _

53

12 Tools and gardening

12.1 TOOLS AND HOME IMPROVEMENT

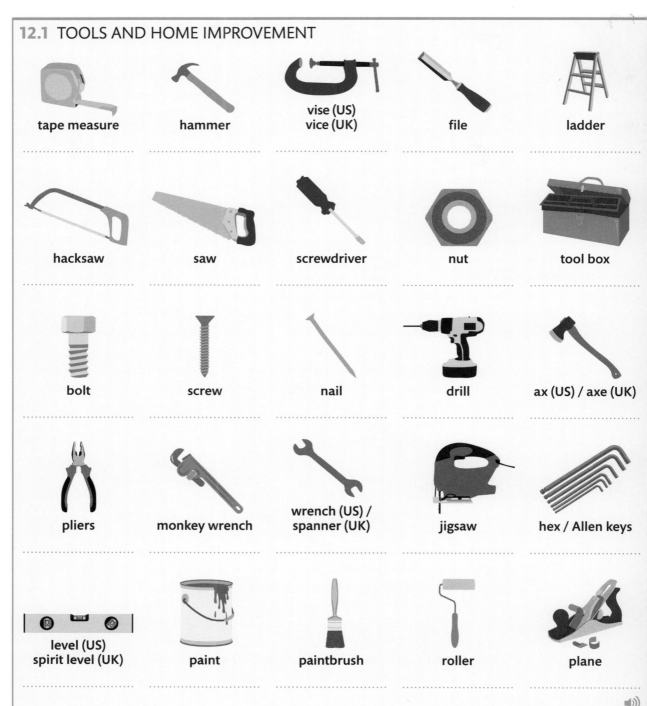

tape measure

hammer

vise (US)
vice (UK)

file

ladder

hacksaw

saw

screwdriver

nut

tool box

bolt

screw

nail

drill

ax (US) / axe (UK)

pliers

monkey wrench

wrench (US) /
spanner (UK)

jigsaw

hex / Allen keys

level (US)
spirit level (UK)

paint

paintbrush

roller

plane

12.2 GARDENING EQUIPMENT

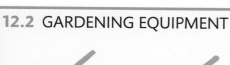
trowel

shears

spade

hoe

rake

fork

wheelbarrow

hose

sprinkler

lawn mower

12.3 HOME IMPROVEMENT VERBS

to paint the house

to paint a room

to plaster the walls

to tile the bathroom

to fit a carpet

to put up shelves

to make curtains

to unclog / unblock the sink

to change a lightbulb

12.4 GARDENING VERBS

to mow the lawn

to do the weeding

to plant bulbs

to prune trees

to trim a hedge

to water the flowers

Aa 12.5 MARK THE CORRECT VERB FOR THE ACTIVITY IN EACH PICTURE

to tile the bathroom ✓
to unblock the sink ☐
to fit a carpet ☐

 **1**

to mow the lawn ☐
to plant bulbs ☐
to trim a hedge ☐

 2

to put up shelves ☐
to prune trees ☐
to change a lightbulb ☐

 **3**

to make curtains ☐
to fit a carpet ☐
to mow the lawn ☐

 **4**

to prune trees ☐
to water the flowers ☐
to do the weeding ☐

 **5**

to make curtains ☐
to plaster the walls ☐
to paint a room ☐

 6

to plaster the walls ☐
to paint the house ☐
to put up shelves ☐

 **7**

to fit a carpet ☐
to do the weeding ☐
to trim a hedge ☐

Aa 12.6 WRITE THE CORRECT WORD UNDER EACH PICTURE

screwdriver

 1 _____

 **2** _____

 **3** _____

 **4** _____

 **5** _____

 **6** _____

 **7** _____

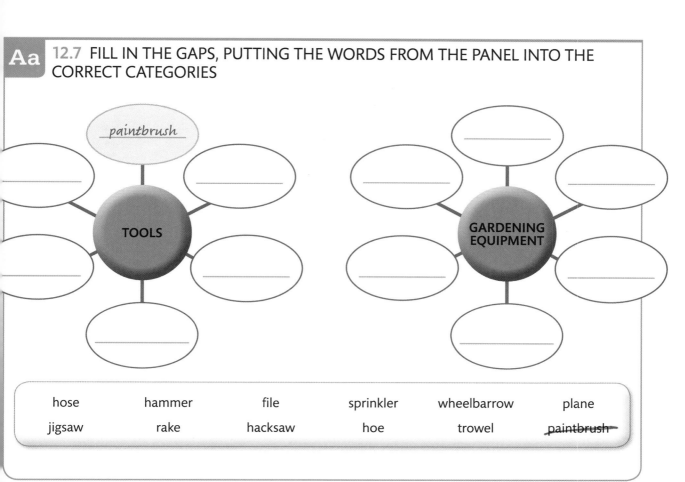

Aa 12.7 FILL IN THE GAPS, PUTTING THE WORDS FROM THE PANEL INTO THE CORRECT CATEGORIES

paintbrush

TOOLS

GARDENING EQUIPMENT

hose	hammer	file	sprinkler	wheelbarrow	plane
jigsaw	rake	hacksaw	hoe	trowel	~~paintbrush~~

12.8 LISTEN TO THE AUDIO AND MARK THE CORRECT PICTURE FOR EACH WORD YOU HEAR

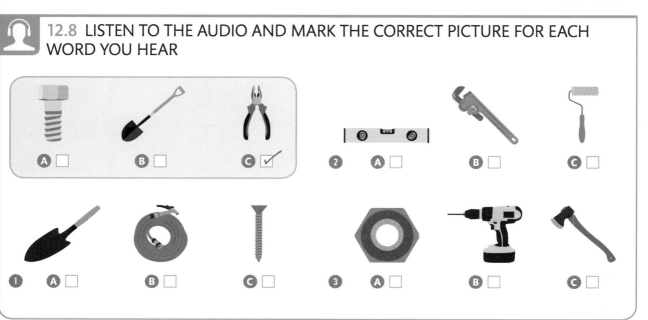

13 Moving and renting

13.1 ACCOMMODATION, MOVING, AND RENTING

apartments (US)
flats (UK)

duplex (US)
semi-detached (UK)

detached houses

row (US) / terraced houses (UK)

ranch house (US)
bungalow (UK)

cottage

furnished

unfurnished

open-plan

parking space

storage

realtor (US)
estate agent (UK)

moving truck (US)
removal van (UK)

boxes

keys

rent

bills

lease / tenancy agreement (UK)

landlord

tenant

to view a house

to pack

to unpack

to move in

to move out

13.2 USEFUL EXPRESSIONS

I had to pay my landlord the equivalent of one month's rent as a deposit.

a deposit
[money that a tenant pays to a landlord before moving into a property]

My new landlord wants a reference from my previous landlord.

a reference
[a letter describing your character and ability to pay your rent]

We had a house-warming party to celebrate buying our new apartment.

a house-warming party
[an informal party that you give after moving into a new house or apartment]

The rent for my new apartment is $500, including utilities.

including utilities
[the rent covers the bills such as electricity, water, and gas]

Real estate is in high demand, so prices are increasing.

real estate (US) / property (UK)
[houses and apartments that are for sale or rented out]

We live in an attractive residential area with lots of parks.

a residential area
[a part of town where most buildings are houses or apartments]

The local stores sell a wide selection of food and drinks.

local
[belonging to the area where you live]

My roommate never does the dishes.

a roommate (US) / housemate (UK)
[a person you share your house or apartment with]

We have a roomer who lives in our spare bedroom.

a roomer (US) / a lodger (UK)
[a person who pays to live in your house]

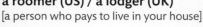

We gave notice to our landlord two months before moving out.

to give notice
[to announce to your landlord that you wish to move out]

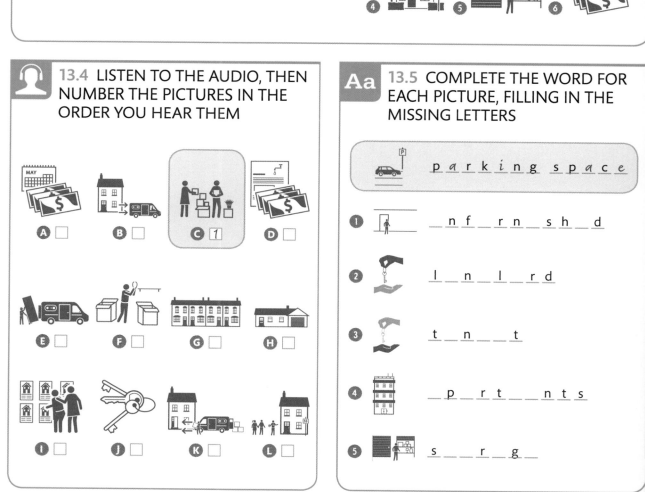

Aa 13.3 LOOK AT THE PICTURE CLUES AND WRITE THE ANSWERS IN THE CORRECT PLACES ON THE GRID

13.4 LISTEN TO THE AUDIO, THEN NUMBER THE PICTURES IN THE ORDER YOU HEAR THEM

A ☐   B ☐   C ☐ 1   D ☐

E ☐   F ☐   G ☐   H ☐

I ☐   J ☐   K ☐   L ☐

Aa 13.5 COMPLETE THE WORD FOR EACH PICTURE, FILLING IN THE MISSING LETTERS

p a r k i n g   s p a c e

1   _ n f _ r n _ s h _ d

2   _ l _ n _ l _ r d

3   t _ n _ t

4   _ p _ r t _ _ n t s

5   s _ _ r _ g _

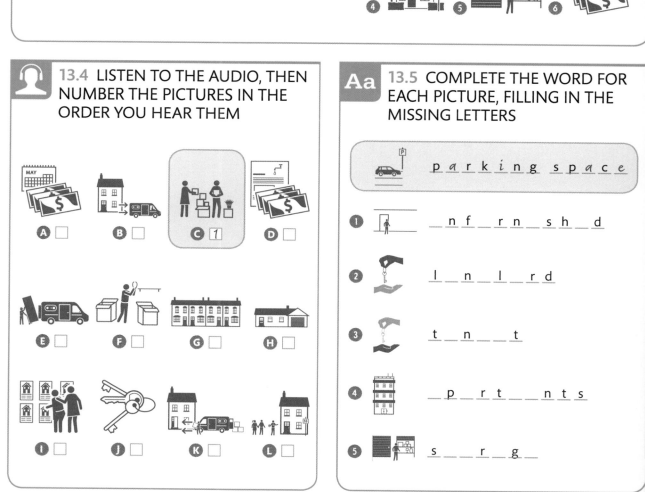

13.6 MATCH THE DEFINITIONS TO THE CORRECT PHRASES

a letter describing your character and ability to pay rent → a reference

1. houses and apartments that are for sale or rented out

2. a part of town where most buildings are houses or apartments

3. belonging to the area where you live

4. money that a tenant pays to a landlord before moving into a property

5. the rent covers the bills such as electricity, water, and gas

a residential area

a reference

a deposit

including utilities

real estate (US) / property (UK)

local

13.7 CROSS OUT THE INCORRECT WORD IN EACH SENTENCE

 I had to pay my landlord the equivalent of one month's rent as a deposit / ~~notice~~.

1. We had a house-heating / house-warming party to celebrate buying our new apartment.

2. We have a landlord / roomer who lives in our spare bedroom.

3. My roommate / deposit never does the dishes.

4. We took / gave notice to our landlord two months before moving out.

5. We live in an attractive residence / residential area with lots of parks.

14 The body

14.1 PARTS OF THE BODY

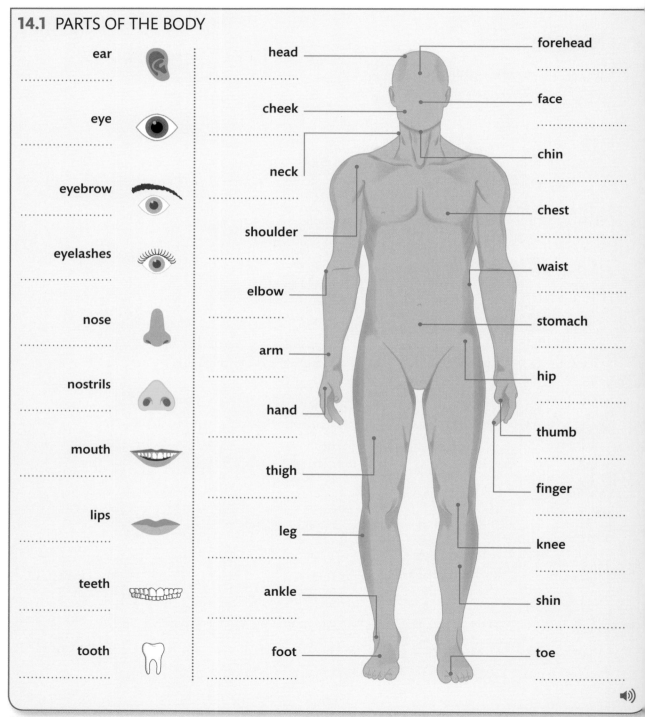

ear

....

eye

....

eyebrow

....

eyelashes

....

nose

....

nostrils

....

mouth

....

lips

....

teeth

....

tooth

....

head

....

cheek

....

neck

....

shoulder

....

elbow

....

arm

....

hand

....

thigh

....

leg

....

ankle

....

foot

....

forehead

....

face

....

chin

....

chest

....

waist

....

stomach

....

hip

....

thumb

....

finger

....

knee

....

shin

....

toe

....

14.2 VERBS

 to smile

 to frown

to grin

 to laugh

 to cry

 to yawn

 to cough

 to sigh

 to lick

 to suck

 to breathe

 to hold your breath

  to wink

 to blink

 to blush

  to sweat / to perspire

to shiver

 to snore

 to sneeze

to wave

 to clap

 to shrug

 to bow

 to nod

 to shake your head

63

14.3 LOOK AT THE PICTURE AND WRITE THE CORRECT WORD FROM THE PANEL FOR EACH LABEL

1 _____

2 _____

3 _____

arm _____

4 _____

5 _____

6 _____

7 _____

8 _____

9 _____

10 _____

11 _____

12 _____

13 _____

chest

waist

toe

shoulder

hip

~~arm~~

thigh

head

knee

chin

finger

foot

shin

neck

14.4 MARK THE BEGINNING AND ENDING OF EACH WORD IN THE CHAIN OF LETTERS

eyelashes|teethnosemoutheyebrownostrilsearankleIipsforeheadthighfingerstomachchinhip

Aa 14.5 MARK THE CORRECT VERB FOR THE ACTIVITY IN EACH PICTURE

to laugh ☑
to cry ☐
to blush ☐

 1

to grin ☐
to wave ☐
to clap ☐

 2

to shiver ☐
to sneeze ☐
to blink ☐

 3

to bow ☐
to shrug ☐
to wink ☐

  4

to yawn ☐
to frown ☐
to cry ☐

 5

to blush ☐
to breathe ☐
to sneeze ☐

 6

to lick ☐
to shiver ☐
to clap ☐

 7

to yawn ☐
to blink ☐
to frown ☐

 8

to smile ☐
to sigh ☐
to snore ☐

 **9**

to wink ☐
to suck ☐
to nod ☐

14.6 LISTEN TO THE AUDIO AND MARK THE CORRECT PICTURE FOR EACH WORD YOU HEAR

A ☐ **B** ☑ **C** ☐

3 **A** ☐ **B** ☐ **C** ☐

1  **A** ☐ **B** ☐ **C** ☐ **4** **A** ☐ **B** ☐ **C** ☐

2 **A** ☐ **B** ☐ **C** ☐ **5** **A** ☐ **B** ☐ **C** ☐

65

15.1 CLOTHES

cuff
collar
sleeve
button

shirt

t-shirt

blouse

suit

uniform

dress

skirt

pants (US)
trousers (UK)

jeans

jacket

raincoat

socks

shorts

tie

pajamas (US)
pyjamas (UK)

zipper (US)
zip (UK)

hood

pocket

sweater (US)
jumper (UK)

bra

panties (US)
knickers (UK)

coat

bathrobe / dressing gown

boxer shorts

jockey shorts (US) pants (UK)

pantyhose (US) tights (UK)

leggings

15.2 VERBS

to wear

to suit (someone)

to fit

to put on

to take off

to do up / fasten

to undo / unfasten

to change / to get changed

15.3 DESCRIBING CLOTHES AND STYLES

leather

cotton

woolen (US) woollen (UK)

polka dot (US) spotted (UK)

striped

checkered (US) checked (UK)

plain

silk

denim

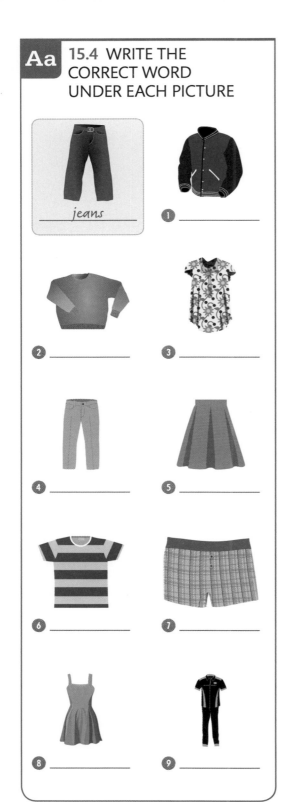

Aa 15.4 WRITE THE CORRECT WORD UNDER EACH PICTURE

jeans

1 _____

2 _____

3 _____

4 _____

5 _____

6 _____

7 _____

8 _____

9 _____

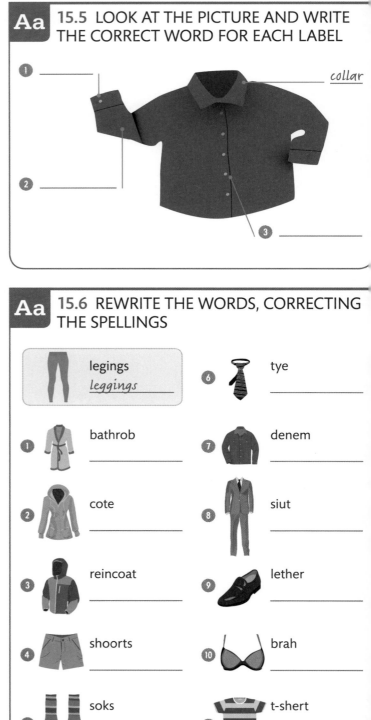

Aa 15.5 LOOK AT THE PICTURE AND WRITE THE CORRECT WORD FOR EACH LABEL

collar

1 _____

2 _____

3 _____

Aa 15.6 REWRITE THE WORDS, CORRECTING THE SPELLINGS

legings
leggings

1 bathrob
_____

2 cote
_____

3 reincoat
_____

4 shoorts
_____

5 soks
_____

6 tye
_____

7 denem
_____

8 siut
_____

9 lether
_____

10 brah
_____

11 t-shert
_____

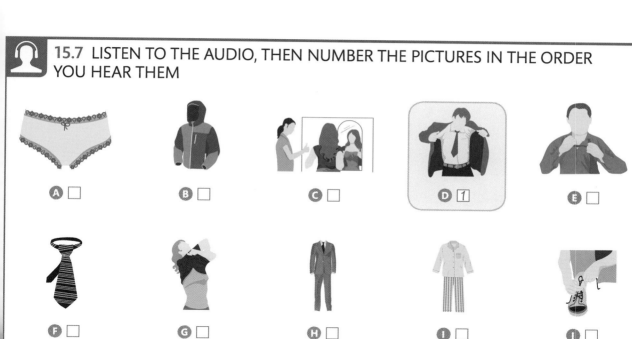

15.7 LISTEN TO THE AUDIO, THEN NUMBER THE PICTURES IN THE ORDER YOU HEAR THEM

Ⓐ ☐ Ⓑ ☐ Ⓒ ☐ Ⓓ 1 Ⓔ ☐

Ⓕ ☐ Ⓖ ☐ Ⓗ ☐ Ⓘ ☐ Ⓙ ☐

Aa **15.8** FIND EIGHT MORE WORDS FOR DESCRIBING CLOTHES IN THE GRID THAT MATCH THE PICTURES

```
C H E C K E R E D S C
T W V P Q H K Q V T O
A O D E N I M M D R T
P O I N T E R T I I T
L L B P L A I N Z P O
E E D I H T U A D E N
A N Z L O L A O Z D O
T A S D C E B Q T Z T
H Q T K P R D M E S X
E M A S T T Z T M I A
R T P R A E S X A L O
P O L K A D O T Q K Q
```

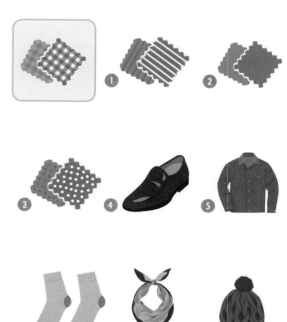

16.1 ACCESSORIES

scarf

hat

cap

gloves

belt

purse (US)
handbag (UK)

briefcase

backpack
rucksack (UK)

jewelry (US)
jewellery (UK)

necklace

bracelet

earrings

ring

brooch

pin (US)
badge (UK)

cufflinks

watch

handkerchief

bow tie

umbrella

hair band (US)
Alice band (UK)

glasses

sunglasses

wallet

wallet (US)
purse (UK)

16.2 SHOES

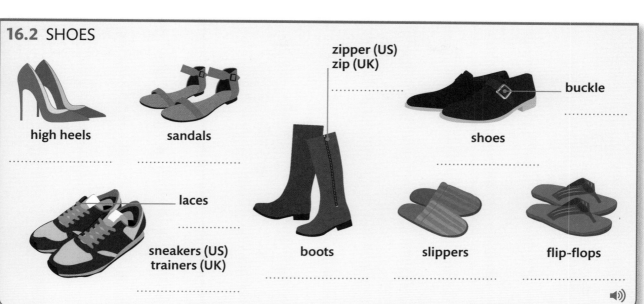

high heels

sandals

zipper (US)
zip (UK)

buckle

shoes

laces

sneakers (US)
trainers (UK)

boots

slippers

flip-flops

16.3 MAKE-UP AND BEAUTY PRODUCTS

lipstick

foundation

mascara

blush (US)
blusher (UK)

eyeliner

eyeshadow

hair dye

hair gel

hair spray

nail polish

perfume

aftershave

moisturizer

hairbrush

comb

Aa 16.4 COMPLETE THE WORD FOR EACH PICTURE, FILLING IN THE MISSING LETTERS

 b r i e f c a s e

① h a __ __ k __ r c __ __ e f

② s __ n __ a l __

③ b __ __ c k __ __ a __ __ k

④ __ c a __ f

⑤ w __ __ l __ e __

Aa 16.5 CIRCLE THE WORD THAT DOES NOT BELONG IN EACH LIST

sandals	high heels	(eyeliner)
① earrings	necklace	shoes
② mascara	belt	blush
③ hair band	boots	sneakers
④ hat	cap	eyeliner
⑤ handkerchief	hairbrush	comb
⑥ laces	scarf	buckle
⑦ moisturizer	perfume	umbrella

16.6 LISTEN TO THE AUDIO, THEN NUMBER THE PICTURES IN THE ORDER YOU HEAR THEM

 A ☐

 B ☐

 C ☐

 D ☐ 1

 E ☐

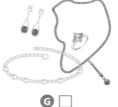 F ☐

 G ☐

 H ☐

 I ☐

 J ☐

72

Aa 16.7 MATCH THE PICTURES TO THE CORRECT WORDS

high heels

perfume

lipstick

nail polish

bow tie

purse (US)
handbag (UK)

hat

flip-flops

ring

Aa 16.8 REWRITE THE WORDS, CORRECTING THE SPELLINGS

breislet
bracelet

1 broach

2 earings

3 umbrela

4 combe

5 parfume

6 sunglases

7 neklace

17 Appearance

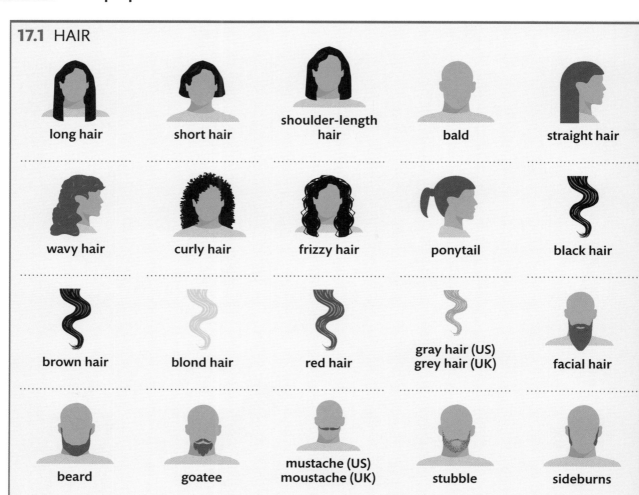

17.1 HAIR

long hair	short hair	shoulder-length hair	bald	straight hair
wavy hair	curly hair	frizzy hair	ponytail	black hair
brown hair	blond hair	red hair	gray hair (US) grey hair (UK)	facial hair
beard	goatee	mustache (US) moustache (UK)	stubble	sideburns

17.2 VERBS

to style your hair · to have / get your hair cut · to tie your hair back · to shave · to grow your hair

17.3 EYES

 blue

 brown

 green

 hazel

 gray (US) / grey (UK)

17.4 APPEARANCE AND STYLE

 short

 medium height

 tall

 beautiful

 handsome

 young

 middle-aged

 old

 formal (US) smart (UK)

 casual

 elegant

 glamorous

 dark skin

 tan skin (US) tanned skin (UK)

 olive skin

 fair skin

 pale skin

 freckles

 wrinkles

 mole

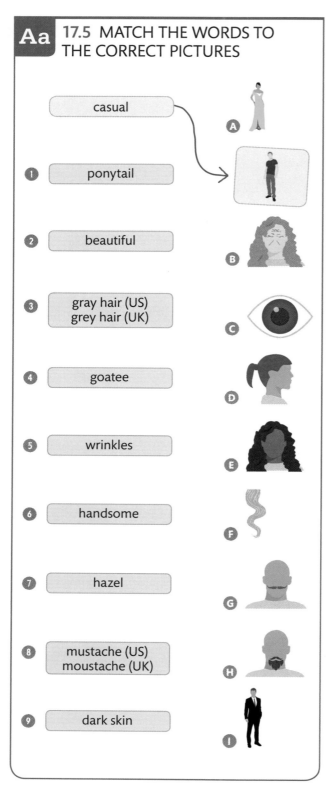

Aa 17.5 MATCH THE WORDS TO THE CORRECT PICTURES

casual — **A**

1. ponytail
2. beautiful
3. gray hair (US) / grey hair (UK)
4. goatee
5. wrinkles
6. handsome
7. hazel
8. mustache (US) / moustache (UK)
9. dark skin

Aa 17.6 WRITE THE CORRECT WORDS UNDER EACH PICTURE

freckles

1. _____
2. _____
3. _____
4. _____
5. _____
6. _____
7. _____
8. _____
9. _____

elegant _____

① _____

② _____

③ _____

④ _____

⑤ _____

⑥ _____

⑦ _____

⑧ _____

⑨ _____

⑩ _____

⑪ _____

Aa **17.8 MARK THE CORRECT PICTURE FOR EACH WORD**

young

Ⓐ ☑ Ⓑ ☐ Ⓒ ☐

③ shoulder-length hair

Ⓐ ☐ Ⓑ ☐ Ⓒ ☐

① brown hair

Ⓐ ☐ Ⓑ ☐ Ⓒ ☐

④ short

Ⓐ ☐ Ⓑ ☐ Ⓒ ☐

② glamorous

Ⓐ ☐ Ⓑ ☐ Ⓒ ☐

⑤ brown

Ⓐ ☐ Ⓑ ☐ Ⓒ ☐

18 Personality traits

18.1 DESCRIBING PERSONALITY

friendly

unfriendly

talkative

enthusiastic

serious

assertive

critical

caring

sensitive

insensitive

reasonable

unreasonable

kind

unkind

secretive

mature

immature

cautious

generous

mean

brave

funny

patient

impatient

lazy

78

 **laid-back**

 **optimistic**

 **outgoing**

 passionate

 **polite**

 rude

 **shy**

 intelligent

 **nervous**

 **silly**

 **selfish**

 **eccentric**

 **calm**

 **confident**

 **honest**

 **dishonest**

 supportive

 **reliable**

 **unreliable**

 talented

 arrogant

 **considerate**

 **impulsive**

 approachable

 **unapproachable**

79

Aa 18.2 CIRCLE THE WORD THAT DOES NOT BELONG IN EACH LIST

calm	laid-back	(impulsive)
❶ shy	assertive	nervous
❷ rude	caring	supportive
❸ friendly	impatient	approachable
❹ unreliable	generous	kind
❺ confident	outgoing	lazy
❻ considerate	selfish	mean
❼ dishonest	talented	unreliable
❽ mean	rude	approachable
❾ funny	insensitive	silly

Aa 18.3 COMPLETE THE WORD FOR EACH PICTURE, FILLING IN THE MISSING LETTERS

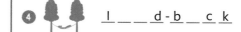 u n r e l i a b l e

❶ 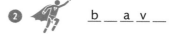 o _ t _ m i _ t _ c

❷ 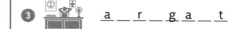 b _ _ a v _

❸ a _ r _ g a _ t

❹ l _ _ d - b _ c k

❺ _ s _ e r _ _ v e

❻ _ n s _ n s _ t _ v e

Aa 18.4 WRITE THE CORRECT WORD UNDER EACH PICTURE

 intelligent

❶  _____

❷ _____

❸ _____

❹ _____

❺ _____

❻ _____

❼  _____

❽  _____

❾  _____

18.5 LISTEN TO THE AUDIO AND MARK THE CORRECT PICTURE FOR EACH WORD YOU HEAR

A □ B ☑ C □

1 A □ B □ C □

2 A □ B □ C □

3 A □ B □ C □

4 A □ B □ C □

5 A □ B □ C □

6 A □ B □ C □

18.6 LOOK AT THE PICTURE CLUES AND WRITE THE ANSWERS IN THE CORRECT PLACES ON THE GRID

1 s
e
c
r
e
t
8 i
v
e

19 Feelings and moods

19.1 FEELINGS AND MOODS

calm

relaxed

pleased

cheerful

happy

delighted

ecstatic

grateful

lucky

amused

interested

curious

intrigued

surprised

shocked

excited

thrilled

amazed

confident

proud

sad

unhappy

upset

miserable

depressed

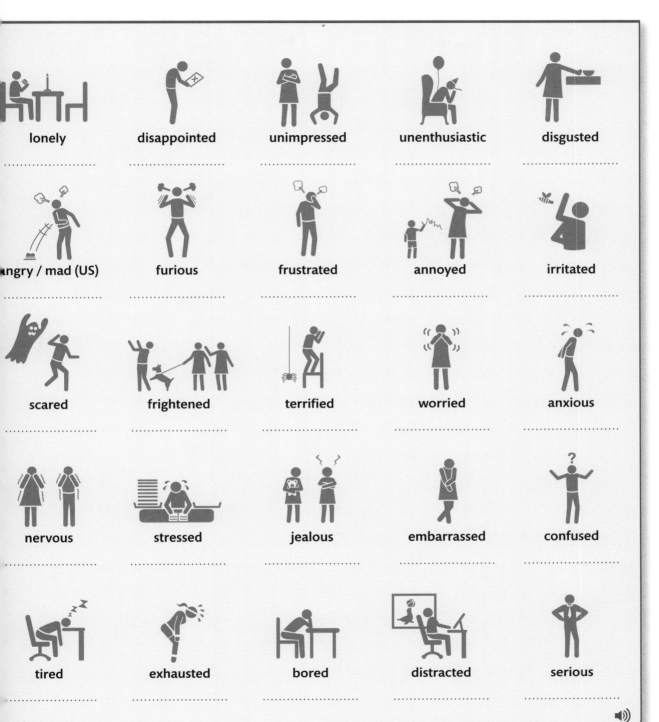

lonely

disappointed

unimpressed

unenthusiastic

disgusted

angry / mad (US)

furious

frustrated

annoyed

irritated

scared

frightened

terrified

worried

anxious

nervous

stressed

jealous

embarrassed

confused

tired

exhausted

bored

distracted

serious

Aa 19.2 WRITE THE CORRECT WORD UNDER EACH PICTURE

unimpressed

 1 _____

 2 _____

 3 _____

 4 _____

 5 _____

 6 _____

 7 _____

 8 _____

 9 _____

 10 _____

 11 _____

 12 _____

 13 _____

 14 _____

 15 _____

 16 _____

 17 _____

 18 _____

 19 _____

Aa 19.3 MARK THE BEGINNING AND ENDING OF EACH WORD IN THE CHAIN OF LETTERS

delighted/annoyedgratefulembarrassedecstaticworriedcuriousunenthusiasticjealousconfused

Aa 19.4 CIRCLE THE WORD THAT DOES NOT BELONG IN EACH LIST

| unhappy | (amused) | miserable |

1. disgusted / happy / cheerful
2. angry / furious / grateful
3. amazed / unimpressed / unenthusiastic
4. calm / scared / relaxed
5. frightened / terrified / interested
6. disappointed / curious / intrigued
7. happy / pleased / depressed
8. tired / annoyed / exhausted
9. bored / thrilled / excited
10. anxious / worried / proud
11. relaxed / irritated / annoyed
12. happy / miserable / ecstatic

Aa 19.5 WRITE THE WORDS FROM THE PANEL NEXT TO THEIR OPPOSITES

relaxed	_stressed_
1. unhappy	
2. bored	
3. confident	
4. anxious	
5. cheerful	
6. disappointed	
7. serious	

proud   ~~stressed~~   amused   interested

nervous   miserable   happy   calm

19.6 LISTEN TO THE AUDIO, THEN NUMBER THE PICTURES IN THE ORDER YOU HEAR THEM

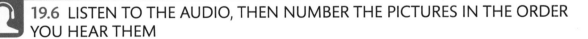

 A ☐

 B ☐1

 C ☐

 D ☐

 E ☐

 F ☐

 G ☐

 H ☐

 I ☐

 J ☐

 K ☐

 L ☐

 M ☐

 N ☐

 O ☐

 P ☐

20.1 JAMAL'S FAMILY

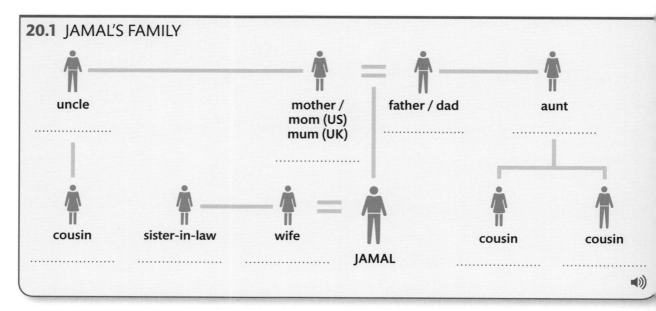

uncle

mother / mom (US) mum (UK)

father / dad

aunt

cousin

sister-in-law

wife

JAMAL

cousin

cousin

20.2 DEBBIE'S FAMILY

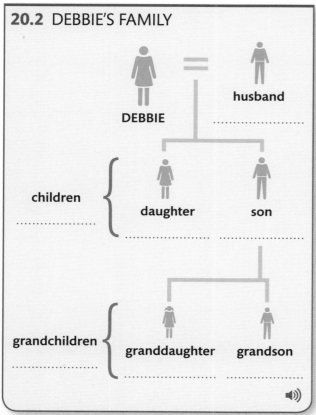

husband

DEBBIE

children

daughter

son

grandchildren

granddaughter

grandson

20.3 ANA'S FAMILY

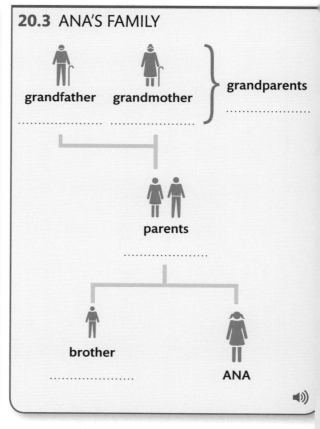

grandfather

grandmother

grandparents

parents

brother

ANA

20.4 GROWING UP

baby

....

toddler

....

girl

....

boy

....

teenagers

....

adults

....

20.5 ROGER'S FAMILY

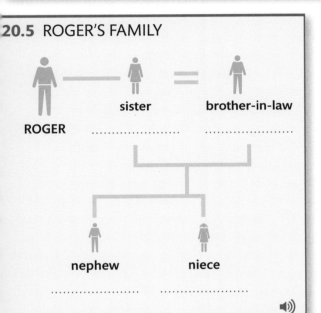

ROGER   sister   brother-in-law

....

nephew   niece

....

20.6 LOGAN'S FAMILY

stepmother /
stepmom (US)
stepmum (UK)

father / dad

....

stepsister   stepbrother

....

LOGAN

20.7 RELATIONSHIPS

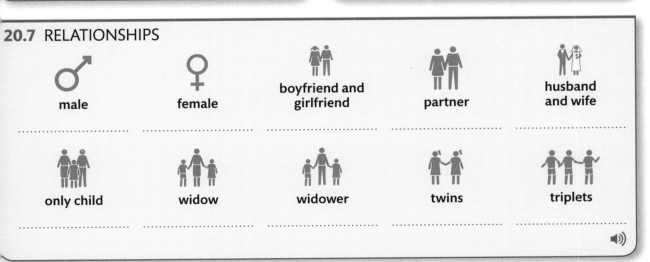

male

....

female

....

boyfriend and
girlfriend

....

partner

....

husband
and wife

....

only child

....

widow

....

widower

....

twins

....

triplets

....

20.8 FILL IN THE GAPS ON JAMAL'S FAMILY TREE

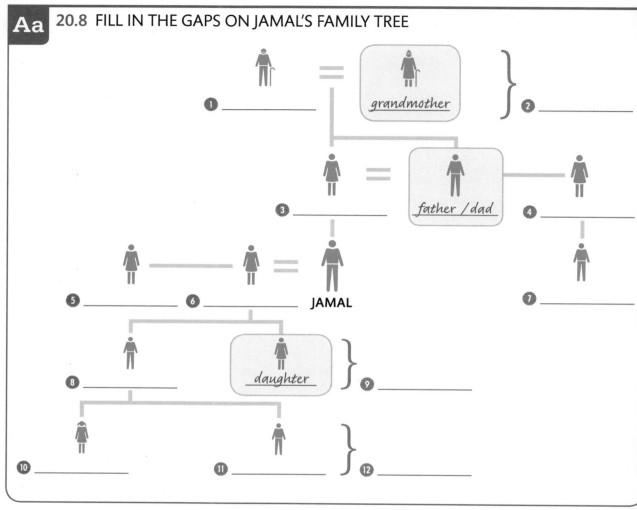

20.9 MATCH THE PICTURES TO THE CORRECT WORDS

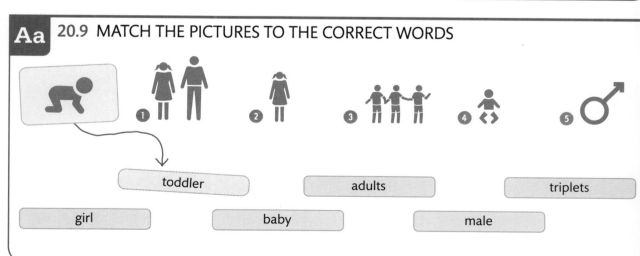

toddler

adults

triplets

girl

baby

male

20.10 LISTEN TO THE AUDIO AND WRITE THE WORD THAT IS SHOWN IN EACH PICTURE

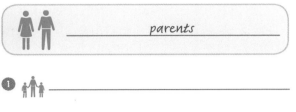 *parents*

1 _____

2 _____

3 _____

4 _____

5 _____

Aa 20.11 FILL IN THE GAPS ON LOGAN'S FAMILY TREE

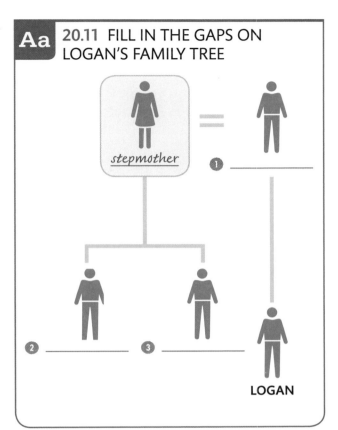

stepmother

1 _____

2 _____

3 _____

LOGAN

Aa 20.12 REWRITE THE WORDS, CORRECTING THE SPELLINGS

neice
niece

1 femeil _____

2 partener _____

3 nehpew _____

4 dauhgter _____

5 husbend _____

6 widou _____

7 girlfreind _____

21 Family and relationships

21.1 USEFUL EXPRESSIONS

Caroline looks up to her eldest brother.

to look up to someone
[to have respect and admiration for someone]

Sadie takes after her mother. They are both very kind.

to take after someone
[to have characteristics of a parent or relative]

We're bringing up our children to work hard at school.

to bring up someone / bring someone up
[to care for a child and teach them how to behave]

I hope my grandson will grow up to enjoy books.

to grow up
[to develop from a child to an adult]

Jo gets along with her boss.

to get along / get on with someone
[to have a good relationship with someone]

My siblings are always falling out with each other.

to fall out with someone
[to stop being friends with someone, often after an argument]

I fell in love with him while we were backpacking in India.

to fall in love with someone
[to begin to love someone]

We broke up because I didn't love him any more.

to break up with someone
[to end a romantic relationship]

They stopped working together last year, so they have drifted apart.

to drift apart
[to slowly become less friendly or close to someone]

I made friends with Miguel after he moved to my town.

to make friends with someone
[to become friendly with a person]

We've been close friends since
we shared an apartment.

a close friend
[a friend who you know very well]

Everyone says how much my
wife and I have in common.

to have something in common
[to share an interest or opinion]

My cousin gave birth
to a baby boy last year.

to give birth to someone
[to have a child]

My sisters and I all have curly
hair. It runs in the family.

to run in the family
[to be a common feature of a family]

We see eye to eye about
most important issues.

to see eye to eye with someone
[to agree with or have similar opinions
to someone]

Jared was really friendly, and I clicked
with him immediately.

to click with someone
[to like someone quickly
and easily]

We often bump into Mary
at the local store.

to bump into someone
[to meet someone unexpectedly]

I always put my foot down
if my son is naughty.

to put your foot down
[to be strict about something]

I stick up for my friends if
people are mean to them.

to stick up for someone
[to speak out in support of someone]

I love playing with my grandson.
I think the world of him.

to think the world of someone
[to have a very high opinion
of someone]

21.2 MATCH THE PICTURES TO THE CORRECT SENTENCES

I love playing with my grandson. I think the world of him.

① We're bringing up our children to work hard at school.

② We see eye to eye about most important issues.

③ My siblings are always falling out with each other.

④ We often bump into Mary at the local store.

21.3 CROSS OUT THE INCORRECT WORDS IN EACH SENTENCE

I always put my foot ~~up~~ / ~~on~~ / down if my son is naughty.

③ My cousin had / made / gave birth to a baby boy last year.

① Caroline sees / looks / takes up to her eldest brother.

④ I stick up / in / through for my friends if people are mean to them.

② Sadie takes onto / after / into her mother. They are both very kind.

⑤ I made / took / put friends with Miguel after he moved to my town.

A   I fell in love with him while we were backpacking in India.   ☐

B   I hope my grandson will grow up to enjoy books.   ☐

C   My sisters and I all have curly hair. It runs in the family.   ☐

D   They stopped working together last year, so they have drifted apart.   ☐

E   Jared was really friendly, and I clicked with him immediately.   1

F   Everyone says how much my wife and I have in common.   ☐

Aa 21.5 REWRITE THE SENTENCES, CORRECTING THE ERRORS

We **see eyes to eyes** about most important issues.
We see eye to eye about most important issues.

❶ Jo **takes along with** her boss.

_____

❷ We've been **near friends** since we shared an apartment.

_____

❸ I love playing with my grandson. I **think the earth of** him.

_____

❹ We **broke in** because I didn't love him any more.

_____

❺ My siblings are always **falling apart with** each other.

_____

Baby equipment and toys

22.1 EQUIPMENT AND CLOTHES

changing mat

changing table

teddy bear

nursery

mobile

crib (US)
cot (UK)

potty

diaper (US)
nappy (UK)

high chair

pacifier (US)
dummy (UK)

stroller (US)
buggy (UK)

baby carriage (US)
pram (UK)

bottle

wet wipe

moses basket

playpen

stair gate

baby monitor

romper suit

snowsuit

bib

booties

bodysuit (US)
babygro (UK)

rattle

22.2 TOYS AND GAMES

toy

**stuffed animal (US)
soft toy (UK)**

doll

board game

playing cards

**dollhouse (US)
doll's house (UK)**

**building blocks /
bricks**

ball

spinning top

yo-yo

**jump rope (US)
skipping rope (UK)**

jigsaw puzzle

train set

puppet

kite

swings

**climbing
frame**

slide

seesaw   **playground**   **sandbox (US)
sandpit (UK)**

balloon

marbles

95

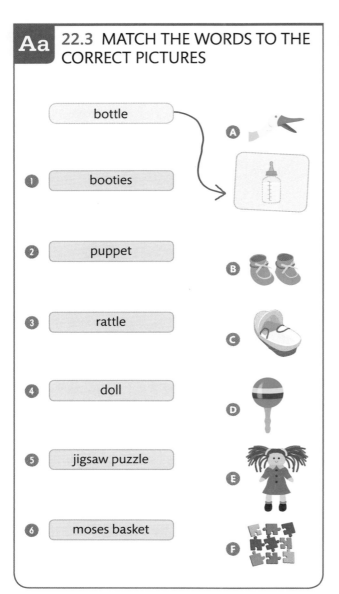

Aa 22.3 MATCH THE WORDS TO THE CORRECT PICTURES

bottle

1. booties
2. puppet
3. rattle
4. doll
5. jigsaw puzzle
6. moses basket

A
B
C
D
E
F

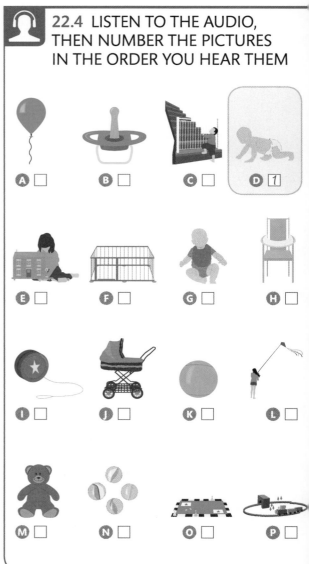

22.4 LISTEN TO THE AUDIO, THEN NUMBER THE PICTURES IN THE ORDER YOU HEAR THEM

A ☐ B ☐ C ☐ D 1

E ☐ F ☐ G ☐ H ☐

I ☐ J ☐ K ☐ L ☐

M ☐ N ☐ O ☐ P ☐

Aa 22.5 MARK THE BEGINNING AND ENDING OF EACH WORD IN THE CHAIN OF LETTERS

booties/nurserytoysandboxswingstrainsetdollmarblesbottlekitepuppetchangingtablerattle

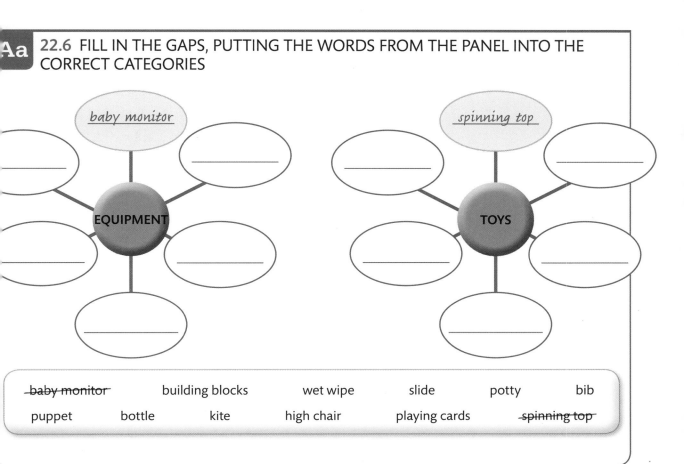

Aa **22.6 FILL IN THE GAPS, PUTTING THE WORDS FROM THE PANEL INTO THE CORRECT CATEGORIES**

baby monitor

EQUIPMENT

spinning top

TOYS

~~baby monitor~~	building blocks	wet wipe	slide	potty	bib
puppet	bottle	kite	high chair	playing cards	~~spinning top~~

Aa **22.7 LOOK AT THE PICTURE CLUES AND WRITE THE ANSWERS IN THE CORRECT PLACES ON THE GRID**

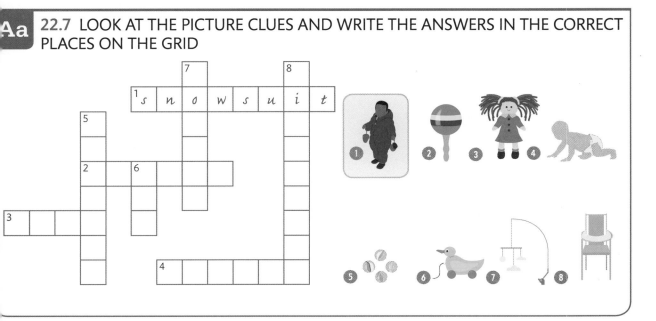

23 Education

23.1 SUBJECTS

English

art

history

geography

science

biology

physics

chemistry

math (US)
maths (UK)

medicine

economics

law

business studies

engineering

architecture

psychology

philosophy

music

drama

languages

design and technology

information technology

physical education

veterinary medicine

geology

23.2 STUDYING AND EXAMS (NOUNS)

 school

 college (US) university (UK)

 library

 classroom

 laboratory

 class

 exam

 essay

 homework

 exercise book

 textbook

 thesis

 lecture

 test

 diploma (US) qualification (UK)

 degree

 teacher

 professor / lecturer

 student

 graduate

23.3 STUDYING AND EXAMS (VERBS)

 to study a subject

 to review (US) to revise (UK)

 to sit an exam

 to pass

 to fail

 to resit

99

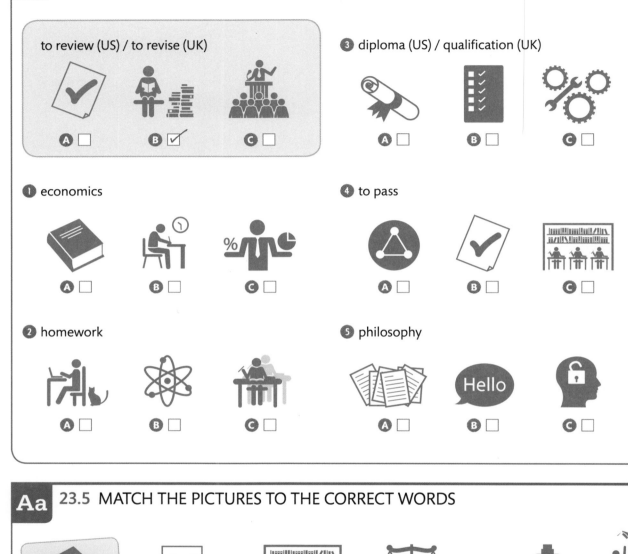

Aa 23.4 MARK THE CORRECT PICTURE FOR EACH WORD

to review (US) / to revise (UK)

A ☐ B ☑ C ☐

❸ diploma (US) / qualification (UK)

A ☐ B ☐ C ☐

❶ economics

A ☐ B ☐ C ☐

❹ to pass

A ☐ B ☐ C ☐

❷ homework

A ☐ B ☐ C ☐

❺ philosophy

A ☐ B ☐ C ☐

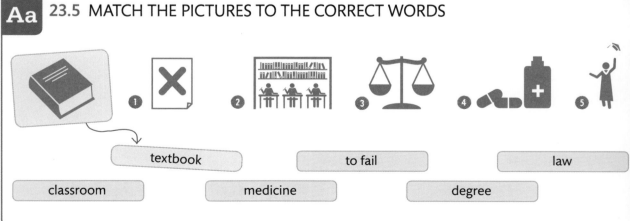

Aa 23.5 MATCH THE PICTURES TO THE CORRECT WORDS

❶ ❷ ❸ ❹ ❺

textbook

to fail

law

classroom

medicine

degree

23.6 LISTEN TO THE AUDIO AND WRITE THE WORD THAT IS SHOWN IN EACH PICTURE

chemistry

1. _____
2. _____
3. _____
4. _____
5. _____
6. _____
7. _____
8. _____
9. _____
10. _____
11. _____
12. _____
13. _____

Aa 23.7 WRITE THE CORRECT WORD UNDER EACH PICTURE

library

1. _____
2. _____
3. _____
4. _____
5. _____
6. _____
7. _____
8. _____
9. _____

24 Studying

24.1 USEFUL EXPRESSIONS

Rowena is taking a year off before she starts college.

to take a year off (US) / take a year out (UK)
[to have a year away from education or work]

Matt enrolled in a computer science course last month.

to enroll in (US) / enrol on (UK)
[to register to start something]

Many undergraduates live in a dormitory in their first year of college.

an undergraduate
[someone studying for a first degree at college or university]

Amira is studying for a graduate degree in chemistry.

graduate (US) / postgraduate (UK)
[study carried out following graduation from a first degree]

When Gavin was a freshman, he was very nervous about starting college.

a freshman (US) / fresher (UK)
[a student in their first year at college or university]

I have to write five essays this semester, so I'm doing lots of research.

a semester (US) / term (UK)
[a period of time in an academic calendar, during which classes are held]

Millie's parents were really proud when she got a degree.

to get a degree
[to be awarded a diploma / qualification after college or university]

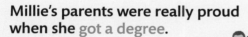

I expect my students to attend classes every week.

to attend classes
[to go to lessons or lectures]

Emma took her driving test last week, and she passed.

to take a test / take an exam
[to answer questions or perform actions to show how much you know about something]

It's important to give students regular feedback on their work.

to give someone feedback on something
[to provide comments and advice on how somebody is doing something]

Tyson is working all day to meet the deadline for his essay.

to meet a deadline
[to finish something within a given time]

Boris almost missed the deadline for his research project.

to miss a deadline
[to fail to finish something within a given time]

I like continuous assessment more than just taking final exams.

continuous assessment
[grading based on work done over a long period]

Chris passed his final college exams with flying colors.

to pass with flying colors (US) / colours (UK)
[to perform excellently on a test]

I've finished the first draft of my essay, but I'm sure that I'll have to make lots of changes to it.

a first draft
[a first, rough version of a piece of written work]

I'd like you to compare and contrast these two pictures.

to compare and contrast
[to consider and describe the similarities and differences between things]

Their views on teaching a class are polar opposites.

polar opposites
[completely different]

There is a clear distinction between these two experiments.

a clear distinction
[an obvious difference]

Kate and Helen take strikingly different after-school classes.

strikingly different
[surprisingly not alike]

Practicing for her class presentation made a world of difference.

a world of difference
[a significant level of difference]

24.2 MARK THE SENTENCES THAT ARE CORRECT

Tyson is working all day to meet the deadline for his essay. ☑
Tyson is working all day to reach the deadline for his essay. ☐

① Rowena is taking a year off before she starts college. ☐
Rowena is taking a year away before she starts college. ☐

② Practicing for her class presentation made a mountain of difference. ☐
Practicing for her class presentation made a world of difference. ☐

③ I expect my students to appear in classes every week. ☐
I expect my students to attend classes every week. ☐

④ Their views on teaching a class are polar opposites. ☐
Their views on teaching a class are Arctic opposites. ☐

⑤ Chris passed his final college exams with burning colors. ☐
Chris passed his final college exams with flying colors. ☐

Aa 24.3 FILL IN THE GAPS USING THE WORDS IN THE PANEL

Kate and Helen take _____*strikingly different*_____ after-school classes.

① When Gavin was a _____, he was very nervous about starting college.

② There is a _____ between these two experiments.

③ Emma _____ last week, and she passed.

④ It's important to give students _____ on their work.

⑤ Amira is studying for a _____ in chemistry.

⑥ Boris almost _____ for his research project.

freshman	took her driving test	graduate degree	clear distinction
	missed the deadline	regular feedback	~~strikingly different~~

Aa 24.4 WRITE THE CORRECT PHRASE NEXT TO ITS DEFINITION

to fail to finish something within a given time	=	*to miss a deadline*

1. someone studying for a first degree at college or university = _____
2. a first, rough version of a piece of written work = _____
3. a student in their first year at college or university = _____
4. grading based on work done over a long period = _____
5. to perform excellently on a test = _____

24.5 LISTEN TO THE AUDIO AND COMPLETE THE SENTENCES THAT DESCRIBE EACH PICTURE

 Millie's parents were really proud when she _got a degree_ .

 ③ Matt _____ a computer science course last month.

 ① I like _____ _____ more than just taking final exams.

 ④ I'd like you to _____ _____ these two pictures.

 ② I've finished the _____ _____ of my essay, but I'm sure that I'll have to make lots of changes to it.

 ⑤ Many _____ live in a dormitory in their first year of college.

25 Speaking a foreign language

25.1 USEFUL EXPRESSIONS

I speak conversational German, but my grammar is awful.

conversational
[language that is not technically perfect, but clear enough for basic communication]

My uncle is fluent in five different languages.

fluent in
[able to use a language easily, without making many mistakes]

I was taught French by a native speaker from Marseilles.

a native speaker
[a person who speaks a language as their first language]

My wife is bilingual; she speaks English and Japanese.

bilingual
[able to speak two languages fluently]

Zara's Portuguese is a bit rusty. She hasn't spoken it in years.

rusty
[not as fluent in a language as you used to be]

Maria's strong accent is impossible to understand.

an accent
[the way in which people from a country or region pronounce a word]

Juan finds the pronunciation of the word "squirrel" impossible.

pronunciation
[the way a specific word is spoken]

Dan's spoken Mandarin isn't bad, but he needs to improve his grammar.

grammar
[the way in which you make sentences from separate words]

I bought a dictionary to improve my Spanish vocabulary.

vocabulary
[the set of words that make up a language]

Watching French TV helps you improve your listening skills.

listening
[the ability to understand spoken language]

The best way to improve your speaking skills is to talk to native speakers.

speaking
[the ability to communicate using spoken language]

The language barrier stopped me from talking to Wen.

the language barrier
[difficulty communicating with someone who speaks another language]

Looking at American websites can help you improve your English reading skills.

reading
[the ability to understand written materials]

After only a few weeks living in Italy, I was able to make myself understood.

to make yourself understood
[to be able to express basic information and ideas to people]

I understand some Hebrew, but find the writing impossible.

writing
[the ability to communicate using written words]

Although Pedro has a strong accent, he does speak accurately.

to speak accurately
[to speak without making mistakes]

English acts as a lingua franca for the people at the conference.

a lingua franca
[a shared language that allows people from various countries to understand each other]

Living in Cairo, I managed to pick up Arabic quickly.

to pick something up quickly
[to be able to learn something in little time]

The translation of the contract was full of mistakes.

a translation
[a piece of writing that has been changed from one language to another]

I have a good ear for languages. I learned Swahili in six months.

to have a good ear for languages
[to be able to understand languages without difficulty]

Aa 25.2 CROSS OUT THE INCORRECT WORD IN EACH SENTENCE

 Living in Cairo, I managed to pick ~~off~~ / up Arabic quickly.

① After only a few weeks living in Italy, I was able to make / take myself understood.

④ My uncle is fluent of / in five different languages.

② I have a good ear / nose for languages. I learned Swahili in six months.

⑤ I speak conversational / conversing German, but my grammar is awful.

③ The language wall / barrier stopped me from talking to Wen.

⑥ Juan finds the pronounce / pronunciation of the word "squirrel" impossible.

Aa 25.3 WRITE THE CORRECT EXPRESSION NEXT TO ITS DEFINITION

the way in which you make sentences from separate words = _grammar_

① the way people from a country or region pronounce a word = _____

② able to speak two languages fluently = _____

③ a person who speaks a language as their first language = _____

④ the ability to communicate using spoken language = _____

⑤ to speak without making mistakes = _____

⑥ the set of words that make up a language = _____

⑦ able to use a language easily, without making many mistakes = _____

Aa 25.4 FILL IN THE GAPS, PUTTING THE WORDS IN THE CORRECT ORDER

your improve reading English

Looking at American websites can help you _improve_ _your_ _English_ _reading_ skills.

speaker a by from native

① I was taught French _____ _____ _____ _____ _____ Marseilles.

as for a franca acts lingua

② English _____ _____ _____ _____ _____ _____ the people at the conference.

writing the find but

③ I understand some Hebrew, _____ _____ _____ _____ impossible.

accent, a he speak strong does

④ Although Pedro has _____ _____ _____ _____ _____ _____ accurately.

25.5 LISTEN TO THE AUDIO, THEN NUMBER THE SENTENCES IN THE ORDER YOU HEAR THEM

Ⓐ The translation of the contract was full of mistakes. ☐

Ⓓ Maria's strong accent is impossible to understand. ☐

Ⓑ I bought a dictionary to improve my Spanish vocabulary. ☐

Ⓔ My wife is bilingual; she speaks English and Japanese. 1

Ⓒ Watching French TV helps you improve your listening skills. ☐

Ⓕ The best way to improve your speaking skills is to talk to native speakers. ☐

26 Communication and beliefs

26.1 USEFUL EXPRESSIONS

Jenna told a white lie and said she liked Barry's new suit.

to tell a white lie
[to say something that is not true to avoid upsetting someone]

Tara is dropping a hint that she would like new shoes for her birthday.

to drop a hint
[to say something indirectly]

Farah started a rumor that Kerry stole a car.

to start / to spread a rumor
[to start / continue saying things that may or may not be true]

Martin loves to gossip about other people's relationships.

to gossip
[to talk about other people, often in a negative way]

We have a sneaking suspicion that Tim won't come to the party with us.

to have a sneaking suspicion
[to have an idea about something with little evidence]

Do you really believe in ghosts?

to believe in something
[to think that something exists or is true]

I have never lost my keys. Knock on wood!

to knock on wood (US)
to touch wood (UK)
[to wish for good luck, or avoid bad luck]

Make a wish when you cut your birthday cake!

to make a wish
[to hope for something to happen]

I have serious misgivings about accepting this job offer.

to have serious misgivings / doubts
[to have a strong feeling that something is not right]

You shouldn't be a tattletale at school.

a tattletale (US) / telltale (UK)
[somebody who tells an authority figure when another person has done something wrong]

...often find out about new products
...y word of mouth.

...ord of mouth
...formation or news transmitted
...y people telling other people]

I really enjoy reading fairy tales
to my grandchildren.

a fairy tale
[a traditional story with magic,
usually written for children]

...don't think the park is haunted.
...hat's just an urban myth.

...n urban myth
...modern story that is untrue,
...t believed by many]

To some people, a black cat is a good
omen; to others, a bad omen.

a good / bad omen
[a positive / negative sign about
something that will happen]

...was such a stroke of luck
...o win that new car.

...stroke of luck
...single piece of good fortune]

I've never played this game, so
I'm hoping for beginner's luck.

beginner's luck
[good fortune the first
time you do something]

...nyone can win this game.
...'s a game of pure luck.

...ure luck
...ood fortune with no skill involved]

That book about Chinese
folklore was really interesting.

folklore
[stories, sayings, and traditions
from a certain area or culture]

...e has a very old-fashioned
...et of beliefs.

...set of beliefs
...group of values]

Rosa has an unshakable belief
in the importance of
being kind.

an unshakable belief
[a firm and unchangeable conviction]

26.2 FILL IN THE GAPS, PUTTING THE WORDS IN THE CORRECT ORDER

| about | have | misgivings | serious |

I ___have___ ___serious___ ___misgivings___ ___about___ accepting this job offer.

| ghosts | in | believe | really |

1 Do you _____ _____ _____ _____ ?

| tales | my | reading | to | fairy |

2 I really enjoy _____ _____ _____ _____ _____ grandchildren.

| a | that | suspicion | have | sneaking |

3 We _____ _____ _____ _____ _____ Tim won't come to the party with us.

| rumor | a | started |

4 Farah _____ _____ _____ that Kerry stole a car.

26.3 CROSS OUT THE INCORRECT WORDS IN EACH SENTENCE

 It was such a **stroke** / ~~strike~~ / ~~stoke~~ of luck to win that new car.

 Tara is **falling** / **throwing** / **dropping** a hint that she would like new shoes for her birthday.

 Jenna told a **clean** / **white** / **kind** lie and said she liked Barry's new suit.

 I've never played this game, so I'm hoping for **beginner's** / **starter's** / **opener's** luck.

 He has a very old-fashioned **set** / **collection** / **box** of beliefs.

Aa 26.4 WRITE THE CORRECT PHRASE NEXT TO ITS DEFINITION, FILLING IN THE MISSING LETTERS

to wish for good luck, or avoid bad luck = t o k n o c k o n w o o d

1 to hope for something to happen = t _ _ m _ _ _ _ a w _ _ _ h

2 good fortune with no skill involved = _ u r _ l _ _ k

3 a modern story that is untrue, but believed by many = a _ _ u _ b _ _ _ m _ _ h

4 stories, sayings, and traditions from a certain area or culture = f _ l _ _ _ o _ _

5 to talk about other people, often in a negative way = t _ _ g _ _ s _ _ _ _

26.5 LISTEN TO THE AUDIO AND COMPLETE THE SENTENCES THAT DESCRIBE EACH PICTURE

Rosa has an _unshakable_ _belief_ in the importance of being kind.

3 You shouldn't be a _____ at school.

1 I often find out about new products _____ .

4 To some people, a black cat is a _____ ; to others, a _____ .

2 Anyone can win this game. It's a game of _____ .

5 Martin loves _____ about other people's relationships.

27.1 CRIME

robbery

burglary

mugging

car theft

shoplifting

pickpocketing

vandalism

graffiti

fraud

hacking

hooliganism

drug dealing

smuggling

speeding

bribery

27.2 PUNISHMENT AND THE LAW

police

law court

judge

lawyer

jury

trial

witness

fine

prison

criminal record

27.3 USEFUL EXPRESSIONS

The burglar wouldn't admit he had committed a crime.

to commit a crime
[to break the law]

Austin served a sentence of two years before he was released from prison.

to serve a sentence
[to spend time in prison]

The police officer arrested Tina for shoplifting.

to arrest somebody
[to use the power of the law to take and question somebody]

It's a police officer's job to enforce the law.

to enforce the law
[to make people obey a rule or a law]

After discussing all the evidence, the jury reached a verdict.

to reach a verdict
[to come to a decision about somebody's guilt or innocence]

The recent crime wave in my home town is very worrying.

a crime wave
[a lot of crimes happening suddenly in the same area]

The jury found Colin guilty of car theft.

to find somebody (not) guilty
[to decide officially that someone has (not) broken the law]

Street crime, such as mugging, can be a problem in our cities.

street crime
[crime committed in a public place]

Paula was sentenced to 100 hours of community service.

to sentence somebody to something
[to decide on a punishment in accordance with the law]

André is trained to deal with white-collar crime, such as fraud.

white-collar crime
[financial, nonviolent crime]

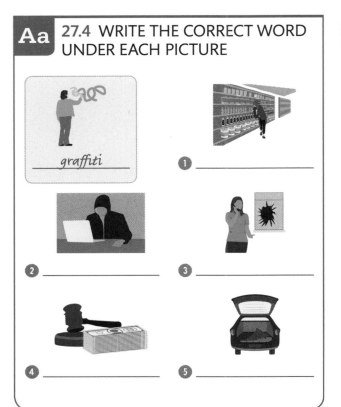

Aa 27.4 WRITE THE CORRECT WORD UNDER EACH PICTURE

graffiti

❶ _____

❷ _____

❸ _____

❹ _____

❺ _____

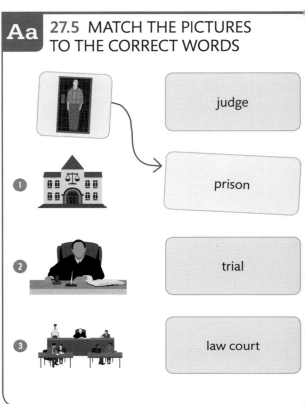

Aa 27.5 MATCH THE PICTURES TO THE CORRECT WORDS

judge

❶ prison

❷ trial

❸ law court

27.6 LISTEN TO THE AUDIO AND MARK THE CORRECT PICTURE FOR EACH WORD YOU HEAR

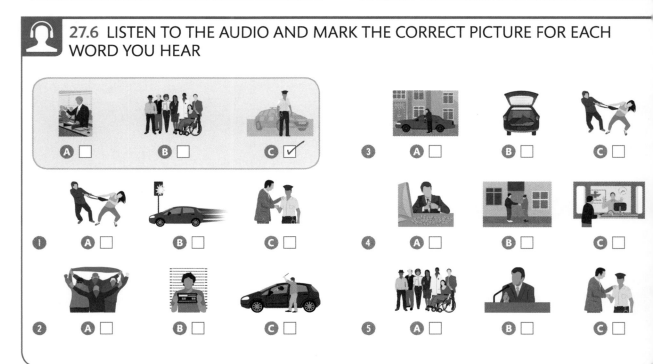

A ☐   B ☐   C ☑

❶ A ☐   B ☐   C ☐

❷ A ☐   B ☐   C ☐

❸ A ☐   B ☐   C ☐

❹ A ☐   B ☐   C ☐

❺ A ☐   B ☐   C ☐

Aa 27.7 MARK THE SENTENCES THAT ARE CORRECT

Street crime, such as mugging, can be a problem in our cities. ✓
Street criminal, such as mugging, can be a problem in our cities. ☐

① The recent crime wave in my home town is very worrying. ☐
The recent crime flood in my home town is very worrying. ☐

② The jury revealed Colin guilty of car theft. ☐
The jury found Colin guilty of car theft. ☐

③ The burglar wouldn't admit he had performed a crime. ☐
The burglar wouldn't admit he had committed a crime. ☐

④ After discussing all the evidence, the jury reached a verdict. ☐
After discussing all the evidence, the jury touched a verdict. ☐

⑤ It's a police officer's job to enforce the law. ☐
It's a police officer's job to cause the law. ☐

Aa 27.8 FILL IN THE GAPS USING THE WORDS IN THE PANEL

Austin served a ___sentence___ of two years before he was released from prison.

① The police officer _____ Tina for shoplifting.

② It's a police officer's job to _____ the law.

③ _____ , such as mugging, can be a problem in our cities.

④ Paula was _____ to 100 hours of community service.

⑤ André is trained to deal with _____ , such as fraud.

enforce   white-collar crime   Street crime   arrested   sentenced   ~~sentence~~

28 Meat, fish, dairy, and snacks

28.1 MEAT

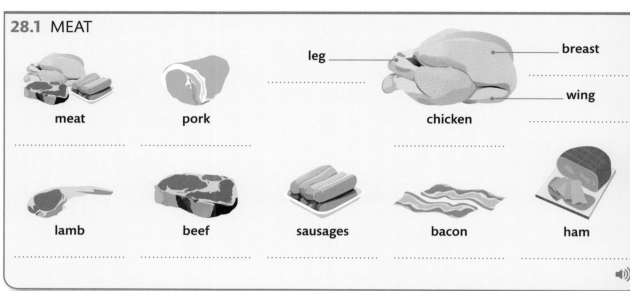

meat

pork

leg

breast

wing

chicken

lamb

beef

sausages

bacon

ham

28.2 FISH AND SEAFOOD

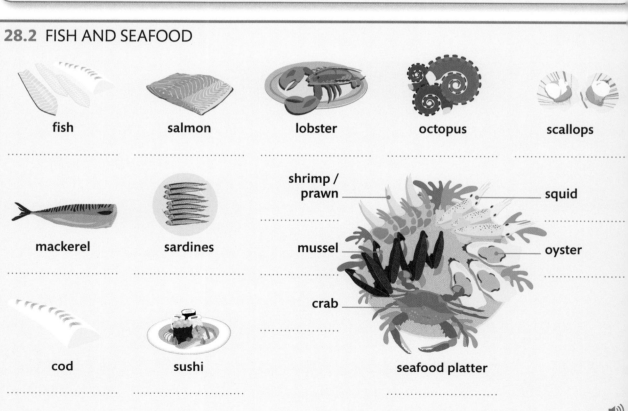

fish

salmon

lobster

octopus

scallops

mackerel

sardines

shrimp / prawn

squid

mussel

oyster

crab

cod

sushi

seafood platter

28.3 DAIRY

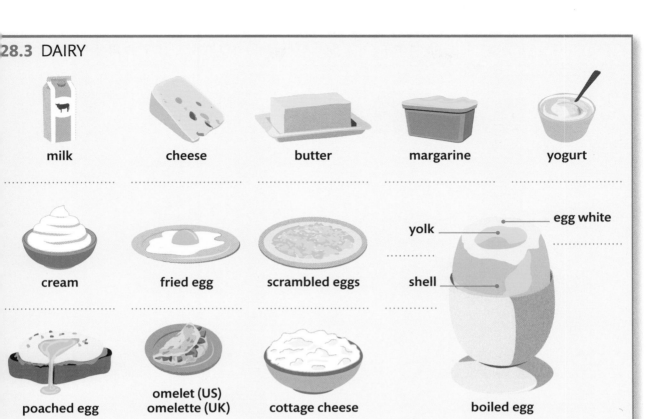

milk

cheese

butter

margarine

yogurt

cream

fried egg

scrambled eggs

yolk

egg white

shell

poached egg

omelet (US)
omelette (UK)

cottage cheese

boiled egg

28.4 FAST FOOD AND LIGHT SNACKS

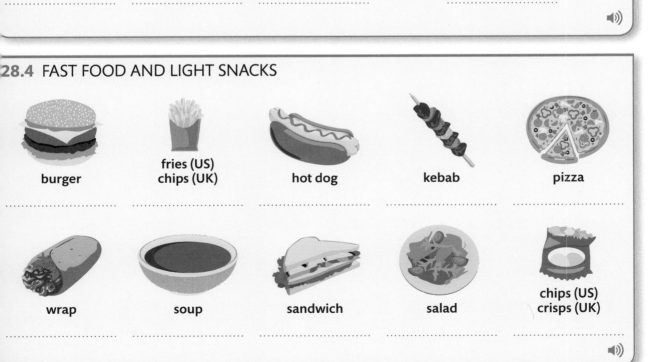

burger

fries (US)
chips (UK)

hot dog

kebab

pizza

wrap

soup

sandwich

salad

chips (US)
crisps (UK)

Aa 28.5 LOOK AT THE PICTURES BELOW, THEN WRITE THE ANSWERS UNDER THE CORRECT HEADING

MEAT	SEAFOOD	DAIRY	FAST FOOD
sausages			

Aa 28.6 FIND FIVE MORE WORDS IN THE GRID THAT MATCH THE PICTURES

```
S G C R E A M A C B
T A M A C K E R E L
O C T O P U S M D K
P S X O J E R T I B
L O B C X W G V S E
E U D W Q R H A D E
R P B A C O N O Z F
```

Aa 28.7 MATCH THE PICTURES TO THE CORRECT WORDS

soup

1 → sandwich

2 wrap

3 scrambled eggs

4 cottage cheese

5 salad

6 chips (US) crisps (UK)

7 burger

8 scallops

28.8 LISTEN TO THE AUDIO, THEN NUMBER THE PICTURES IN THE ORDER YOU HEAR THEM

A ☐   B ☐

C ☐ 1   D ☐

E ☐   F ☐

G ☐   H ☐

I ☐   J ☐

121

29 Fruit and nuts

29.1 FRUIT

apple

orange

banana

strawberries

mango

pineapple

lemon

melon

raspberries

peach

pear

grapes

mandarin

grapefruit

lime

nectarine

apricot

plum

cherries

blackberries

blueberries

cranberries

blackcurrants

watermelon

papaya

guava   starfruit   lychees   coconut   passion fruit

pomegranate   kiwi fruit   redcurrants   gooseberries   quince

29.2 NUTS AND DRIED FRUIT

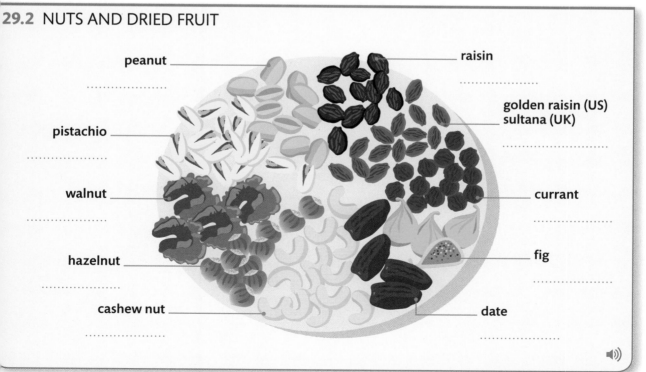

peanut

raisin

golden raisin (US)
sultana (UK)

pistachio

walnut

currant

hazelnut

fig

cashew nut

date

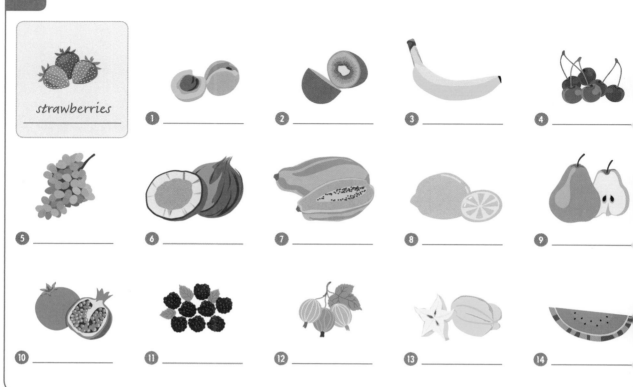

strawberries

1 _____

2 _____

3 _____

4 _____

5 _____

6 _____

7 _____

8 _____

9 _____

10 _____

11 _____

12 _____

13 _____

14 _____

Aa 29.4 LOOK AT THE PICTURE AND WRITE THE CORRECT WORD FOR EACH LABEL

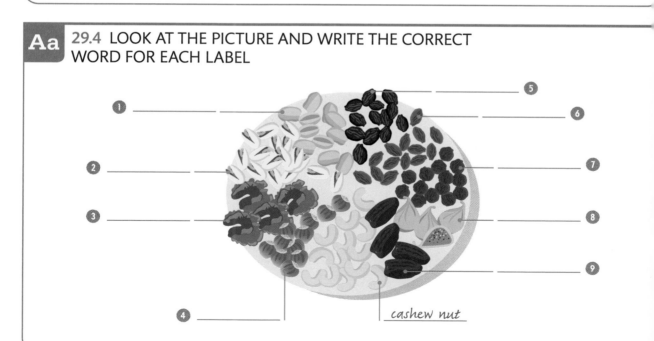

1 _____

2 _____

3 _____

4 _____

5 _____

6 _____

7 _____

8 _____

9 _____

cashew nut

Aa 29.5 CIRCLE THE WORD THAT DOES NOT BELONG IN EACH LIST

walnut	~~pork~~	cashew nut

1. fries   blackcurrants   cranberries
2. hazelnut   quince   peanut
3. guava   gooseberries   salmon
4. pistachio   pomegranate   redcurrants

5. pineapple   peach   yolk
6. soup   plum   watermelon
7. lamb   fig   date
8. raisin   pizza   currant

29.6 LISTEN TO THE AUDIO, THEN NUMBER THE PICTURES IN THE ORDER YOU HEAR THEM

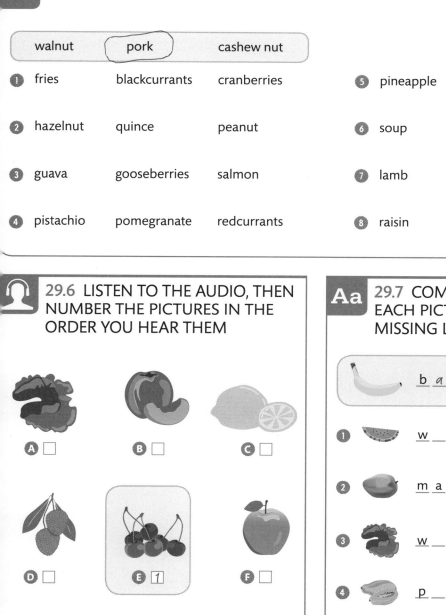

A ☐   B ☐   C ☐

D ☐   E 1   F ☐

G ☐   H ☐   I ☐

Aa 29.7 COMPLETE THE WORD FOR EACH PICTURE, FILLING IN THE MISSING LETTERS

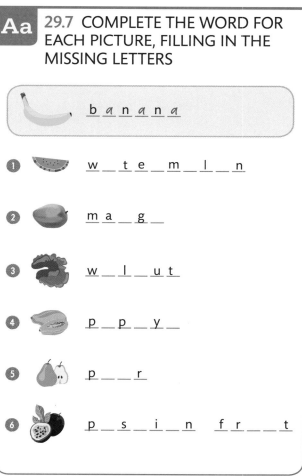

b a n a n a

1. w _ t e _ m _ l _ n
2. m a _ g _
3. w _ l _ u t
4. p _ p _ y _
5. p _ _ r
6. p _ s _ i _ n   f r _ _ t

30.1 VEGETABLES

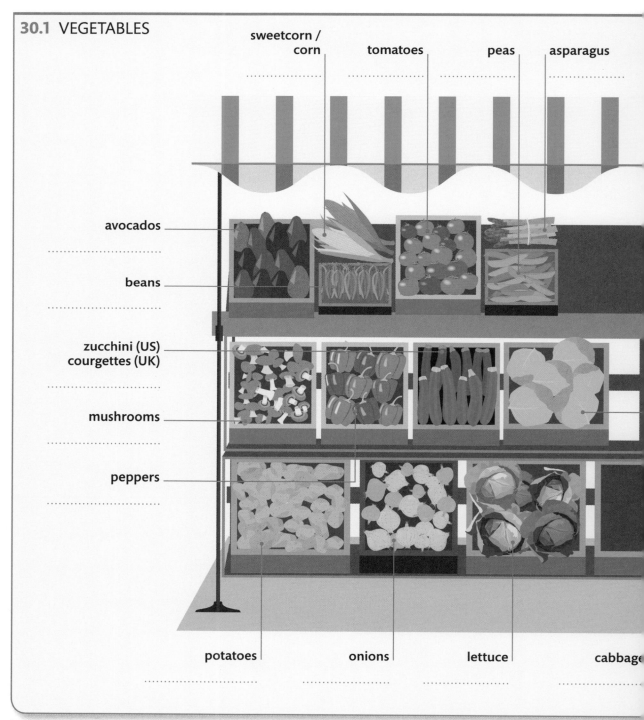

sweetcorn / corn

tomatoes

peas

asparagus

avocados

beans

zucchini (US) courgettes (UK)

mushrooms

peppers

potatoes

onions

lettuce

cabbage

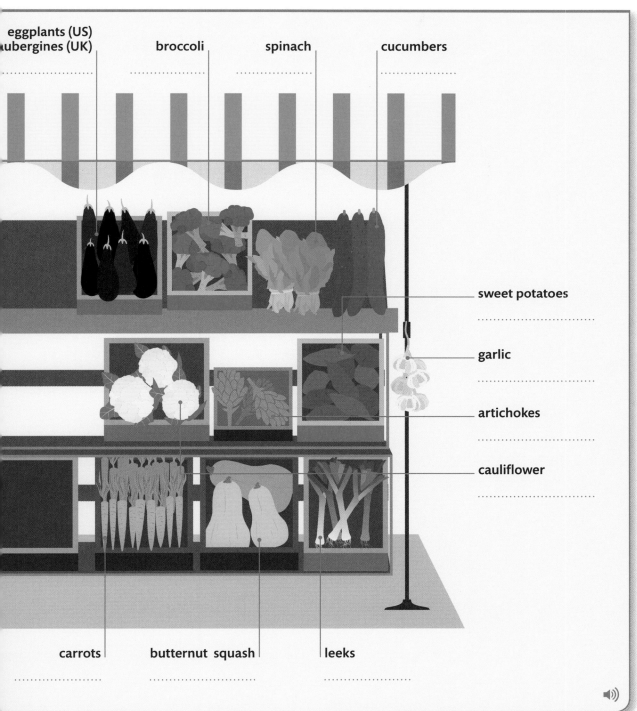

eggplants (US)
aubergines (UK)

broccoli

spinach

cucumbers

sweet potatoes

garlic

artichokes

cauliflower

carrots

butternut squash

leeks

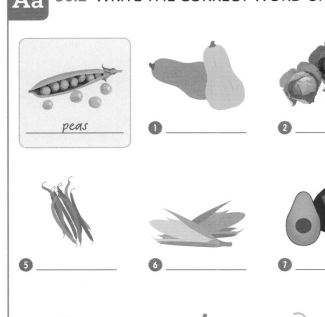

_____ peas

1  _____

2 _____

3 _____

4  _____

5  _____

6 _____

7  _____

8  _____

9 _____

10 _____

11 _____

12  _____

13 _____

14 _____

Aa 30.3 MARK THE BEGINNING AND ENDING OF EACH WORD IN THE CHAIN OF LETTERS, THEN WRITE THE WORDS YOU FIND

garlic|artichokesspinachmushroomscauliflowercucumberseggplantsasparagussweetcorn

_____ garlic

1 _____

2 _____

3 _____

4 _____

5 _____

6 _____

7 _____

8 _____

30.4 LISTEN TO THE AUDIO AND MARK THE CORRECT PICTURE FOR EACH WORD YOU HEAR

A ☐   B ☑   C ☐

③ A ☐   B ☐   C ☐

① A ☐   B ☐   C ☐

④ A ☐   B ☐   C ☐

② A ☐   B ☐   C ☐

⑤ A ☐   B ☐   C ☐

30.5 COMPLETE THE WORD FOR EACH PICTURE, FILLING IN THE MISSING LETTERS

   p o t a t o e s

①   c _ _ b _ g _

②   _ o m _ _ o _ _

③   l _ _ k _

④   c _ _ u _ b _ r _

⑤   _ _ t _ _ r n _ t _ s _ _ a _ h

⑥   m _ s h _ _ o _ _

⑦   _ p _ _ a _ h

⑧   a _ _ _ _ c h _ k _ _ _

⑨   s _ e _ t _ _ o t _ _ o _ _

31.1 BREAD, PASTA, AND DESSERTS

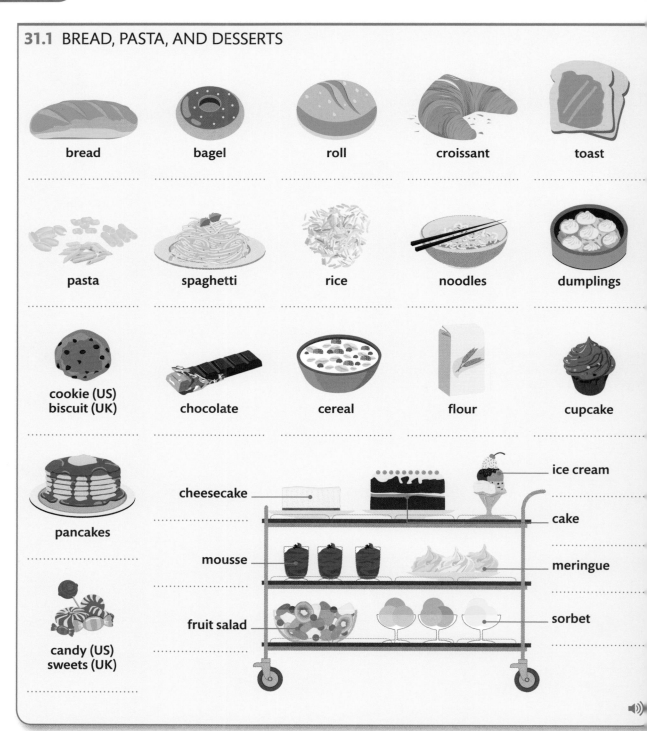

bread

bagel

roll

croissant

toast

pasta

spaghetti

rice

noodles

dumplings

cookie (US)
biscuit (UK)

chocolate

cereal

flour

cupcake

pancakes

cheesecake

ice cream

cake

mousse

meringue

candy (US)
sweets (UK)

fruit salad

sorbet

31.2 FLAVORINGS AND CONDIMENTS

sugar

salt

pepper

oil

vinegar

ginger

jam

marmalade

honey

mayonnaise

ketchup

mustard

chutney

peanut butter

chili flakes (US)
chilli flakes (UK)

spices

herbs

parsley

basil

mint

soy sauce

cilantro (US)
coriander (UK)

chives

dill

lemongrass

31.3 MARK THE CORRECT PICTURE FOR EACH WORD

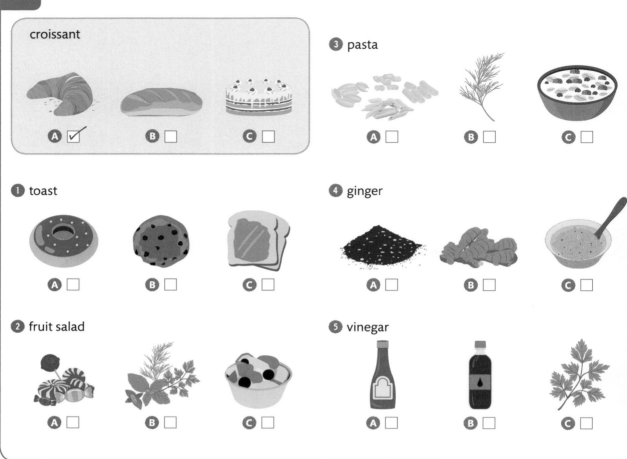

croissant

A ✓ B ☐ C ☐

3 pasta

A ☐ B ☐ C ☐

1 toast

A ☐ B ☐ C ☐

4 ginger

A ☐ B ☐ C ☐

2 fruit salad

A ☐ B ☐ C ☐

5 vinegar

A ☐ B ☐ C ☐

31.4 MATCH THE PICTURES TO THE CORRECT WORDS

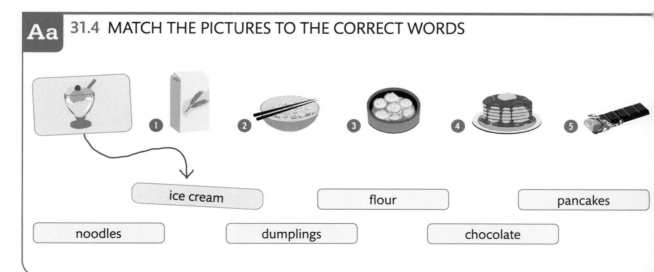

1 2 3 4 5

ice cream

flour

pancakes

noodles

dumplings

chocolate

31.5 LISTEN TO THE AUDIO AND WRITE THE WORD THAT IS SHOWN IN EACH PICTURE

cookie

1 _____

2 _____

3 _____

4 _____

5 _____

6 _____

7 _____

8 _____

9 _____

10 _____

11 _____

12 _____

13 _____

14 _____

15 _____

16 _____

17 _____

31.6 REWRITE THE WORDS, CORRECTING THE SPELLINGS

suger
sugar

1 marmelaid
_____

2 spageti
_____

3 role
_____

4 mayonais
_____

5 cuppcake
_____

6 cheelie flakes
_____

7 merange
_____

32 Drinking and eating

32.1 DRINKS

coffee	tea	hot chocolate	herbal tea	juice
water	ice tea	lemonade	orangeade	cola
beer	wine	milkshake	smoothie	sports drink / energy drink

32.2 FOOD AND DRINK CONTAINERS

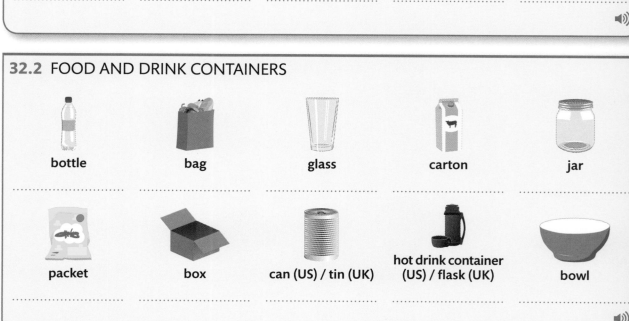

bottle	bag	glass	carton	jar
packet	box	can (US) / tin (UK)	hot drink container (US) / flask (UK)	bowl

32.3 FOOD AND DRINK: ADJECTIVES

sweet

savory (US)
savoury (UK)

tasty

iced / chilled

salty

bitter

spicy / hot

fresh

off / gone off

strong

sour

carbonated /
sparkling

non-carbonated /
still

delicious

disgusting

32.4 EATING AND DRINKING

to eat

to dine

to chew

to taste

to nibble

to bite

to swallow

to drink

to sip

to gulp

Aa 32.5 MATCH THE WORDS TO THE CORRECT PICTURES

lemonade

1. wine
2. ice tea
3. smoothie
4. hot chocolate
5. cola
6. coffee
7. tea
8. water
9. herbal tea

Aa 32.6 FILL IN THE MISSING LETTERS FOR EACH WORD

s a l t y

1. s _ _ r _ n _
2. _ o n _ _ _ f _
3. s _ _ r
4. f _ _ s _
5. i _ _ d
6. s w _ _ t
7. t _ s _ _
8. d _ _ l _ _ c _ _ _ _ s
9. s _ v _ r _
10. _ i _ _ e _
11. d _ _ g _ s _ _ n _
12. _ p _ c _

32.7 LISTEN TO THE AUDIO AND MARK THE CORRECT PICTURE FOR EACH WORD YOU HEAR

A ☐ B ☑ C ☐

4 A ☐ B ☐ C ☐

1 A ☐ B ☐ C ☐

5 A ☐ B ☐ C ☐

2 A ☐ B ☐ C ☐

6 A ☐ B ☐ C ☐

3 A ☐ B ☐ C ☐

7 A ☐ B ☐ C ☐

 ## 32.8 WRITE THE CORRECT VERB UNDER EACH PICTURE

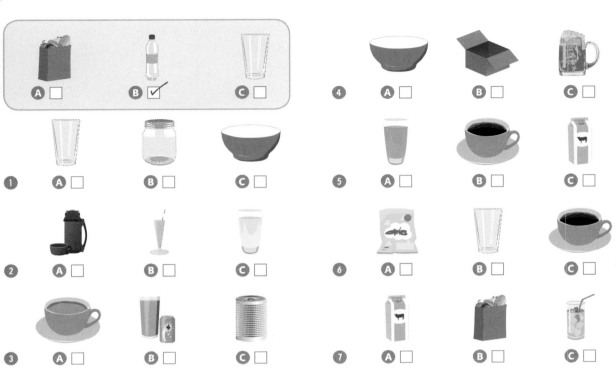

to sip

1 _____

2 _____

3 _____

4 _____

5 _____

6 _____

7 _____

8 _____

9 _____

33.1 MEALS

 breakfast

 brunch

 lunch

 dinner

 snack

33.2 FOOD PREPARATION

 to broil (US) to grill (UK)

 to bake

 to roast

 to boil

  to fry

 to peel

 to slice

 to grate

 to pour

 to mix

 to add

 to whisk

 to roll

 to stir

 to simmer

 to poach

 to mash

 to chop

 to cut

 to mince

33.3 EATING OUT: NOUNS

café

bar

restaurant

food stall

napkin

fast food

chef

waiter

waitress

menu

appetizer (US)
starter (UK)

entrée (US)
main course (UK)

dessert /
pudding (UK)

buffet

fixed menu (US)
set menu (UK)

side / side order

specials

check (US)
bill (UK)

service charge

tip

33.4 EATING OUT: VERBS

to make a
reservation

to order

to take out (US)
to take away (UK)

to pay separately

to split the check
(US) / bill (UK)

Aa 33.5 MARK THE CORRECT VERB FOR THE ACTIVITY IN EACH PICTURE

to cut ☐
to fry ☐
to boil ☑

① to peel ☐
to whisk ☐
to simmer ☐

② to roast ☐
to bake ☐
to mince ☐

③ to roll ☐
to poach ☐
to simmer ☐

④ to mash ☐
to chop ☐
to stir ☐

⑤ to slice ☐
to grate ☐
to add ☐

⑥ to broil ☐
to chop ☐
to bake ☐

⑦ to mix ☐
to fry ☐
to add ☐

⑧ to peel ☐
to pour ☐
to mix ☐

⑨ to roll ☐
to whisk ☐
to cut ☐

Aa 33.6 LOOK AT THE PICTURE CLUES AND WRITE THE ANSWERS IN THE CORRECT PLACES ON THE GRID

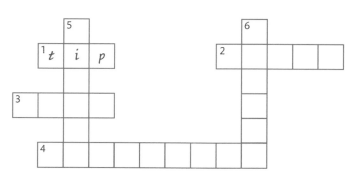

Grid:
¹t i p
3
4

Aa 33.7 WRITE THE CORRECT WORD UNDER EACH PICTURE

waiter

1 _____

2 _____

3 _____

4 _____

5 _____

6 _____

7 _____

8 _____

9 _____

10 _____

FIXED MENU
$9

11 _____

12 _____

13 _____

14 _____

🎧 33.8 LISTEN TO THE AUDIO, THEN NUMBER THE PICTURES IN THE ORDER YOU HEAR THEM

A ☐

B ☐

C 1

D ☐

E ☐

F ☐

G ☐

H ☐

I ☐

J ☐

K ☐

L ☐

Specials

M ☐

N ☐

O ☐

141

34 Jobs

waiter

waitress

chef

butcher

farmer

scientist

hairdresser /
stylist

gardener

cleaner / janitor

train driver

taxi driver

librarian

lawyer

teacher

judge

police officer

firefighter

security guard

driver

electrician

construction
worker

plumber

engineer

architect

mechanic

 businessman

 businesswoman

 sales assistant

 receptionist

 personal assistant / PA

 surgeon

 doctor

 nurse

 dentist

 paramedic

 psychologist

 child-care provider

 vet

 pilot

 flight attendant

 travel agent

 tour guide

 journalist

 writer

 designer

 photographer

 actor

 artist

 musician

 fashion designer

143

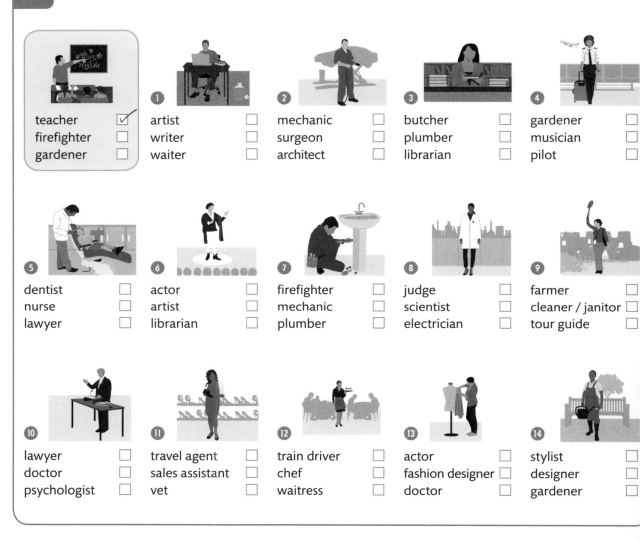

Aa 34.2 MARK THE CORRECT JOB FOR THE PERSON IN EACH PICTURE

teacher ✓
firefighter ☐
gardener ☐

1
artist ☐
writer ☐
waiter ☐

2
mechanic ☐
surgeon ☐
architect ☐

3
butcher ☐
plumber ☐
librarian ☐

4
gardener ☐
musician ☐
pilot ☐

5
dentist ☐
nurse ☐
lawyer ☐

6
actor ☐
artist ☐
librarian ☐

7
firefighter ☐
mechanic ☐
plumber ☐

8
judge ☐
scientist ☐
electrician ☐

9
farmer ☐
cleaner / janitor ☐
tour guide ☐

10
lawyer ☐
doctor ☐
psychologist ☐

11
travel agent ☐
sales assistant ☐
vet ☐

12
train driver ☐
chef ☐
waitress ☐

13
actor ☐
fashion designer ☐
doctor ☐

14
stylist ☐
designer ☐
gardener ☐

Aa 34.3 MARK THE BEGINNING AND ENDING OF EACH WORD IN THE CHAIN OF LETTERS

psychologistjudgedriverphotographerparamedicbusinessmanjournalistengineerscientist

34.4 MATCH THE WORDS TO THE CORRECT PICTURES

doctor

② chef

④ security guard

① firefighter

③ police officer

⑤ journalist

A   B   C   D   E

34.5 CIRCLE THE WORD THAT DOES NOT BELONG IN EACH LIST

journalist	dentist	writer
① flight attendant	pilot	lawyer
② doctor	teacher	paramedic
③ musician	actor	scientist
④ artist	plumber	mechanic
⑤ farmer	gardener	train driver
⑥ police officer	butcher	firefighter
⑦ scientist	engineer	librarian
⑧ mechanic	travel agent	tour guide
⑨ chef	surgeon	nurse
⑩ sales assistant	psychologist	butcher
⑪ waitress	designer	chef
⑫ doctor	vet	architect

34.6 LISTEN TO THE AUDIO AND CIRCLE THE WORDS YOU HEAR

actor	artist	architect
① vet	chef	judge
② businessman	nurse	gardener
③ doctor	dentist	driver
④ surgeon	scientist	psychologist
⑤ writer	waitress	waiter
⑥ nurse	musician	judge
⑦ teacher	taxi driver	designer
⑧ artist	architect	actor
⑨ plumber	photographer	psychologist
⑩ lawyer	farmer	librarian
⑪ firefighter	taxi driver	train driver

35 Working conditions

35.1 EMPLOYMENT

company

headquarters

staff

employer

employee

manager

permanent

temporary

co-worker / colleague

assistant

intern

apprentice

annual vacation (US) / leave (UK)

nine-to-five job

client

35.2 VERBS

to work part-time

to work full-time

to work from home

to work shifts

to have a day off

to retire

to get fired

to earn

to call in sick

to go on maternity leave

35.3 PAY AND CONDITIONS

The store pays its staff an hourly rate of $15.

an hourly rate
[an amount of money paid per hour]

Benefits include gym membership and health insurance.

benefits
[extras given to employees in addition to their usual pay]

My new job is much more interesting, but I had to take a pay cut.

a pay cut
[a reduction in pay]

Our profits are up, so your wages will increase by $100 per week.

wages
[an amount of money paid per week or month]

My boss is really pleased with my work, so I'm hoping to get a raise next year.

a raise (US) / a pay rise (UK)
[an increase in pay]

I'm looking for a job with a salary of at least $25,000.

a salary
[a fixed, regular payment, often expressed as an annual sum]

My bonus this year was $1,000, so I'm going to go on vacation.

a bonus
[money added to a person's salary as a reward for good performance]

I got a promotion after working for the company for only six months.

a promotion
[a new job at the same company that is more senior or better paid]

We will pay overtime to all staff who are willing to work weekends.

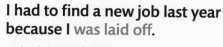

overtime
[additional pay for extra hours worked]

I had to find a new job last year because I was laid off.

to be laid off (US) / made redundant (UK)
[to lose your job because it is no longer necessary]

Aa 35.4 FIND SEVEN MORE WORDS IN THE GRID THAT MATCH THE PICTURES

```
S D M Y U I R A C S A H A
T A P P R E N T I C E P Q
Y S T I M T A O T A A E T
B L I N T E R N E P S N E
C O L L E A G U E L S C M
L E Y E P A O C A R I I P
I M A N A G E R Q B S S L
E Y Q A B F R S T H T V O
N M P L N Y T T A P A D Y
T J S X S M T A E N I E
P R Z W T B M F U L T S E
L F E R G A V F I M F W X
```

1

2 3

4 5

6 7

Aa 35.5 WRITE THE CORRECT VERB UNDER EACH PICTURE

to retire

1 _____

2 _____

3 _____

4 _____

5 _____

6 _____

7 _____

8 _____

9 _____

148

35.6 LISTEN TO THE AUDIO AND COMPLETE THE SENTENCES THAT DESCRIBE EACH PICTURE

 My boss is really pleased with my work, so I'm hoping to get a _raise_ next year.

 4 _____ include gym membership and health insurance.

 1 The store pays its staff an _____ of $15.

 5 My _____ this year was $1,000, so I'm going to go on vacation.

 2 We will pay _____ to all staff who are willing to work weekends.

6 I had to find a new job last year because I _____.

 3 I'm looking for a job with a _____ of at least $25,000.

 7 I got a _____ after working for the company for only six months.

35.7 WRITE THE CORRECT WORD OR PHRASE NEXT TO ITS DEFINITION, FILLING IN THE MISSING LETTERS

additional pay for extra hours worked	=	o v e r t i m e
1 extras given to employees in addition to their usual pay	=	b _ n _ f _ _ s
2 an amount of money paid per week or month	=	w _ _ _ _ s
3 a reduction in pay	=	a p _ _ _ c _ _ _
4 an increase in pay	=	a r _ _ s _
5 an amount of money paid per hour	=	a n h _ _ _ _ _ _ _ _ _ t _

36 Industries and departments

36.1 INDUSTRIES

education

healthcare

catering / food

chemical

construction

agriculture / farming

energy

electronics

entertainment

fashion

finance

fishing

hospitality

journalism

manufacturing

advertising

mining

petroleum engineering

pharmaceutical

real estate (US) property (UK)

recycling

shipping

tourism

transportation

aerospace

Administration

[deals with organization and internal and external communication]

Production

[ensures that all manufacturing stages run smoothly]

Research and Development (R&D)

[researches and develops future products for a company]

Purchasing

[buys goods and raw materials for manufacturers and other companies]

Human Resources (HR)

[deals with employee relations and matters such as hiring staff]

Sales

[sells products to buyers and outside markets]

Accounts / Finance

[deals with money matters, from paying bills to projecting sales]

Facilities / Office Services

[carries out cleaning, maintenance, and building operation services]

Marketing

[promotes products for companies to the market]

Legal

[ensures that all contracts and company activities are legal]

Public Relations (PR)

[presents and maintains a positive public image for a company]

Information Technology (IT)

[sets up and maintains all technological systems in an organization]

Aa 36.3 MATCH THE WORDS TO THE CORRECT PICTURES

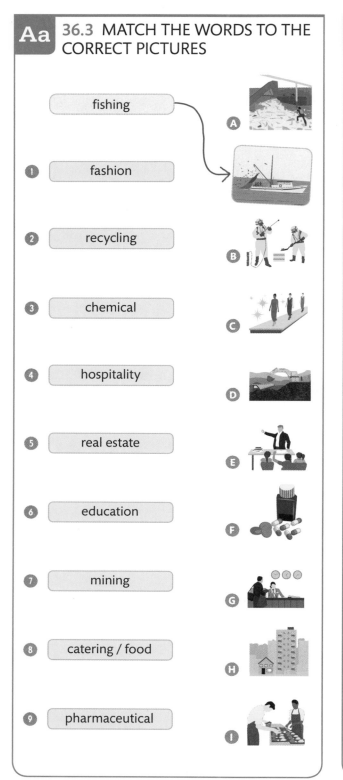

fishing —  **A**

1 fashion → **A** (image)

2 recycling — **B**

3 chemical — **C**

4 hospitality — **D**

5 real estate — **E**

6 education — **F**

7 mining — **G**

8 catering / food — **H**

9 pharmaceutical — **I**

Aa 36.4 COMPLETE THE WORD FOR EACH PICTURE, FILLING IN THE MISSING LETTERS

 e l e c t r o n i c s

1  h _ _ l t h c _ r _

2 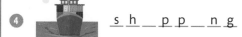 _ g r _ c _ l t _ r _

3  f _ n _ n c _

4  s h _ p p _ n g

5  _ n _ r g y

6  _ d v _ r t _ s _ n g

7 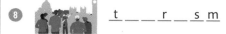 j _ _ r n _ l _ s m

8  t _ _ r _ s m

9 _ _ r _ s p _ c _

36.5 LISTEN TO THE AUDIO, THEN NUMBER THE PICTURES IN THE ORDER THEY ARE MENTIONED

A ☐

B ☐

C ☐

D ☐

E ☐

F 1

G ☐

H ☐

I ☐

J ☐

K ☐

L ☐

36.6 WRITE THE NAME OF THE DEPARTMENT NEXT TO ITS DEFINITION

ensures that all manufacturing stages run smoothly = *Production*

1 deals with employee relations and matters such as hiring staff = _____

2 deals with money matters, from paying bills to projecting sales = _____

3 ensures that all contracts and company activities are legal = _____

4 deals with organization and internal and external communication = _____

5 presents and maintains a positive public image for a company = _____

6 sells products to buyers and outside markets = _____

7 promotes products for companies to the market = _____

37 Office equipment

37.1 IN THE OFFICE

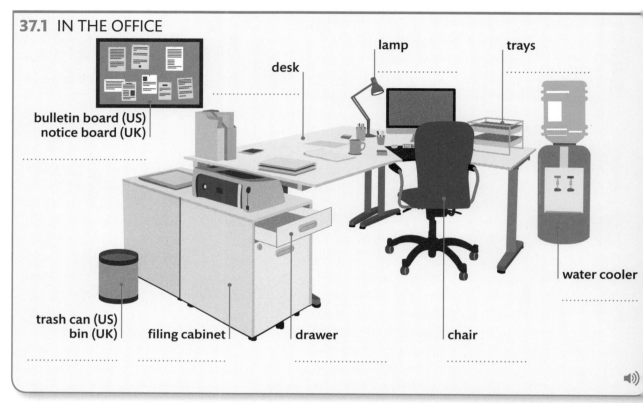

bulletin board (US)
notice board (UK)

desk

lamp

trays

water cooler

trash can (US)
bin (UK)

filing cabinet

drawer

chair

37.2 EQUIPMENT

photocopier

telephone / phone

printer

projector

shredder

scanner

computer

laptop

cell phone (US)
mobile phone (UK)

headset

37.3 STATIONERY

letter

envelope

calendar

planner (US)
diary (UK)

clipboard

files / folders

hole punch

stapler

staples

pencil sharpener

pencil

pen

highlighter

adhesive tape

notepad

paper clips

eraser (US)
rubber (UK)

ruler

paper

correction fluid

sticky notes

rubber bands

binder clip

thumbtack (US)
drawing pin (UK)

scissors

155

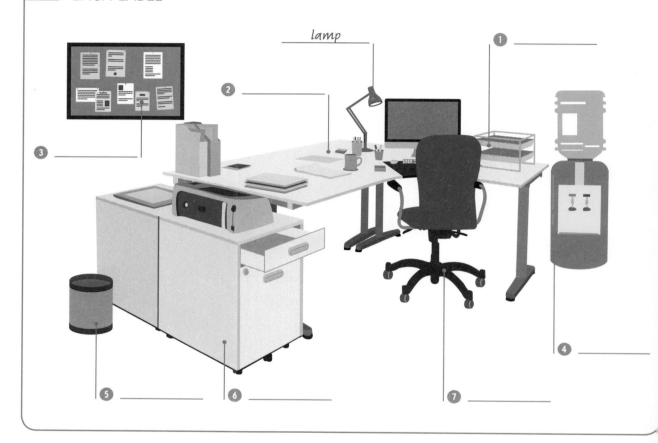

Aa **37.4** LOOK AT THE PICTURE AND WRITE THE CORRECT WORD FOR EACH LABEL

lamp

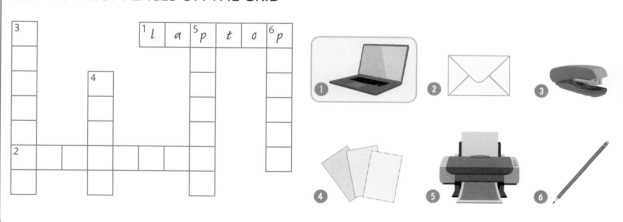

Aa **37.5** LOOK AT THE PICTURE CLUES AND WRITE THE ANSWERS IN THE CORRECT PLACES ON THE GRID

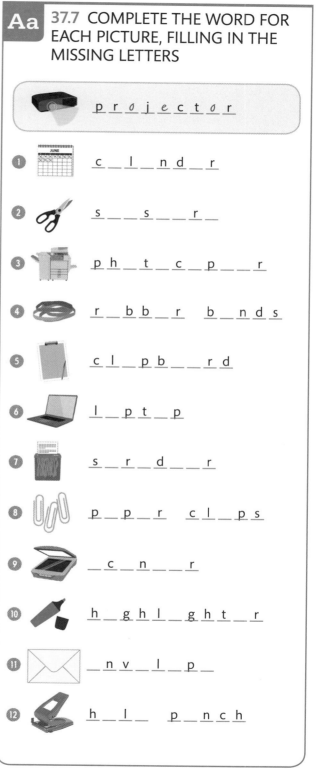

p r o j e c t o r

1. c _ l _ n d _ r
2. s _ _ s _ _ r _
3. p h _ t _ c _ p _ _ r
4. r _ b b _ r _ b _ n d s
5. c l _ p b _ _ r d
6. l _ p t _ p
7. s _ r _ d _ _ r
8. p _ p _ r _ c l _ p s
9. _ c _ n _ _ r
10. h _ g h l _ g h t _ _ r
11. _ n v _ l _ p _
12. h _ l _ _ p _ n c h

38.1 MONEY

bills (US)
notes (UK)

coins

wallet

wallet (US)
purse (UK)

credit card

debit card

cash machine /
ATM

bank

bank statement

online banking

mobile banking

receipt

currency

cash register (US)
till (UK)

invoice

check (US)
cheque (UK)

mortgage

bank loan

PIN

stock exchange

interest rate

to withdraw
money

to change money

to transfer money

to save

Our income fell after we lost an important client.

income
[money coming into a business]

If we can't sell more products, we will get into debt.

to get into debt
[to get into a situation where you owe people money]

We have a large marketing budget, so there's no excuse for poor sales.

a budget
[the amount of money that is available to spend on something]

We've made a loss because we haven't sold any pineapples.

to make a loss
[to lose money by spending more than you earn]

The bank charges $10 per month for overdrafts.

an overdraft
[extra money the bank allows you to spend]

The exchange rate has made trips to some countries more expensive.

the exchange rate
[the amount of one currency that you get when you change it for another]

We have to sell these cars if we're going to break even.

to break even
[to earn just enough to cover the costs of producing a product]

The store has gone out of business because most people download movies now.

to go out of business
[to no longer be able to exist as a business]

The expenditure on these laptops was huge, but now we can work from home.

expenditure / outlay
[an amount of money spent]

We might lose our jobs because of the economic downturn.

an economic downturn
[a major decline in economic activity]

Aa 38.3 MARK THE CORRECT WORD FOR EACH PICTURE

Example
- receipt ✓
- PIN ☐
- bank ☐

1
- currency ☐
- mortgage ☐
- purse ☐

2
- online banking ☐
- cash machine ☐
- invoice ☐

3
- bank loan ☐
- stock exchange ☐
- coins ☐

4
- credit card ☐
- bank ☐
- check ☐

5
- stock exchange ☐
- interest rate ☐
- bills ☐

6
- mortgage ☐
- bank statement ☐
- receipt ☐

7
- interest rate ☐
- to change money ☐
- currency ☐

8
- to save ☐
- mobile banking ☐
- bank loan ☐

9
- mobile banking ☐
- stock exchange ☐
- PIN ☐

10
- mobile banking ☐
- credit card ☐
- cash register ☐

11
- wallet ☐
- invoice ☐
- coins ☐

12
- mortgage ☐
- stock exchange ☐
- bank ☐

13
- bank loan ☐
- credit card ☐
- cash register ☐

14
- coins ☐
- invoice ☐
- bills ☐

Aa 38.4 MARK THE BEGINNING AND ENDING OF EACH WORD IN THE CHAIN OF LETTERS

mortgage/cashmachineinvoicewalletcoinsbankreceiptcheckmobilebankingstockexchange

38.5 MARK THE SENTENCES THAT ARE CORRECT

We've made a loss because we haven't sold any pineapples. ☑
We've made a lose because we haven't sold any pineapples. ☐

① The store has gone out for business because most people download movies now. ☐
The store has gone out of business because most people download movies now. ☐

② The bank charges $10 per month for underdrafts. ☐
The bank charges $10 per month for overdrafts. ☐

③ The exchange rate has made trips to some countries more expensive. ☐
The exchange rata has made trips to some countries more expensive. ☐

④ If we can't sell more products, we will get into debit. ☐
If we can't sell more products, we will get into debt. ☐

⑤ Our income fell after we lost an important client. ☐
Our incomings fell after we lost an important client. ☐

38.6 LISTEN TO THE AUDIO AND MARK THE CORRECT PICTURE FOR EACH WORD YOU HEAR

Ⓐ ☑   Ⓑ ☐   Ⓒ ☐

③ Ⓐ ☐   Ⓑ ☐   Ⓒ ☐

① Ⓐ ☐   Ⓑ ☐   Ⓒ ☐

④ Ⓐ ☐   Ⓑ ☐   Ⓒ ☐

② Ⓐ ☐   Ⓑ ☐   Ⓒ ☐

⑤ Ⓐ ☐   Ⓑ ☐   Ⓒ ☐

39.1 USEFUL EXPRESSIONS

I don't work a nine-to-five job because I have two young children.

a nine-to-five
[a job with regular hours]

It's very important to create a positive working environment.

a working environment
[the conditions in which you work]

All our employees are fully trained and have hands-on experience.

hands-on experience
[knowledge and skill gained through doing something yourself]

Elena's chosen career path involves a lot of travel.

a career path
[progression within a profession, in a job, or through a series of jobs]

Bruno's career took off after he won an important new client.

to take off
[to suddenly become more successful]

I have held a position in management for five years.

to hold a position
[to have a job]

My boss started working here at the bottom of the career ladder.

the bottom of the career ladder
[a position with the lowest level of responsibility or pay]

Lucas has been stuck in a dead-end job for two years.

a dead-end job
[a position without many prospects for promotion]

Some of the factory workers were laid off after our profits fell.

to be laid off / made redundant (UK)
[to lose your job because the company can no longer give you work]

Gavin was fired because he was caught stealing from the warehouse.

to be fired
[to be forced to leave your job for doing something wrong]

I'm stepping down from this job because I need more training.

step down
[stop doing a job voluntarily]

I need to tackle this problem head-on or it will get worse.

to tackle something head-on
[to deal with something directly]

We've set our sights on winning more industry awards.

set your sights on something
[aim to achieve a particular goal]

If they don't stop arguing, they'll never get ahead in this company.

to get ahead
[to make more progress than others]

We've taken on three new employees for the busy summer months.

take someone on / take on someone
[employ someone]

Can I call you back later? I'm snowed under right now.

snowed under
[very busy with too much work]

People who work in childcare have their hands full all day.

have your hands full
[be busy with a task or many tasks]

Don't disturb Harry today! He's up to his eyeballs with work.

up to your eyeballs / ears (UK)
[extremely busy]

We always goes the extra mile to deliver our products on time.

go the extra mile
[do more than you are required to do]

Working well with clients involves a lot of give and take.

give and take
[compromise]

Aa 39.2 WRITE THE CORRECT PHRASE NEXT TO ITS DEFINITION, FILLING IN THE MISSING LETTERS

a job with regular hours	=	a n i n e-t o-f i v e

1 to make more progress than others = t _ _ g _ _ _ a _ _ _ _ _

2 to suddenly become more successful = t _ _ t _ _ _ _ o _

3 to employ someone = t _ _ t _ _ _ _ s _ _ _ _ _ _ _ o _ _

4 compromise = g _ _ _ _ a _ _ t _ _ _ _

5 to stop doing a job voluntarily = t _ _ s _ _ _ _ d _ _ _

39.3 LISTEN TO THE AUDIO AND COMPLETE THE SENTENCES THAT DESCRIBE EACH PICTURE

It's very important to create a positive *working environment*.

1 All our employees are fully trained and have _____.

2 Gavin _____ because he was caught stealing from the warehouse.

3 Bruno's career _____ after he won an important new client.

4 People who work in childcare _____ _____ all day.

5 We've _____ _____ winning more industry awards.

6 I need to _____ _____ or it will get worse.

7 Working well with clients involves a lot of _____.

Aa 39.4 FILL IN THE GAPS, PUTTING THE WORDS IN THE CORRECT ORDER

position   held   in   a

I have _held_ _a_ _position_ _in_ management for five years.

of   career   the   at   bottom   the

1 My boss started working here _____ _____ _____ _____ _____ _____ ladder.

a   in   job   dead   -end   stuck

2 Lucas has been _____ _____ _____ _____ _____ _____ for two years.

job   five   -to-   nine   a

3 I don't work _____ _____ _____ _____ _____ because I have two young children.

job   down   stepping   this   from

4 I'm _____ _____ _____ _____ _____ because I need more training.

Aa 39.5 CROSS OUT THE INCORRECT WORD IN EACH SENTENCE

Don't disturb Harry today! He's up to his eyeballs / ~~nose~~ with work.

1 Elena's chosen career path / route involves a lot of travel.

2 Can I call you back later? I'm rained / snowed under right now.

3 Clive always goes the extra inch / mile to deliver our products on time.

4 Some of the factory workers were laid off / up after our profits fell.

40 Meeting and presenting

40.1 USEFUL EXPRESSIONS

Carla will attend the team meeting tomorrow afternoon.

to attend a meeting
[to go to a meeting]

Emir is giving a presentation on his team's latest research.

to give a presentation
[to present a formal talk to an audience]

Our poor sales figures will be on the agenda today.

on the agenda
[included in a list of things to discuss]

Stefan is on vacation and will be absent from this meeting.

absent
[not present]

We're having a conference call with our clients in Japan this morning.

a conference call
[a telephone call with a number of people at the same time]

Deepak has been promoted, so now he's on the board of directors.

the board of directors
[a group of people who manage a business or organization]

Let me see a show of hands. How many of you agree with my proposal?

a show of hands
[a vote made by raising hands in the air to show agreement]

We reached a unanimous agreement on the budget.

a unanimous agreement
[when everyone agrees]

I'll talk through the report and then I'll take questions.

to take questions
[to answer questions]

Cameron is going to take minutes during our finance meeting.

to take minutes
[to write a record of what is said during a meeting]

We easily reached a consensus on the best poster design.

to reach a consensus
[to come to an agreement about an issue]

We've gone through the agenda. Is there any other business?

any other business (AOB)
[any matter discussed in a meeting that is not on the agenda]

The main objective of this meeting is to discuss product ideas.

the main objective
[the primary aim]

This is my strategy for selling more products overseas.

strategy
[a plan for achieving a particular goal]

There were three clear action points arising from today's meeting.

action points
[proposals for specific action to be taken]

To sum up, sales of our older products have fallen this year.

to sum up
[to give a brief summary]

Ellen has reviewed the minutes from our meeting last week.

to review the minutes
[to look again at the written record of a past meeting]

Let's wrap up this meeting. It's almost one o'clock.

to wrap up
[to conclude or finish something]

I'm sorry to interrupt, but your client is waiting in reception.

to interrupt
[to disturb a meeting or say something before someone else has finished speaking]

We can't discuss the new computer system because we've run out of time.

to run out of time
[to have no time left for something]

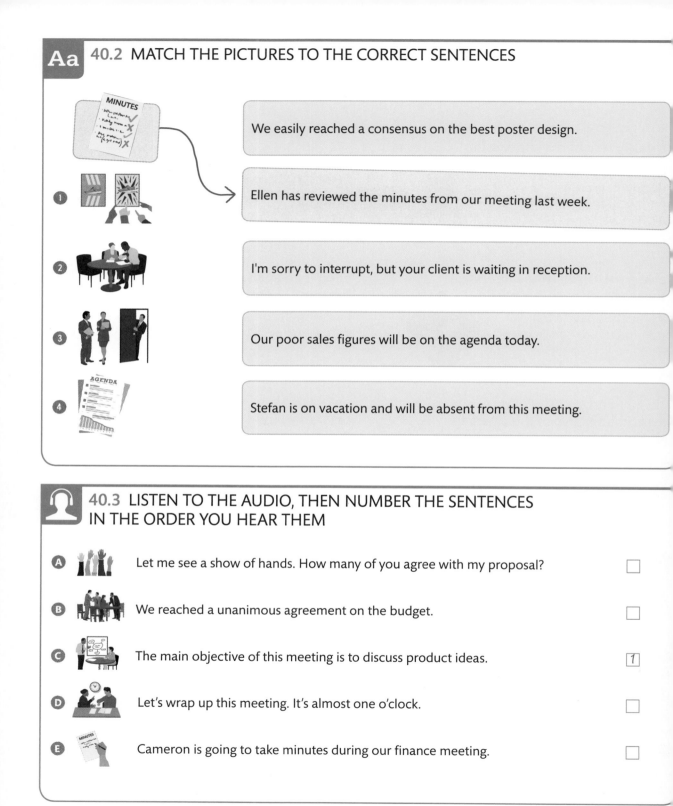

Aa 40.2 MATCH THE PICTURES TO THE CORRECT SENTENCES

We easily reached a consensus on the best poster design.

Ellen has reviewed the minutes from our meeting last week.

I'm sorry to interrupt, but your client is waiting in reception.

Our poor sales figures will be on the agenda today.

Stefan is on vacation and will be absent from this meeting.

40.3 LISTEN TO THE AUDIO, THEN NUMBER THE SENTENCES IN THE ORDER YOU HEAR THEM

A   Let me see a show of hands. How many of you agree with my proposal? ☐

B   We reached a unanimous agreement on the budget. ☐

C   The main objective of this meeting is to discuss product ideas. ☐ 1

D   Let's wrap up this meeting. It's almost one o'clock. ☐

E   Cameron is going to take minutes during our finance meeting. ☐

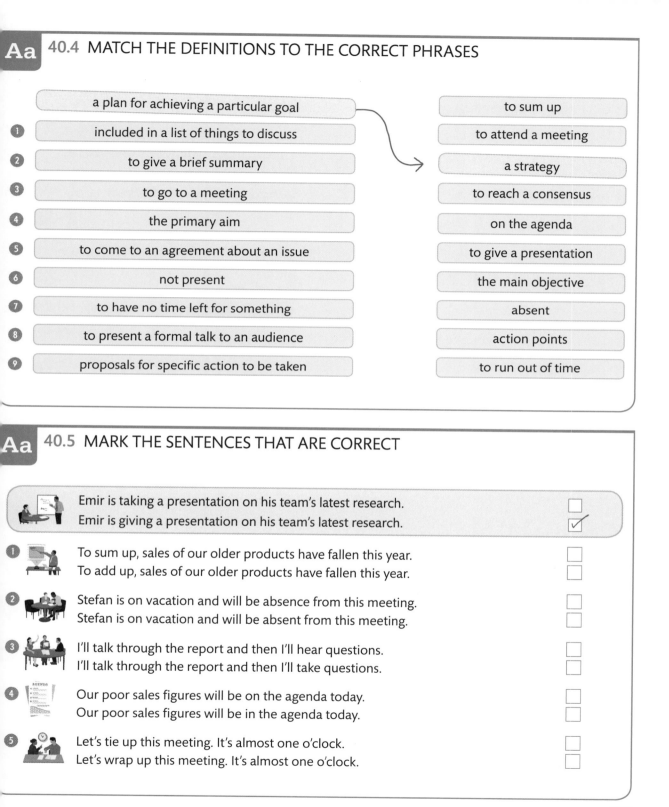

Aa 40.4 MATCH THE DEFINITIONS TO THE CORRECT PHRASES

a plan for achieving a particular goal → a strategy

1. included in a list of things to discuss
2. to give a brief summary
3. to go to a meeting
4. the primary aim
5. to come to an agreement about an issue
6. not present
7. to have no time left for something
8. to present a formal talk to an audience
9. proposals for specific action to be taken

to sum up
to attend a meeting
a strategy
to reach a consensus
on the agenda
to give a presentation
the main objective
absent
action points
to run out of time

Aa 40.5 MARK THE SENTENCES THAT ARE CORRECT

Emir is taking a presentation on his team's latest research. ☐
Emir is giving a presentation on his team's latest research. ☑

1. To sum up, sales of our older products have fallen this year. ☐
   To add up, sales of our older products have fallen this year. ☐

2. Stefan is on vacation and will be absence from this meeting. ☐
   Stefan is on vacation and will be absent from this meeting. ☐

3. I'll talk through the report and then I'll hear questions. ☐
   I'll talk through the report and then I'll take questions. ☐

4. Our poor sales figures will be on the agenda today. ☐
   Our poor sales figures will be in the agenda today. ☐

5. Let's tie up this meeting. It's almost one o'clock. ☐
   Let's wrap up this meeting. It's almost one o'clock. ☐

41 Work and business idioms

41.1 WORKPLACE IDIOMS

The store was closed for remodeling, but it's business as usual now.

business as usual
[the normal daily routine at a company]

Health and safety in the warehouse involves a lot of red tape.

red tape
[administration, paperwork, or rules and regulations]

We're in the red after losing three of our clients this year.

in the red
[owing money or making a loss]

This is the best deal we can offer. The ball is in your court now.

the ball is in your court
[it is your turn to do or say something]

Let's get the ball rolling. What do you all think of this logo design?

to get the ball rolling
[to start something]

This product will never sell. We're throwing money down the drain.

to throw money down the drain
[to waste money]

The client loves our cars and we've agreed on a great price. It's a win-win situation.

a win-win situation
[a situation with no negative outcome]

You need to think outside the box to come up with good designs.

to think outside the box
[to think about something in an original way]

This client will never be satisfied because he keeps moving the goalposts.

to move the goalposts
[to change the desired end result]

Let's get down to business. I have to leave by 5 o'clock.

to get down to business
[to start work on something that needs doing]

41.2 BUSINESS IDIOMS

We're really ahead of the game with these great new products.

ahead of the game
[ahead of your competitors in a certain field]

Great! We're all on the same page about this marketing campaign.

on the same page
[in agreement about something]

This is a difficult job. Make sure you do everything by the book.

to do something by the book
[to do something strictly according to the rules]

Could I touch base with you for a quick update on this project?

to touch base
[to talk to someone briefly in order to catch up or get an update]

Rohit clinched the deal after offering the clients a discount.

to clinch the deal
[to confirm or settle an agreement or contract]

We don't know the exact costs, but here's a ballpark figure.

a ballpark figure
[a rough estimate]

They've cornered the market with their new range of sports shoes.

to corner the market
[to dominate a particular market]

We expected a change of pace after we received several large orders.

a change of pace
[an increase or decrease in speed from what is normal]

We're losing money, so we need a game plan for increasing sales.

a game plan
[a strategy worked out beforehand]

I'm so busy today. Please tell me the facts in a nutshell.

in a nutshell
[simply and quickly]

41.3 REWRITE THE SENTENCES, CORRECTING THE ERRORS

> The store was closed for remodeling, but it's business like usual now.
> *The store was closed for remodeling, but it's business as usual now.*

❶ This is a difficult job. Make sure you do everything by the instructions.

_____

❷ Great! We're all on the same chapter about this marketing campaign.

_____

❸ This client will never be satisfied because he keeps moving the net.

_____

❹ Health and safety in the warehouse involves a lot of red papers.

_____

Aa **41.4 MATCH THE PICTURES TO THE CORRECT SENTENCES**

We're losing money, so we need a game plan for increasing sales.

❶

We're really ahead of the game with these great new products.

❷

Could I touch base with you for a quick update on this project?

❸

We don't know the exact costs, but here's a ballpark figure.

❹

Rohit clinched the deal after offering the clients a discount.

Aa 41.5 MATCH THE BEGINNINGS OF THE SENTENCES TO THE CORRECT ENDINGS

I'm so busy today. Please tell me	throwing money down the drain.
1 We expected a change of pace	market with their new range of shoes.
2 This product will never sell. We're	the facts in a nutshell.
3 This client will never be satisfied because	sure you do everything by the book.
4 They've cornered the	after we received several large orders.
5 This is a difficult job. Make	he keeps moving the goalposts.

41.6 LISTEN TO THE AUDIO, THEN NUMBER THE SENTENCES IN THE ORDER YOU HEAR THEM

A Let's get down to business. I have to leave by 5 o'clock. ☐

B The store was closed for remodeling, but it's business as usual now. ☐

C We're in the red after losing three of our clients this year. ☐ 1

D Let's get the ball rolling. What do you all think of this logo design? ☐

E You need to think outside the box to come up with good designs. ☐

F This is the best deal we can offer. The ball is in your court now. ☐

G The client loves our cars and we've agreed on a great price. It's a win-win situation. ☐

H Health and safety in the warehouse involves a lot of red tape. ☐

42 Applying for a job

42.1 RÉSUMÉ HEADINGS

Adriana Pires

275 Main Street, Minneapolis, MN 55401
addi123@pires456.com · 612-555-1746

PERSONAL STATEMENT
A highly motivated individual, with a proven track record
in hotel reception and front-of-house work.

PROFESSIONAL ACHIEVEMENTS
Won an award for the Best Hotel Receptionist
in the Midwestern Region.

CAREER SUMMARY
Hotel Deluxe Cite
FRONT DESK MANAGER · May 2014–Present
• Working in a service-oriented environment.
• Gained in-depth knowledge of the hospitality industry,
  and hands-on experience in customer service.

EDUCATION
• BA in Tourism and Hospitality
• Minor in Spanish

KEY SKILLS
• Fluent in Portuguese, Spanish, and English
• Proficient in IT use, including most types of reservation systems

INTERESTS
Cooking, traveling, paragliding, scuba diving

REFERENCES
Available upon request

résumé (US)
CV (UK)

job ad (US) / advert (UK)

application form

portfolio

cover letter (US)
covering letter (UK)

recruitment agency

42.2 VERBS

to apply for a job

to fill out a form

to have an interview

to manage

to negotiate

to coordinate

to collaborate

to volunteer

to organize

to supervise

42.3 USEFUL EXPRESSIONS

I have a proven track record in the catering industry.

a proven track record
[a long list of achievements]

I am proficient in all major types of accounting software.

proficient in
[highly skilled at something]

As an ex-car salesman, I have a service-oriented background.

service-oriented
[having a lot of contact with customers]

All our staff are fully trained in first aid.

trained in
[taught how to do something]

I have an in-depth knowledge of hair-coloring techniques.

an in-depth knowledge
[an expert understanding of something]

I am responsible for six other staff members.

responsible for
[having control over someone or something]

42.4 LOOK AT THE RÉSUMÉ AND WRITE THE CORRECT WORD FROM THE PANEL FOR EACH LABEL

Adriana Pires

275 Main Street, Minneapolis, MN 55401
addi123@pires456.com · 612-555-1746

Personal statement
A highly motivated individual, with a proven track record in hotel reception and front-of-house work.

❶ _____

Won an award for the Best Hotel Receptionist in the Midwestern Region.

❷ _____

Hotel Deluxe Cite
FRONT DESK MANAGER · May 2014–Present
• Working in a service-oriented environment.
• Gained in-depth knowledge of the hospitality industry, and hands-on experience in customer service.

❸ _____

• BA in Tourism and Hospitality
• Minor in Spanish

❹ _____

• Fluent in Portuguese, Spanish, and English
• Proficient in IT use, including most types of reservation systems

❺ _____

Cooking, traveling, paragliding, scuba diving

❻ _____

Available upon request

Career summary

Key skills

~~Personal statement~~

Interests

References

Professional achievements

Education

42.5 WRITE THE CORRECT WORD UNDER EACH PICTURE

application form

❶ _____

❷ _____

❸ _____

❹ _____

42.6 WRITE THE CORRECT WORD UNDER EACH PICTURE

to volunteer

1 _____

2 _____

3 _____

4 _____

5 _____

6 _____

7 _____

8 _____

9 _____

42.7 LISTEN TO THE AUDIO AND COMPLETE THE SENTENCES THAT DESCRIBE EACH PICTURE

All our staff are fully
trained in first aid.

3 I have a _____
in the catering industry.

1 I am _____
six other staff members.

4 As an ex-car salesman,
I have a _____
background.

2 I have an _____
of hair-coloring techniques.

5 I am _____ all major
types of accounting software.

43 Workplace skills and abilities

43.1 PROFESSIONAL ATTRIBUTES

organized

patient

accurate

creative

honest

practical

professional

adaptable

ambitious

calm

confident

punctual

reliable

customer-focused

independent

efficient

energetic

flexible

hardworking

responsible

innovative

motivated

determined

team player

competitive

43.2 FOR THE WORKPLACE

organization

IT / computing

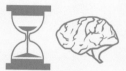
administration

problem-solving

data analysis

decision-making

teamwork

fast learner

numeracy

customer service

interpersonal skills

leadership

research

fluent in languages

attention to detail

negotiating

public speaking

written
communication

initiative

telephone manner

work well
under pressure

able to drive

project
management

time
management

businesslike
attitude

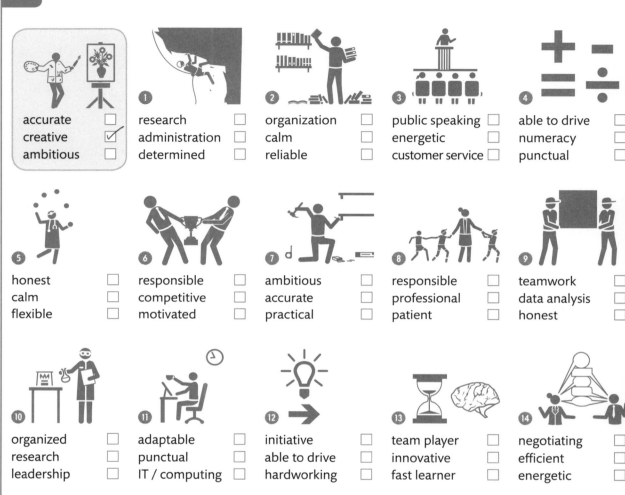

Aa 43.3 MARK THE CORRECT WORD FOR EACH PICTURE

accurate	☐
creative	☑
ambitious	☐

1
research	☐
administration	☐
determined	☐

2
organization	☐
calm	☐
reliable	☐

3
public speaking	☐
energetic	☐
customer service	☐

4
able to drive	☐
numeracy	☐
punctual	☐

5
honest	☐
calm	☐
flexible	☐

6
responsible	☐
competitive	☐
motivated	☐

7
ambitious	☐
accurate	☐
practical	☐

8
responsible	☐
professional	☐
patient	☐

9
teamwork	☐
data analysis	☐
honest	☐

10
organized	☐
research	☐
leadership	☐

11
adaptable	☐
punctual	☐
IT / computing	☐

12
initiative	☐
able to drive	☐
hardworking	☐

13
team player	☐
innovative	☐
fast learner	☐

14
negotiating	☐
efficient	☐
energetic	☐

Aa 43.4 MARK THE BEGINNING AND ENDING OF EACH WORD IN THE CHAIN OF LETTERS

professional reliable hardworking responsible administration motivated research organized calm

43.5 MATCH THE PICTURES TO THE CORRECT WORDS

leadership

problem-solving

customer-focused

time management

fluent in languages

attention to detail

43.6 LISTEN TO THE AUDIO AND CIRCLE THE WORDS YOU HEAR

teamwork	energetic	team player
① confident	calm	creative
② punctual	practical	patient
③ organized	honest	accurate
④ research	reliable	responsible
⑤ administration	innovative	motivated
⑥ independent	adaptable	ambitious
⑦ leadership	efficient	initiative
⑧ data analysis	professional	fast learner
⑨ organization	ambitious	flexible
⑩ negotiating	competitive	confident
⑪ decision-making	determined	teamwork

43.7 REWRITE THE WORDS, CORRECTING THE SPELLINGS

inovative
innovative

① ambicious

② teem pleyer

③ ennergetic

④ interpersonnel skils

⑤ eficient

44.1 FORMS OF TRANSPORTATION

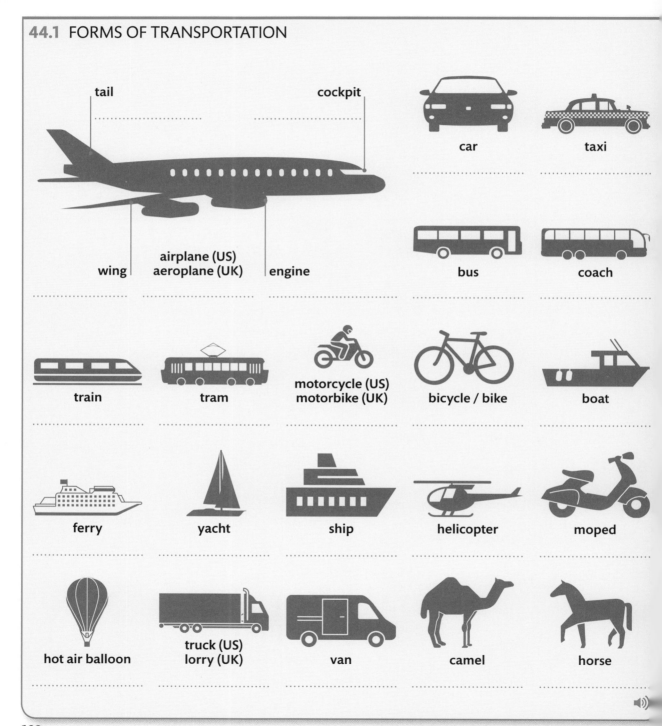

tail

cockpit

car

taxi

wing

airplane (US)
aeroplane (UK)

engine

bus

coach

train

tram

motorcycle (US)
motorbike (UK)

bicycle / bike

boat

ferry

yacht

ship

helicopter

moped

hot air balloon

truck (US)
lorry (UK)

van

camel

horse

44.2 TRAVEL

passengers

pedestrian

commuters

train station

platform

ticket

bus stop

airport

taxi stand (US)
taxi rank (UK)

port

44.3 VERBS

to ride a bike

to ride a horse

to take a flight

to drive a car

to take the bus

to take the train

to walk

to hitchhike

to get on a bus

to get off a bus

to get in a taxi

to get out of a taxi

to catch a train

to miss a train

to give someone a
ride (US) / lift (UK)

Aa 44.4 MATCH THE VERBS TO THE CORRECT PICTURES

to hitchhike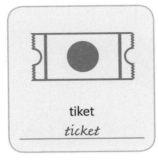

A

1 to give someone a lift

2 to miss a train

B

3 to get on a bus

C

4 to catch a train

D

5 to ride a bike

E

6 to take a flight

F

7 to ride a horse

G

8 to get off a bus

H

9 to get out of a taxi

I

Aa 44.5 REWRITE THE WORDS, CORRECTING THE SPELLINGS

tiket
ticket

1 passagers

2 platforma

3 bycicle

 4 pedesstrien

5 comutters

 6 couch

7 jacht

 8 mopped

9 ven

Aa 44.6 FIND NINE MORE WORDS IN THE GRID THAT MATCH THE PICTURES

```
A I R P O R T A C T H
T A V P Q H O Q V R E
A E D E M J J M D A L
T A X I T E K T I I I
L T B C X W N X B N C
E E O I C A M E L X O
R M A L O L A O Z B P
A B O A T C R Y C H T
V A N P S V V A V O E
A E D E R D D C D R R
P R I N G I I H I S A
F E R R Y B B T B E O
```

44.7 LISTEN TO THE AUDIO, THEN NUMBER THE PICTURES IN THE ORDER YOU HEAR THEM

 A ☐

 B ☐

 C 1

 D ☐

 E ☐

 F ☐

 G ☐

 H ☐

 I ☐

 J ☐

 K ☐

 L ☐

 M ☐

 N ☐

 O ☐

45 Driving a car

45.1 DRIVING VOCABULARY

driver's license
(US) / licence (UK)

insurance

seatbelt

gas station (US)
petrol station (UK)

engine

turn signal (US)
indicator (UK)

steering wheel

fuel

gasoline (US)
petrol (UK)

diesel

oil

auto repair shop
(US) / garage (UK)

mechanic

flat tire (US)
flat tyre (UK)

wipers

pedestrian
crossing

trunk (US)
boot (UK)

hood (US) / bonnet (UK)

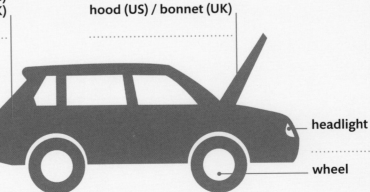

headlight

wheel

traffic lights

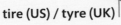
tire (US) / tyre (UK)

car

parking attendant

speed camera

parking meter

wheel clamp

parking ticket

car wash

speed limit

road sign

traffic jam

parking lot (US)
car park (UK)

45.2 VERBS

to park

to set off

to check the oil

to fill up

to check the tires
(US) / tyres (UK)

to service the car

to signal (US)
to indicate (UK)

to brake

to slow down

to speed up

to pick
someone up

to drop
someone off

to have a car
accident

to break down

to pass (US)
to overtake (UK)

45.3 WRITE THE CORRECT EXPRESSION UNDER EACH PICTURE

 mechanic

 1 _____

 2 _____

 3 _____

 4 _____

 5 _____

 6 _____

 7 _____

 8 _____

 9 _____

 10 _____

 11 _____

 12 _____

 13 _____

 14 _____

45.4 MARK THE BEGINNING AND ENDING OF EACH WORD OR EXPRESSION IN THE CHAIN OF LETTERS, THEN WRITE THE WORDS YOU FIND

insurance/trunkdieselmechanicgasolinetrafficjamheadlightsteeringwheelparkingattendant

_____ insurance _____

1 _____

2 _____

3 _____

4 _____

5 _____

6 _____

7 _____

8 _____

Aa 45.5 LOOK AT THE PICTURE AND WRITE THE CORRECT WORD FOR EACH LABEL

headlight

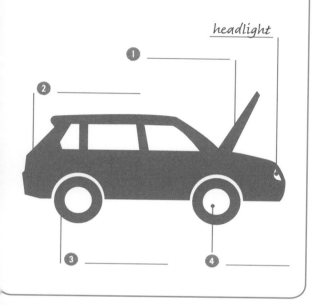

45.6 LISTEN TO THE AUDIO AND CIRCLE THE WORDS YOU HEAR

steering wheel	(headlight)	fuel
① parking meter	parking lot	gas station
② flat tire	turn signal	traffic lights
③ driver's license	gas station	car wash
④ wheel	wipers	tire
⑤ to set off	to speed up	to slow down
⑥ trunk	insurance	road sign
⑦ seatbelt	speed limit	speed camera
⑧ oil	engine	diesel

Aa 45.7 MARK THE CORRECT EXPRESSION FOR EACH PICTURE

to fill up ☑
to pass ☐
to brake ☐

①

driver's license ☐
traffic lights ☐
parking ticket ☐

②

parking lot ☐
headlight ☐
pedestrian crossing ☐

③

to pick someone up ☐
to check the oil ☐
to pass ☐

④

flat tire ☐
parking attendant ☐
wheel clamp ☐

⑤

road sign ☐
parking attendant ☐
mechanic ☐

⑥

to park ☐
to set off ☐
to brake ☐

⑦

speed limit ☐
car wash ☐
insurance ☐

46.1 MAPS AND DIRECTIONS

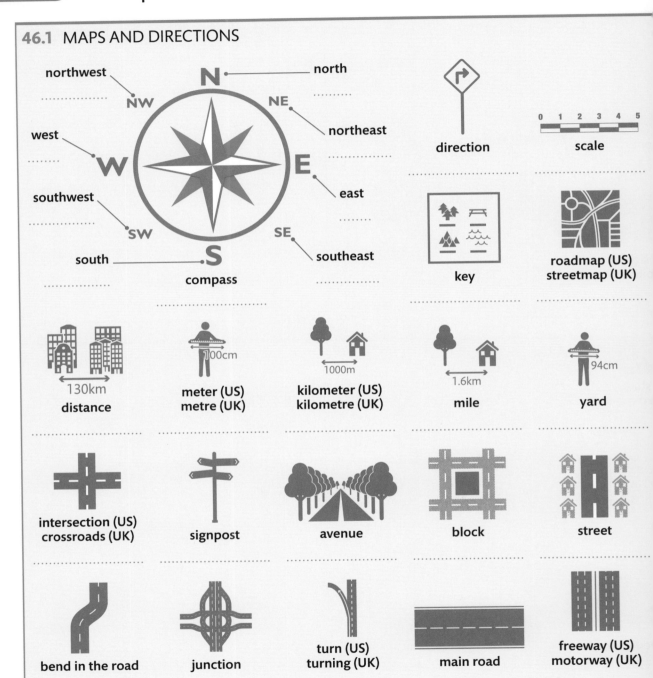

northwest
north
NW
NE
northeast
west
W
E
east
southwest
SW
south
S
SE
southeast
compass

direction

scale

key

roadmap (US)
streetmap (UK)

130km
distance

100cm
meter (US)
metre (UK)

1000m
kilometer (US)
kilometre (UK)

1.6km
mile

94cm
yard

intersection (US)
crossroads (UK)

signpost

avenue

block

street

bend in the road

junction

turn (US)
turning (UK)

main road

freeway (US)
motorway (UK)

one-way street

sidewalk (US)
pavement (UK)

shoulder (US)
hard shoulder (UK)

footpath

pedestrianized
street

46.2 PREPOSITIONS OF PLACE

here

there

next to

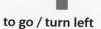

across from (US)
opposite (UK)

between

on the corner

behind

in front of

on the right

on the left

46.3 VERBS

to go / turn left

to go / turn right

to go straight ahead
(US) / on (UK)

to stop at
(the hotel)

to go past (the
restaurant)

to take the
first left

to take the
second right

to read a map

to plan
your route

to ask directions

191

Aa 46.4 LOOK AT THE PICTURE AND WRITE THE CORRECT WORD FOR EACH LABEL

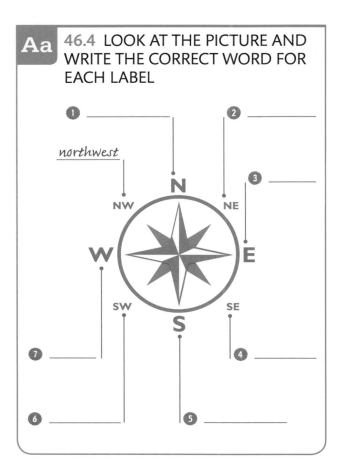

northwest

Aa 46.5 REWRITE THE WORDS, CORRECTING THE SPELLINGS

sinepost
signpost

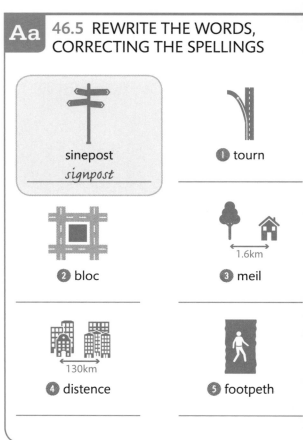

① tourn

② bloc

③ meil

④ distence

⑤ footpeth

Aa 46.6 WRITE THE CORRECT WORD UNDER EACH PICTURE

in front of

① _____

② _____

③ _____

④ _____

⑤ _____

⑥ _____

⑦ _____

⑧ _____

⑨ _____

Aa 46.7 MATCH THE PICTURES TO THE CORRECT VERBS

to go / turn right

to read a map

1

to go / turn left

2

to go straight ahead (US) / on (UK)

3

to take the second right

4

to take the first left

5

to ask directions

6

7

to stop at (the hotel)

46.8 LISTEN TO THE AUDIO AND MARK THE CORRECT PICTURE FOR EACH WORD YOU HEAR

A ☐   B ☑   C ☐

1   A ☐   B ☐   C ☐

2   A ☐   B ☐   C ☐

3   A ☐   B ☐   C ☐

4   A ☐   B ☐   C ☐

5   A ☐   B ☐   C ☐

193

47 Travel and accommodation

47.1 GOING ON VACATION (US) / HOLIDAY (UK)

passport

suitcase

luggage

guidebook

phrasebook

one-way ticket

round-trip (US) /
return (UK) ticket

direct flight

window seat

boarding pass

departure gate

passport control

walking vacation
(US) / holiday (UK)

all-inclusive

guided tour

47.2 VERBS

to go on a vacation
(US) / holiday (UK)

to book a vacation
(US) / holiday (UK)

to pack your bags

to board a plane

to land at the
airport

to be delayed

to go sightseeing

to go abroad

to go on a cruise

to go on an
excursion

47.3 WHERE TO STAY

hotel

apartment

hostel

guesthouse

villa

chalet

cabin

front desk (US)
reception (UK)

single room

double room

twin beds

dorm

en-suite
bathroom (UK)

safe

room service

laundry service

room with a view

no vacancies

vacancies

bed and breakfast

47.4 VERBS

to make a
reservation

to rent a cottage

to stay in a hotel

to check in

to check out

195

Aa 47.5 MATCH THE PICTURES TO THE CORRECT VERBS

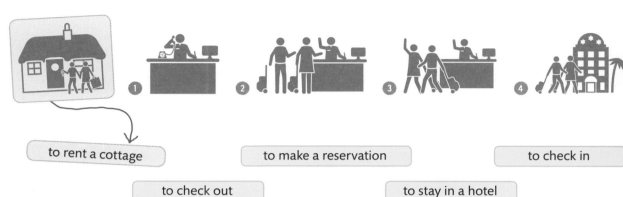

to rent a cottage

to make a reservation

to check in

to check out

to stay in a hotel

Aa 47.6 WRITE THE CORRECT WORD OR EXPRESSION UNDER EACH PICTURE

front desk

1 _____

2 _____

3 _____

4 _____

5 _____

6 _____

7 _____

8 _____

9 _____

10 _____

11 _____

12 _____

13 _____

14 _____

47.7 LISTEN TO THE AUDIO, THEN NUMBER THE PICTURES IN THE ORDER YOU HEAR THEM

 **A** ☐

 **B** 1

 **C** ☐

 **D** ☐

 E ☐

 F ☐

 **G** ☐

 **H** ☐

 **I** ☐

 **J** ☐

 **K** ☐

 L ☐

Aa 47.8 MARK THE CORRECT WORD OR EXPRESSION FOR EACH PICTURE

to go on a cruise ☑
to pack your bags ☐
to rent a cottage ☐

①
to go on an excursion ☐
direct flight ☐
to make a reservation ☐

②
to book a vacation ☐
bed and breakfast ☐
guided tour ☐

③
villa ☐
dorm ☐
phrasebook ☐

④
luggage ☐
all-inclusive ☐
walking vacation ☐

⑤
room service ☐
vacancies ☐
safe ☐

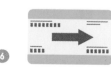
⑥
one-way ticket ☐
boarding pass ☐
window seat ☐

⑦
hostel ☐
single room ☐
safe ☐

48 Travel and tourism

48.1 USEFUL EXPRESSIONS

I love to get away from it all when I'm on vacation.

to get away from it all
[to go somewhere relaxing for a break]

I've won a once-in-a-lifetime trip around the world.

once-in-a-lifetime
[unique and unrepeatable]

This place is so different from home. It's such a culture shock.

a culture shock
[a feeling of confusion or distress when visiting a different place or culture]

This hotel looks very run-down. Let's stay somewhere else.

run-down
[in a bad condition through lack of care or repair]

Tim has gone abroad again. He's always getting itchy feet.

itchy feet
[a desire to travel or move]

The palace is such a tourist trap in the summer.

a tourist trap
[a place that attracts too many tourists]

I don't like going abroad because I feel homesick.

to feel homesick
[to be sad because you miss your home and family]

We like to stay in places that are off the beaten path.

off the beaten path (US) / track (UK)
[a long way from other people, buildings, and roads]

I love going birdwatching in this unspoiled countryside.

unspoiled
[not changed, damaged, or built on by people]

Brendan loves sports and has a real thirst for adventure.

a thirst for adventure
[a desire for exciting experiences]

n taking Clara to look around
e park today.

look around
explore an area or place]

We got hopelessly lost when
we tried to drive into Tokyo.

hopelessly lost
[totally unable to find your way]

t's stop off at the gallery before
e check into our hotel.

stop off
pause a trip in one
ce before continuing]

I save lots of money on train
tickets by booking in advance.

to book in advance
[to book a ticket or accommodation
several days or weeks before you need it]

ike to travel out of season,
en it's nice and quiet.

ut of season
a time of year when a tourist
stination is less popular]

We're checking out the zoo
that you recommended.

**to check out something /
to check something out**
[to find out how interesting
something is]

e first leg of the trip to
ustralia is a flight to Bangkok.

eg of a trip (US) / journey (UK)
stage in a trip from
e place to another]

We don't need another suitcase.
It's just a weekend getaway.

a getaway
[a vacation, particularly a short one]

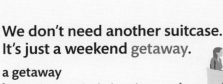

e is really looking forward
visiting the pyramids.

look forward to something
feel excited about something
at is going to happen]

Dan's parents came to the airport
to see him off.

to see off somebody / see somebody off
[to go to the station or airport to
say goodbye to someone]

Aa 48.2 MATCH THE BEGINNINGS OF THE SENTENCES TO THE CORRECT ENDINGS

I've won a once-in-a-lifetime — trip around the world.

1 We like to stay in places that are off

2 Zoe is really looking forward

3 We got hopelessly

4 The palace is such a tourist

5 We're checking out

6 I love to get away

7 I'm taking Clara to look

8 I save lots of money on train tickets

to visiting the pyramids.

trap in the summer.

the beaten path.

from it all when I'm on vacation.

around the park today.

lost when we tried to drive into Tokyo.

by booking in advance.

the zoo that you recommended.

Aa 48.3 REWRITE THE SENTENCES, CORRECTING THE ERRORS

Tim has gone abroad again. He's always getting itchy legs.
Tim has gone abroad again. He's always getting itchy feet.

1 I don't like going abroad because I feel housesick.

_____

2 I save lots of money on train tickets by booking on advance.

_____

3 We got uselessly lost when we tried to drive into Tokyo.

_____

4 We like to stay in places that are off a beaten path.

_____

48.4 MARK THE SENTENCES THAT ARE CORRECT

The first leg of the trip to Australia is a flight to Bangkok. ☑
The first arm of the trip to Australia is a flight to Bangkok. ☐

1. Brendan loves sports and has a real hunger for adventure. ☐
   Brendan loves sports and has a real thirst for adventure. ☐

2. I like to travel away from season, when it's nice and quiet. ☐
   I like to travel out of season, when it's nice and quiet. ☐

3. This place is so different from home. It's such a culture shock. ☐
   This place is so different from home. It's such a culture clash. ☐

4. Let's stop off at the gallery before we check into our hotel. ☐
   Let's stop in at the gallery before we check into our hotel. ☐

5. Dan's parents came to the airport to see him out. ☐
   Dan's parents came to the airport to see him off. ☐

48.5 LISTEN TO THE AUDIO AND COMPLETE THE SENTENCES THAT DESCRIBE EACH PICTURE

I love going birdwatching in this _unspoiled_ countryside.

3 I save lots of money on train tickets by _____ .

1 This hotel looks very _____ . Let's stay somewhere else.

4 I love to _____ from it all when I'm on vacation.

2 I don't like going abroad because I feel _____ .

5 We don't need another suitcase. It's just a weekend _____ .

49 Camping and cycling

49.1 CAMPING

backpack / rucksack (UK)

campsite

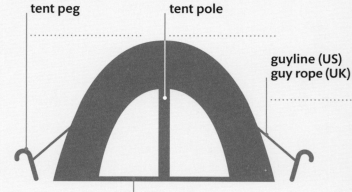

tent peg · tent pole · guyline (US) guy rope (UK) · groundsheet · tent

sleeping bag

to pitch a tent

to build a fire

campfire

camping stove

air bed / air mattress

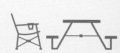
folding chair / table

toilet block

shower block

flashlight (US) torch (UK)

waterproofs

barbecue

hot drink container (US) / flask (UK)

walking boots

insect repellent

caravan

motor home (US) camper van (UK)

49.2 CYCLING

gear

brakes

frame

handlebar

saddle

chain

pedal

bicycle / bike

cycling helmet

mountain bike

racing bike

cycling trails

unicycle

cycle pump

tandem

lock

reflector

tire (US)
tyre (UK)

bike rack

basket

bicycle lane

to get on a bike

to get off a bike

to fix a puncture

pothole

203

Aa 49.3 LOOK AT THE PICTURE AND WRITE THE CORRECT WORD FOR EACH LABEL

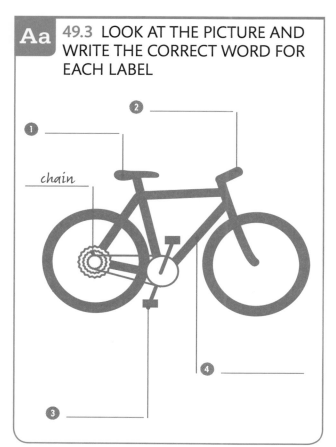

chain

① _____

② _____

③ _____

④ _____

Aa 49.4 MATCH THE PICTURES TO THE CORRECT WORDS

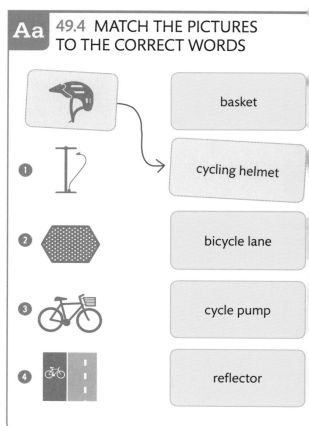

basket

cycling helmet

bicycle lane

cycle pump

reflector

Aa 49.5 WRITE THE CORRECT WORD UNDER EACH PICTURE

sleeping bag

① _____

② _____

③ _____

④ _____

⑤ _____

⑥ _____

⑦ _____

⑧ _____

⑨ _____

49.6 COMPLETE THE WORDS FOR EACH PICTURE, FILLING IN THE MISSING LETTERS

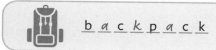
b a c k p a c k

1. s h _ _ e _   b l _ _ k
2. r _ c i g b _ e
3. _ n _ c _ c l _
4. w _ t _ r _ r o f _
5. b _ _ e _ r _ c _
6. t _ n _ _ m
7. _ c _ m p _ _ r _
8. c _ r _ v _ n
9. t _ t
10. b _ c _ c l _ _ l _ n _
11. b _ r b _ c _
12. _ r _ _ e s

49.7 LISTEN TO THE AUDIO, THEN NUMBER THE PICTURES IN THE ORDER YOU HEAR THEM

A ☐   B ☐   C [1]

D ☐   E ☐   F ☐

G ☐   H ☐   I ☐

J ☐   K ☐   L ☐

M ☐   N ☐   O ☐

P ☐   Q ☐   R ☐

50.1 AT THE BEACH

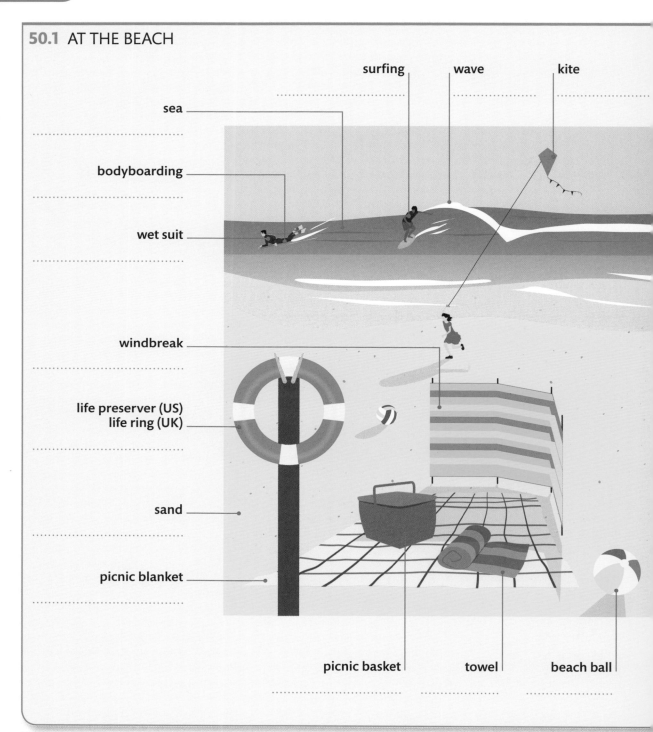

surfing

wave

kite

sea

bodyboarding

wet suit

windbreak

life preserver (US)
life ring (UK)

sand

picnic blanket

picnic basket

towel

beach ball

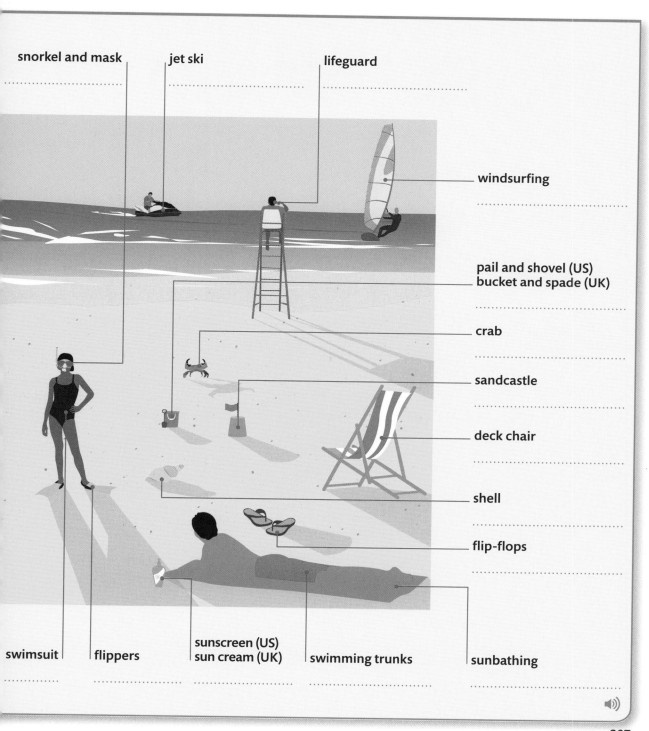

snorkel and mask

jet ski

lifeguard

windsurfing

pail and shovel (US)
bucket and spade (UK)

crab

sandcastle

deck chair

shell

flip-flops

swimsuit

flippers

sunscreen (US)
sun cream (UK)

swimming trunks

sunbathing

Aa 50.2 WRITE THE CORRECT WORD UNDER EACH PICTURE

crab

1 _____

2 _____

3 _____

4 _____

5 _____

6 _____

7 _____

8 _____

9 _____

10 _____

11 _____

12 _____

13 _____

14 _____

Aa 50.3 MARK THE BEGINNING AND ENDING OF EACH WORD OR EXPRESSION IN THE CHAIN OF LETTERS, THEN WRITE THE WORDS YOU FIND

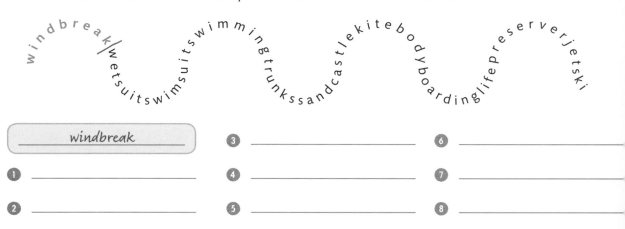

windbreak/wetsuitswimsuitswimmingtrunkssandcastlekitebodyboardinglifepreserverjetski

windbreak

1 _____

2 _____

3 _____

4 _____

5 _____

6 _____

7 _____

8 _____

50.4 REWRITE THE WORDS, CORRECTING THE SPELLINGS

lifegaurd
lifeguard

❶ bodybording

❷ windbrake

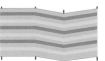

❸ windserfing

❹ see

❺ krab

❻ dek chair

❼ flipers

❽ picknick blanket

❾ sandcassel

50.5 LISTEN TO THE AUDIO AND MARK THE CORRECT PICTURE FOR EACH WORD YOU HEAR

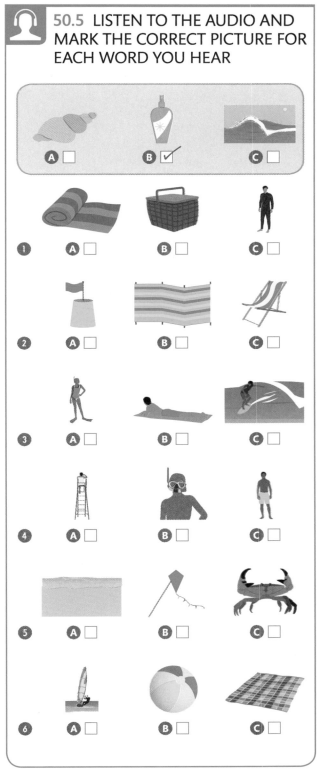

A ☐   B ✓   C ☐

❶ A ☐   B ☐   C ☐

❷ A ☐   B ☐   C ☐

❸ A ☐   B ☐   C ☐

❹ A ☐   B ☐   C ☐

❺ A ☐   B ☐   C ☐

❻ A ☐   B ☐   C ☐

51 Weather and climate

51.1 WEATHER

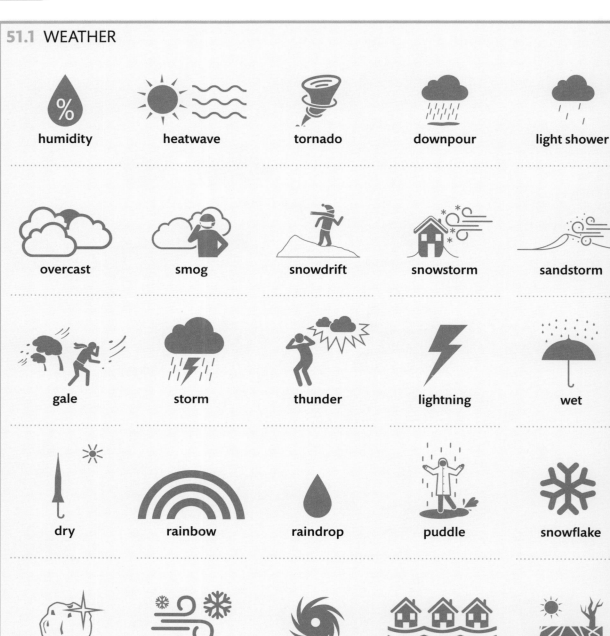

humidity

heatwave

tornado

downpour

light shower

overcast

smog

snowdrift

snowstorm

sandstorm

gale

storm

thunder

lightning

wet

dry

rainbow

raindrop

puddle

snowflake

hailstone

blizzard

hurricane

flood

drought

51.2 TEMPERATURE

freezing

cold

chilly

warm

hot

stifling

freezing point

boiling point

minus 10

cool

mild

boiling

25 degrees

Celsius

Fahrenheit

51.3 ADJECTIVES

sun → sunny

cloud → cloudy

fog → foggy

rain → rainy

snow → snowy

ice → icy

frost → frosty

wind → windy

storm → stormy

thunder → thundery

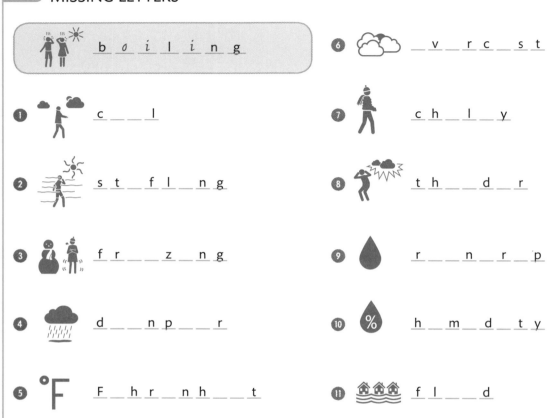

Aa 51.4 COMPLETE THE WORD FOR EACH PICTURE, FILLING IN THE MISSING LETTERS

b _o_ _i_ l _i_ n g

1. c _ _ l

2. s _ _ _ f l _ _ n g

3. f r _ _ z _ n g

4. d _ _ _ n p _ _ r

5. F _ _ h r _ _ n h _ _ t

6. _ _ v _ r c _ _ s t

7. c h _ _ l _ y

8. t h _ _ _ d _ _ r

9. r _ _ _ n _ r _ _ p

10. h _ m _ d _ t y

11. f l _ _ _ d

Aa 51.5 MATCH THE PICTURES TO THE CORRECT WORDS

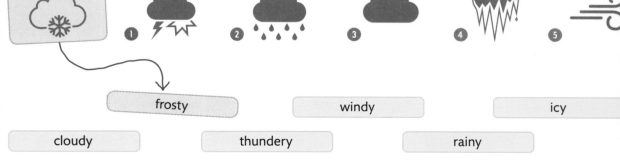

frosty

windy

icy

cloudy

thundery

rainy

Aa 51.6 FIND EIGHT MORE WORDS IN THE GRID THAT MATCH THE PICTURES

```
R A I N B O W A C S A
H A V P L H K Q V N Q
E E G E I J S E L O L
A R A N Z E R T I W I
T T L C Z W D X B S G
W E E I A R Y A P T H
A M Z L R L A O U O T
V E T E D A H V D R N
E N X W T P P D D M I
D R O U G H T I L L N
S N O W F L A K E T G
```

 1

 2

 3

 4

 5

 6

 7

8

51.7 LISTEN TO THE AUDIO, THEN NUMBER THE PICTURES IN THE ORDER YOU HEAR THEM

A ☐

B 1

C ☐

D ☐

E ☐

F ☐

G ☐

H ☐

I ☐

J ☐

K ☐

L ☐

52 Geographical features

52.1 GEOGRAPHICAL FEATURES

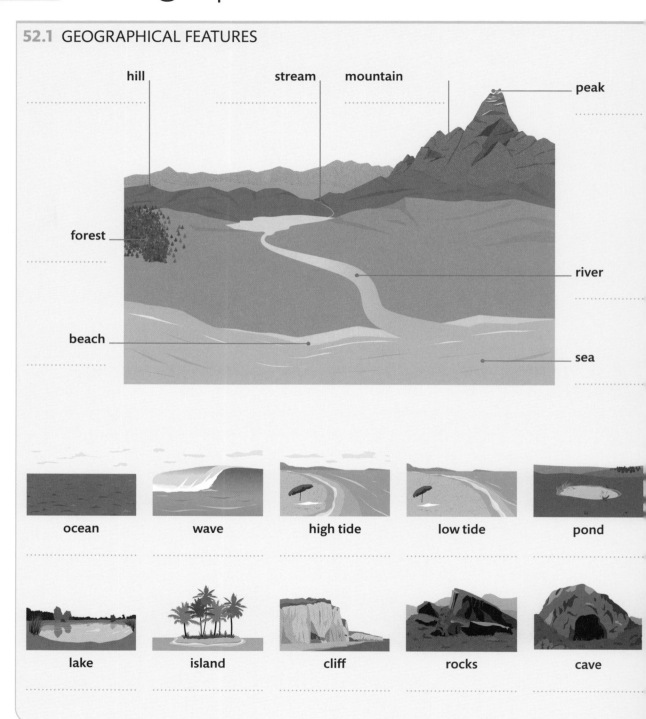

hill · stream · mountain · peak · forest · river · beach · sea

ocean · wave · high tide · low tide · pond

lake · island · cliff · rocks · cave

wood

rain forest (US)
rainforest (UK)

swamp

waterfall

rapids

countryside

field

hill

hedge

farmland

meadow

grassland

plain

desert

oasis

volcano

geyser

mountain range

plateau

valley

canyon

sand dune

polar region

glacier

iceberg

Aa 52.2 WRITE THE CORRECT WORD UNDER EACH PICTURE

island

 ❶ _____

 ❷ _____

 ❸ _____

 ❹ _____

 ❺ _____

 ❻ _____

 ❼ _____

 ❽ _____

 ❾ _____

 ❿ _____

 ⓫ _____

 ⓬ _____

 ⓭ _____

 ⓮ _____

Aa 52.3 MARK THE BEGINNING AND ENDING OF EACH GEOGRAPHICAL FEATURE IN THE CHAIN OF LETTERS, THEN WRITE THE WORDS YOU FIND

hightide/countrysidecanyonplateauvolcanomeadowrainforestmountainrangepolarregion

high tide

❸ _____

❻ _____

❶ _____

❹ _____

❼ _____

❷ _____

❺ _____

❽ _____

52.4 LOOK AT THE PICTURE AND WRITE THE CORRECT WORD FOR EACH LABEL

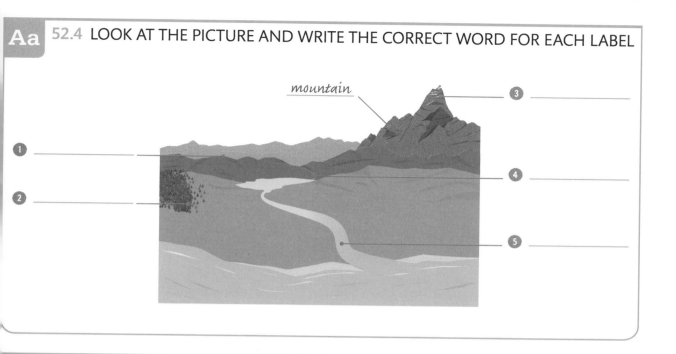

52.5 LISTEN TO THE AUDIO AND MARK THE CORRECT PICTURE FOR EACH WORD YOU HEAR

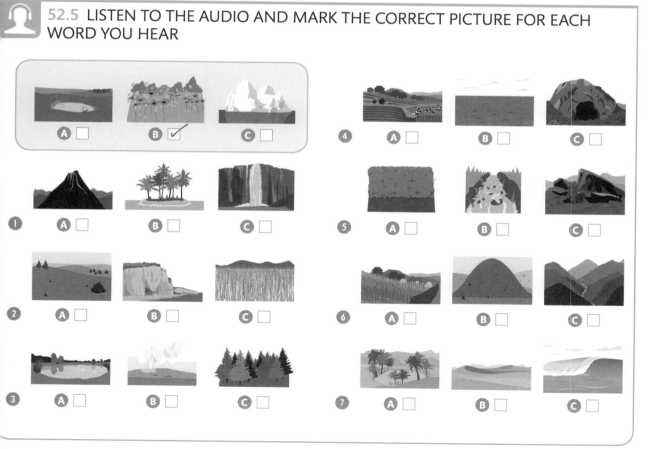

53.1 USEFUL EXPRESSIONS

Factory emissions are a cause of global warming.

global warming
[the increase in the Earth's temperature]

Climate change is a huge threat to many animals.

climate change
[changes in the Earth's weather patterns]

Carbon dioxide is one of the best-known greenhouse gases.

greenhouse gases
[gases that cause the greenhouse effect, heating up the Earth]

Fossil fuels such as coal and oil produce carbon dioxide.

fossil fuels
[fuels based on oil, coal, and gas]

This space rocket consumes a lot of fuel.

to consume
[to use a supply of something, such as fuel or energy]

You can reduce your carbon footprint by flying less.

to reduce your carbon footprint
[to lower the level of carbon dioxide produced by your actions]

We need to tackle pollution in our rivers.

to tackle pollution
[to deal with the problem of pollution]

We can reduce pollution by using more types of alternative energy.

alternative energy
[energy that does not use fossil fuels]

We must use more green energy sources, like wind and solar.

green energy sources
[types of energy that do not damage the environment]

It can be much cheaper to use renewable energy.

renewable energy
[energy from sources that do not run out]

The traffic in our cities is
harmful to the environment.

harmful to the environment
[causing damage to the environment]

Water pollution has dire
consequences for local wildlife.

dire consequences
[very bad results]

You can use solar power
to heat your water.

solar power
[energy created using sunlight]

Solar panels on your house
can help you save electricity.

a solar panel
[a panel that turns
sunlight into electricity]

Some areas use turbines
to turn wind power
into electricity.

wind power
[energy created using the wind]

This wind farm has been
running for several years.

a wind farm
[a place with many turbines for
generating wind power]

Years of poaching have made the
white rhino endangered.

endangered
[at risk of extinction]

Dinosaurs became extinct
millions of years ago.

extinct
[no longer existing]

We must work together to stop the
destruction of our forests.

destruction
[the act of damaging something
so badly that it cannot survive
be repaired]

If we don't reduce pollution, Earth will
undergo irreversible change.

irreversible change
[permanent change that cannot
be undone]

Aa 53.2 MATCH THE PICTURES TO THE CORRECT SENTENCES

Fossil fuels such as coal and oil produce carbon dioxide.

①

Some areas use turbines to turn wind power into electricity.

②

Solar panels on your house can help you save electricity.

③

It can be much cheaper to use renewable energy.

④

Carbon dioxide is one of the best-known greenhouse gases.

⑤

Factory emissions are a cause of global warming.

Aa 53.3 WRITE THE CORRECT PHRASE NEXT TO ITS DEFINITION, FILLING IN THE MISSING LETTERS

very bad results	=	d i r e c o n s e q u e n c e s

① at risk of extinction   =   e _ d a _ _ e r _

② the increase in the Earth's temperature   =   _ l _ _ a l   w _ r _ i n _

③ energy created using the wind   =   w _ n _   _ o _ e _

④ energy created using sunlight   =   _ o _ r   p _ _ e _

⑤ energy that does not use fossil fuels   =   a _ t e _ a _ _ e   _ n _ _ g y

53.4 LISTEN TO THE AUDIO AND COMPLETE THE SENTENCES THAT DESCRIBE EACH PICTURE

This space rocket _consumes_ a lot of fuel.

3 The traffic in our cities is
_____
_____ .

1 We need to _____ in our rivers.

4 We can reduce pollution by using more types of
_____ .

2 Dinosaurs became _____ millions of years ago.

5 _____ is a huge threat to many animals.

Aa 53.5 REWRITE THE SENTENCES, CORRECTING THE ERRORS

You can reduce your carbon fingerprint by flying less.
You can reduce your carbon footprint by flying less.

1 This wind firm has been running for several years.

_____

2 We must work together to stop the destructing of our forests.

_____

3 Weather change is a huge threat to many animals.

_____

4 If we don't reduce pollution, Earth will undergo unreversible change.

_____

54.1 PETS AND FARM ANIMALS

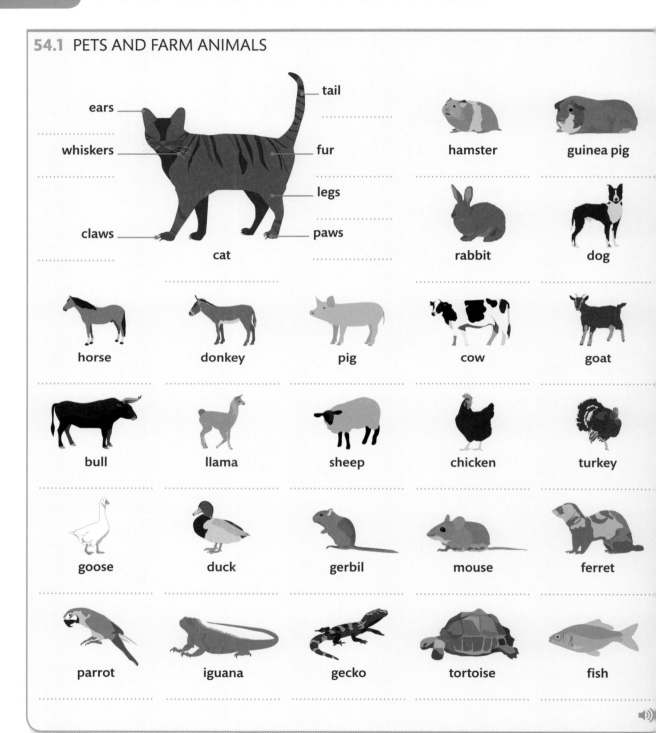

ears

whiskers

tail

fur

legs

paws

claws

cat

hamster

guinea pig

rabbit

dog

horse

donkey

pig

cow

goat

bull

llama

sheep

chicken

turkey

goose

duck

gerbil

mouse

ferret

parrot

iguana

gecko

tortoise

fish

54.2 ANIMAL VERBS

to bark

to meow

to gallop

to purr

to molt (US)
to moult (UK)

to hiss

to scratch

to sniff

to crow

to squeak

to snort

to hop

to bleat

to quack

to croak

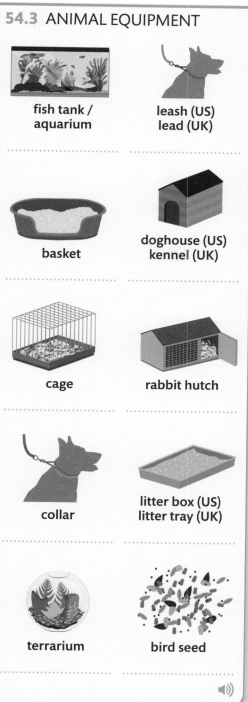

54.3 ANIMAL EQUIPMENT

fish tank /
aquarium

leash (US)
lead (UK)

basket

doghouse (US)
kennel (UK)

cage

rabbit hutch

collar

litter box (US)
litter tray (UK)

terrarium

bird seed

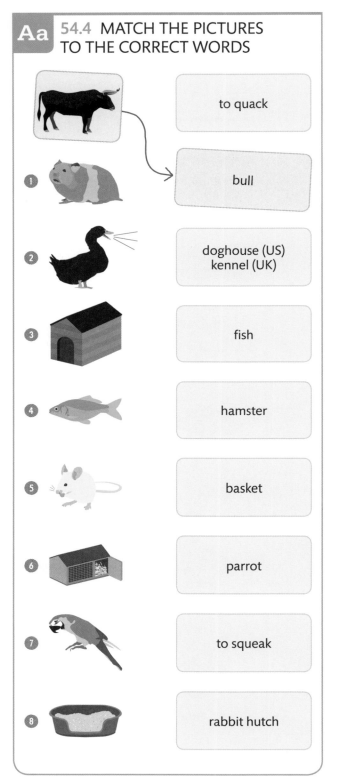

to quack

bull

doghouse (US)
kennel (UK)

fish

hamster

basket

parrot

to squeak

rabbit hutch

1

2

3

4

5

6

7

8

Aa 54.5 REWRITE THE WORDS, CORRECTING THE SPELLINGS

to galop
to gallop

1 hurse

2 terkey

3 shipe

4 to pur

5 to miow

6 mowse

7 to croke

8 donkiy

9 colar

54.6 LOOK AT THE PICTURE AND WRITE THE CORRECT WORD FOR EACH LABEL

fur

1 _____

2 _____

3 _____

4 _____

54.7 COMPLETE THE WORD FOR EACH PICTURE, FILLING IN THE MISSING LETTERS

c h i c k e n

1 t _ _ s _ r _ t _ h

2 g _ _ _ s e

3 t _ r t _ s _

4 _ q u _ _ r _ _ m

5 b _ _ d s _ _ d

54.8 LISTEN TO THE AUDIO, THEN NUMBER THE PICTURES IN THE ORDER YOU HEAR THEM

A ☐

B ☐

C ☐

D 1

E ☐

F ☐

G ☐

H ☐

I ☐

J ☐

225

55 Wild animals

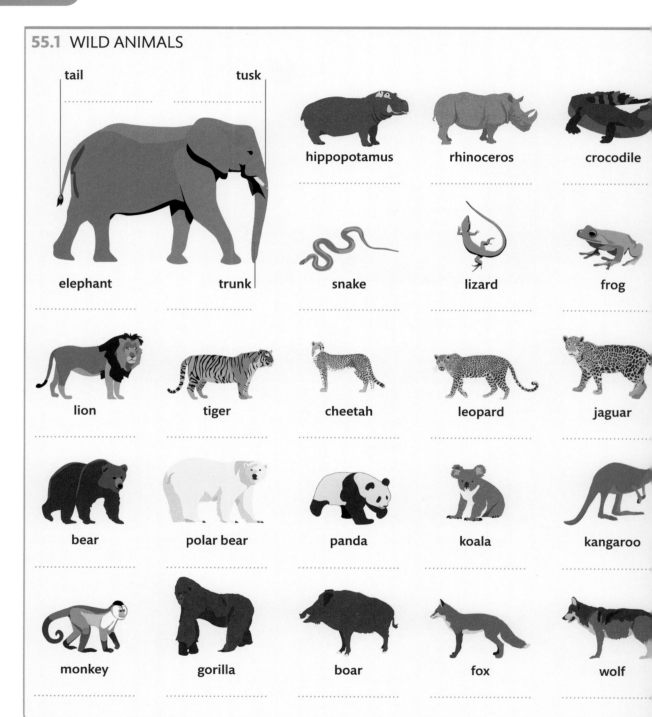

55.1 WILD ANIMALS

tail   tusk

elephant   trunk

hippopotamus

rhinoceros

crocodile

snake

lizard

frog

lion

tiger

cheetah

leopard

jaguar

bear

polar bear

panda

koala

kangaroo

monkey

gorilla

boar

fox

wolf

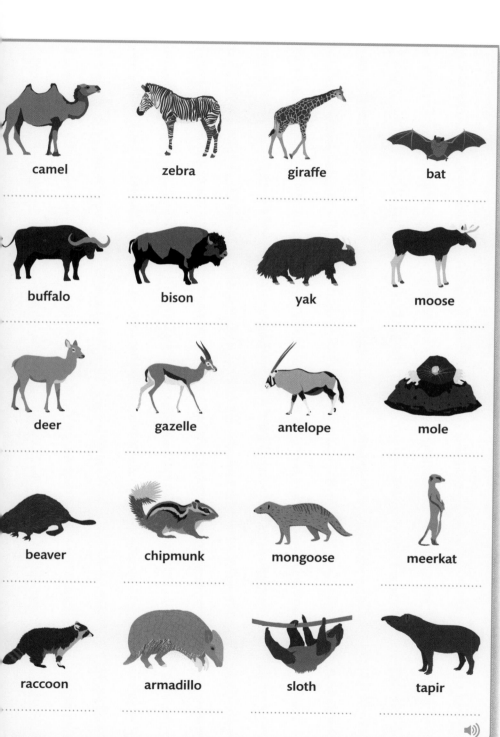

camel

zebra

giraffe

bat

buffalo

bison

yak

moose

deer

gazelle

antelope

mole

beaver

chipmunk

mongoose

meerkat

raccoon

armadillo

sloth

tapir

55.2 VERBS

to roar

to burrow

to hunt

to swing

to prowl

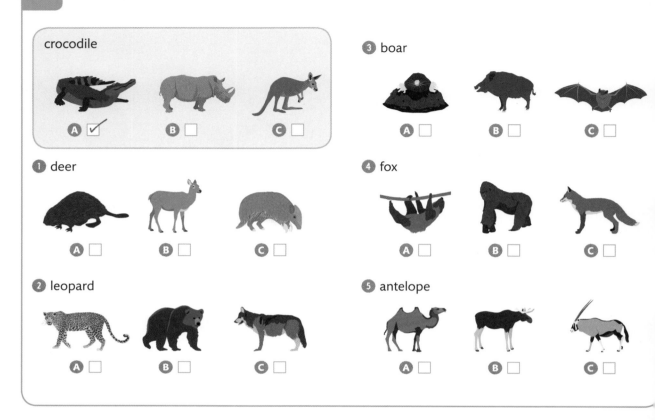

Aa 55.3 MARK THE CORRECT PICTURE FOR EACH WORD

crocodile

A ✓ B ☐ C ☐

❶ deer

A ☐ B ☐ C ☐

❷ leopard

A ☐ B ☐ C ☐

❸ boar

A ☐ B ☐ C ☐

❹ fox

A ☐ B ☐ C ☐

❺ antelope

A ☐ B ☐ C ☐

🎧 55.4 LISTEN TO THE AUDIO AND WRITE THE WORD THAT IS SHOWN IN EACH PICTURE

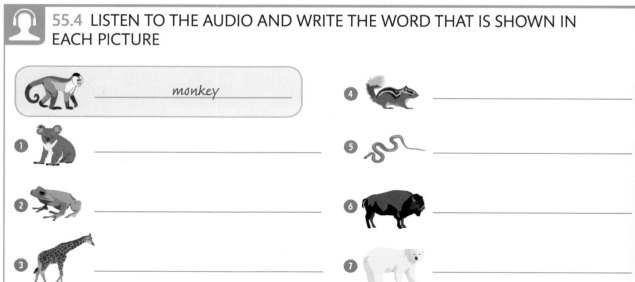

monkey

❶ _____

❷ _____

❸ _____

❹ _____

❺ _____

❻ _____

❼ _____

55.5 FIND EIGHT MORE WORDS IN THE GRID THAT MATCH THE PICTURES

```
C A M E L I R A C S A H
T A V L Q H K Q V W Q P
A E D E M J S M D H B O
H I P P O P O T A M U S
Z T B H X W B X B F F A
P E J A G U A R D W F Y
Q M Z N O L T O Z O A M
L E D T I G E R D L L J
M O N G O O S E Z F O S
```

55.6 WRITE THE CORRECT WORD UNDER EACH PICTURE

lizard

1 _____

2 _____

3 _____

4 _____

5 _____

6 _____

7 _____

8 _____

9 _____

10 _____

11 _____

12 _____

13 _____

14 _____

56.1 BIRDS

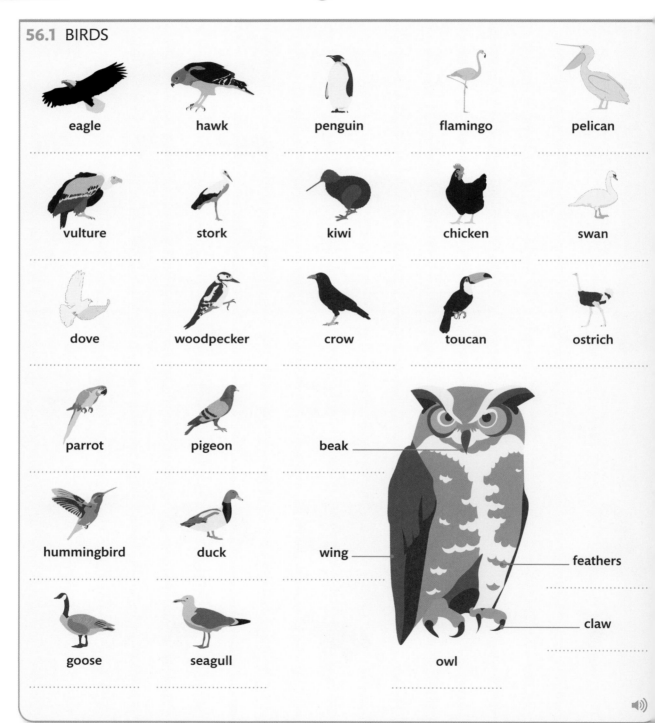

eagle

hawk

penguin

flamingo

pelican

vulture

stork

kiwi

chicken

swan

dove

woodpecker

crow

toucan

ostrich

parrot

pigeon

beak

hummingbird

duck

wing

feathers

claw

goose

seagull

owl

56.2 INSECTS AND BUGS

butterfly

moth

mosquito

bee

fly

wasp

caterpillar

cockroach

locust

ant

ladybug (US)
ladybird (UK)

beetle

spider

worm

snail

56.3 VERBS FOR BIRDS AND BUGS

to fly

to hoot

to swoop

to flap

to glide

to hatch

to peck

to buzz

to sting

to sing

56.4 FILL IN THE GAPS, PUTTING THE WORDS FROM THE PANEL INTO THE CORRECT CATEGORIES

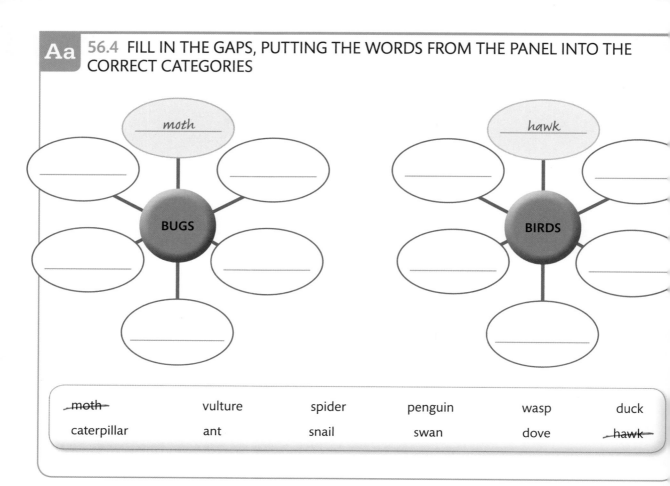

moth

BUGS

hawk

BIRDS

moth   vulture   spider   penguin   wasp   duck

caterpillar   ant   snail   swan   dove   hawk

56.5 MATCH THE PICTURES TO THE CORRECT VERBS

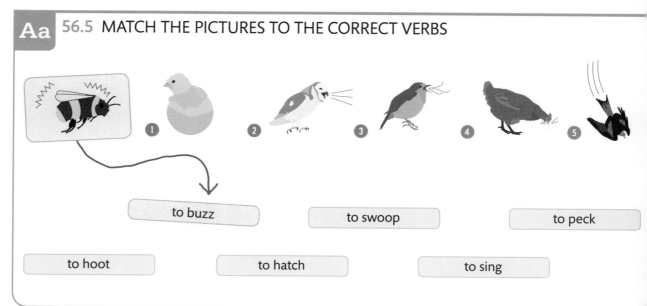

to buzz   to swoop   to peck

to hoot   to hatch   to sing

Aa 56.6 LOOK AT THE PICTURE AND WRITE THE CORRECT WORD FOR EACH LABEL

1 _____

feathers

2 _____   3 _____

56.7 LISTEN TO THE AUDIO AND MARK THE WORDS YOU HEAR

owl ☐	beetle ✓	bee ☐

1 crow ☐	kiwi ☐	claw ☐
2 to fly ☐	to flap ☐	to glide ☐
3 toucan ☐	locust ☐	ostrich ☐
4 stork ☐	wing ☐	dove ☐
5 pigeon ☐	pelican ☐	goose ☐
6 seagull ☐	fly ☐	swan ☐
7 bee ☐	beak ☐	eagle ☐
8 feather ☐	mosquito ☐	caterpillar ☐

Aa 56.8 COMPLETE THE WORD FOR EACH PICTURE, FILLING IN THE MISSING LETTERS

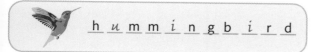 h u m m i n g b i r d

1 w _ _ d p _ c k _ r

2 w _ r _

3 _ _ g l _

4 b _ t _ _ r f l _ _

5 b _ _ t l _

6 c h _ c _ _ n

7 p _ r _ _ t

8 c _ _ k r _ _ _ c _

9 p _ l _ c _ n

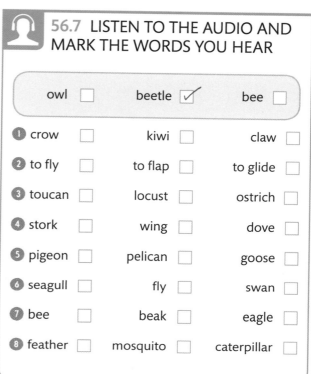

57 Fish, whales, and sea creatures

57.1 FISH AND SEA CREATURES

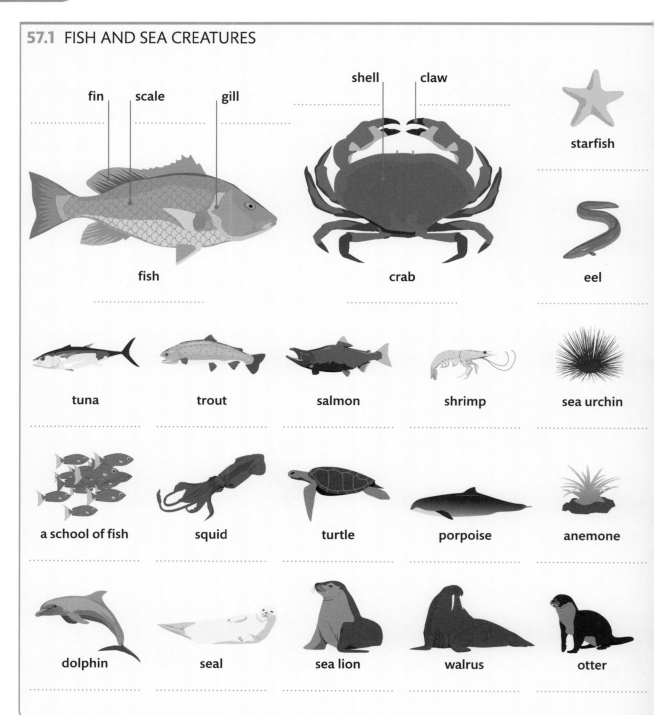

fin   scale   gill

fish

shell   claw

crab

starfish

eel

tuna

trout

salmon

shrimp

sea urchin

a school of fish

squid

turtle

porpoise

anemone

dolphin

seal

sea lion

walrus

otter

octopus

mussel

clam

oyster

shark

lobster

jellyfish

seahorse

swordfish

ray

57.2 WHALES

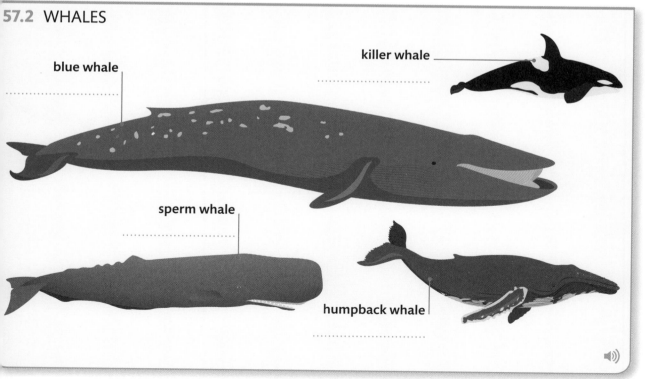

killer whale

blue whale

sperm whale

humpback whale

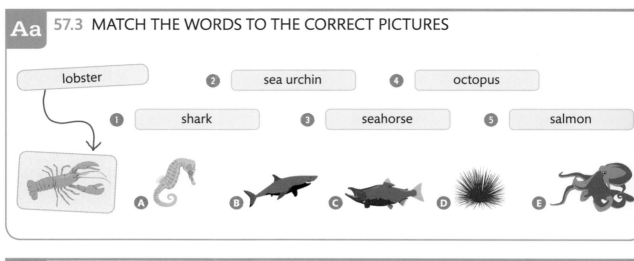

Aa 57.3 MATCH THE WORDS TO THE CORRECT PICTURES

lobster

2 sea urchin

4 octopus

1 shark

3 seahorse

5 salmon

Aa 57.4 LOOK AT THE PICTURE CLUES AND WRITE THE ANSWERS IN THE CORRECT PLACES ON THE GRID

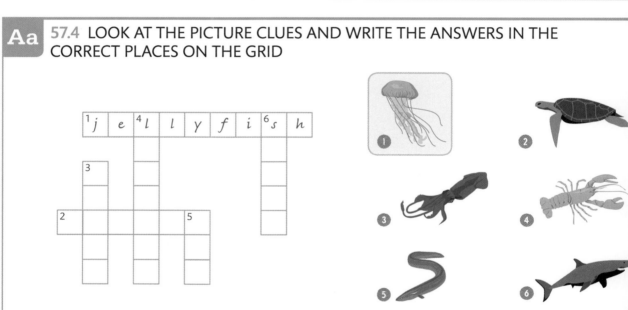

¹j e ⁴l l y f i ⁶s h

Aa 57.5 MARK THE BEGINNING AND ENDING OF EACH WORD IN THE CHAIN OF LETTERS

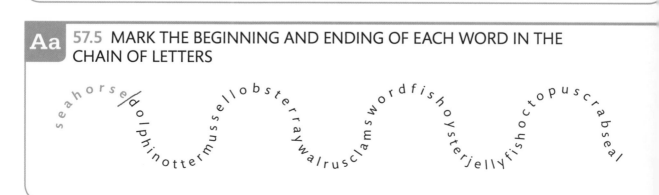

seahorse/dolphinottermussellobsterraywalrusclamswordfishoysterjellyfishoctopuscrabseal

Aa **57.7** WRITE THE CORRECT WORD UNDER EACH PICTURE

A ☐   B ✓   C ☐

1 A ☐   B ☐   C ☐

2 A ☐   B ☐   C ☐

3 A ☐   B ☐   C ☐

4 A ☐   B ☐   C ☐

5 A ☐   B ☐   C ☐

6 A ☐   B ☐   C ☐

swordfish

①

②

③

④

⑤

⑥

⑦

⑧

⑨

58 Free time activities

58.1 FREE TIME ACTIVITIES

 to do puzzles

 to play cards

 to play chess

 to play board games

 to go to a book club

 to play video games

 to read

 to draw

 to write

 to paint

 to take photos

 to play a musical instrument

 to walk / to hike

 to cook

 to bake

 to sew

 to knit

 to go to a party

 to do karaoke

 to watch television

 to watch a movie

 to see a play

 to do exercise

 to go to the gym

 to do yoga

to listen to music

 to go camping

 to go birdwatching

 to go out for a meal

 to do the gardening

 to visit a museum / gallery

 to meet friends

 to go on vacation (US) to go on holiday (UK)

 to go shopping

 to go to a concert

 to stay (at) home

 to have a picnic

 to collect stamps

 to do pottery

 to make models

 to surf / browse the internet

 to call friends

 to go to an evening class

 to go to the beach

 to fly a kite

 to ride a horse

 to go jogging

 to sing in a choir

 to arrange flowers

 to go foraging

Aa 58.2 MARK THE CORRECT VERB FOR THE ACTIVITY IN EACH PICTURE

to draw ☐
to play cards ☑
to collect stamps ☐

1
to meet friends ☐
to make models ☐
to sew ☐

2
to take photos ☐
to go shopping ☐
to do karaoke ☐

3
to collect stamps ☐
to cook ☐
to do puzzles ☐

4
to call friends ☐
to take photos ☐
to paint ☐

5
to read ☐
to go to a party ☐
to go camping ☐

6
to walk / hike ☐
to fly a kite ☐
to ride a horse ☐

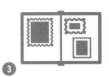

7
to see a play ☐
to bake ☐
to go foraging ☐

8
to have a picnic ☐
to listen to music ☐
to knit ☐

9
to write ☐
to paint ☐
to go jogging ☐

10
to fly a kite ☐
to knit ☐
to play chess ☐

11
to watch television ☐
to sing in a choir ☐
to do puzzles ☐

Aa 58.3 MATCH THE ACTIVITIES TO THE CORRECT PICTURES

to go birdwatching

1 to go to an evening class
2 to watch a movie
3 to go out for a meal
4 to sing in a choir

A **B** **C** **D**

58.4 LISTEN TO THE AUDIO AND WRITE THE ACTIVITY THAT IS SHOWN IN EACH PICTURE

to do pottery

1 _____

2 _____

3 _____

4 _____

5 _____

6 _____

7 _____

8 _____

9 _____

58.5 WRITE THE CORRECT ACTIVITY UNDER EACH PICTURE

to go shopping

1 _____

2 _____

3 _____

4 _____

5 _____

6 _____

7 _____

8 _____

9 _____

10 _____

11 _____

12 _____

13 _____

14 _____

59 Abilities and actions

59.1 ABILITIES AND ACTIONS

to see

to lick

to taste

to smell

to listen

to work

to play

to kick

to throw

to hit

to whisper

to dance

to run

to crawl

to jump

to repair

to shake

to make (a snowman)

to do (homework)

to think

to understand

to spell

to move

to dig

to fall

to carry

 to climb

 to stand up

 to sit down

 to lift

 to add

 to subtract

 to count

 to sing

 to catch

 to talk

 to speak

 to shout

 to push

 to pull

 to act

 to blow

 to copy

 to decide

 to remember

 to hold

 to point

 to pack

 to fly

 to ride

Aa 59.2 WRITE THE CORRECT ACTION UNDER EACH PICTURE

to catch

 1 _____

 2 _____

 3 _____

 4 _____

 5 _____

 6 _____

 7 _____

 8 _____

 9 _____

 10 _____

 11 _____

 12 _____

 13 _____

 14 _____

59.3 LISTEN TO THE AUDIO, THEN NUMBER THE ACTIONS IN THE ORDER YOU HEAR THEM

 A ☐

 B ☐

 C 1

 D ☐

 E ☐

 F ☐

 G ☐

 H ☐

 I ☐

 J ☐

 K ☐

 L ☐

 M ☐

 N ☐

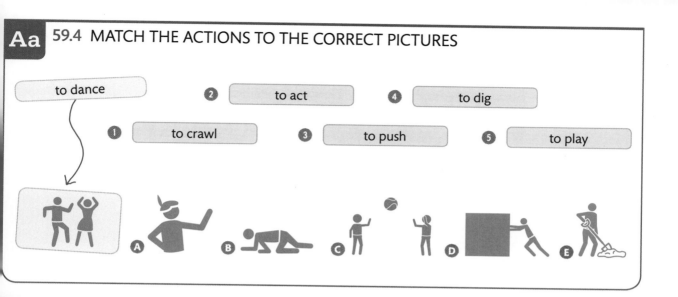

Aa 59.4 MATCH THE ACTIONS TO THE CORRECT PICTURES

to dance

2 to act   4 to dig

1 to crawl   3 to push   5 to play

Aa 59.5 MARK THE CORRECT PICTURE FOR EACH ACTION

to jump

A ☐   B ☐   C ☑

3 to hit

A ☐   B ☐   C ☐

1 to shake

A ☐   B ☐   C ☐

4 to climb

A ☐   B ☐   C ☐

2 to add

A ☐   B ☐   C ☐

5 to throw

A ☐   B ☐   C ☐

60.1 SPORTS

judo

boxing

archery

gymnastics

discus

high jump

long jump

baseball

cricket

field hockey (US)
hockey (UK)

badminton

soccer (US)
football (UK)

rugby

volleyball

basketball

golf

cycling

fishing

pool

roller-skating

canoeing /
kayaking

surfing

swimming

sailing

rowing

javelin

running

running a marathon

hockey (US)
ice hockey (UK)

tennis

squash

football (US)
American football (UK)

horse riding

motor racing

skating

skiing

diving

table tennis

bowling

skateboarding

abseiling

bungee jumping

hang gliding

paragliding

rock climbing

scuba diving

skydiving

snorkeling (US)
snorkelling (UK)

snowboarding

windsurfing

60.3 LOOK AT THE PICTURE CLUES AND WRITE THE ANSWERS IN THE CORRECT PLACES ON THE GRID

| ¹s | k | a | ⁷t | i | n | ⁸g |

6

2

3   9

4

5

60.4 MARK THE BEGINNING AND ENDING OF EACH SPORT IN THE CHAIN OF LETTERS, THEN WRITE THE WORDS YOU FIND

hockey/rockclimbingsurfingjudomotorracingvolleyballparaglidingskydivingskateboarding

_____hockey_____

3 _____   6 _____

❶ _____   4 _____   7 _____

❷ _____   5 _____   8 _____

248

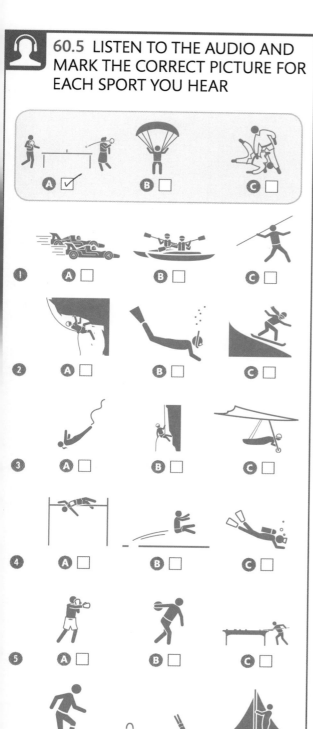

60.5 LISTEN TO THE AUDIO AND MARK THE CORRECT PICTURE FOR EACH SPORT YOU HEAR

A ✓ B ☐ C ☐

1 A ☐ B ☐ C ☐

2 A ☐ B ☐ C ☐

3 A ☐ B ☐ C ☐

4 A ☐ B ☐ C ☐

5 A ☐ B ☐ C ☐

6 A ☐ B ☐ C ☐

60.6 COMPLETE THE WORDS FOR EACH PICTURE, FILLING IN THE MISSING LETTERS

h o r s e   r i d i n g

1 b _ d m _ n t _ n

2 b _ s _ b _ l l

3 g _ m n _ s t _ c s

4 c _ c l _ n g

5 s q _ _ s h

6 s k _ t _ b _ _ _ r d _ n g

7 s c _ b _   d _ _ v _ n g

8 t _ b l _   t _ n n _ s

9 s k _ d _ v _ _ n g

10 v _ l l _ y b _ l l

11 _ b s _ _ l _ n g

12 _ w _ m _ i _ g

61 Soccer

61.1 SOCCER GAME

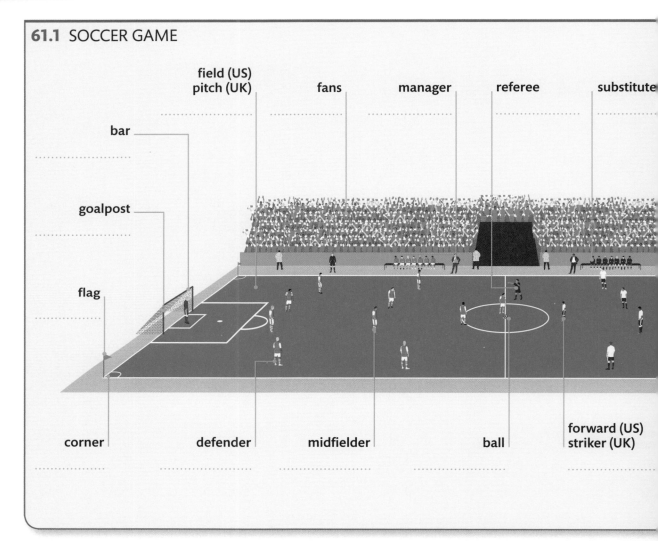

bar

goalpost

flag

corner

field (US)
pitch (UK)

fans

manager

referee

substitute

defender

midfielder

ball

forward (US)
striker (UK)

61.3 TIMINGS AND RULES

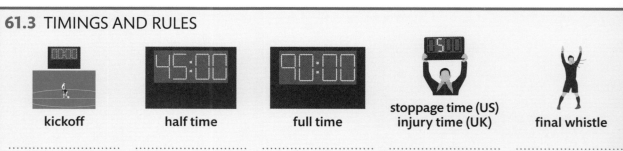

kickoff

half time

full time

stoppage time (US)
injury time (UK)

final whistle

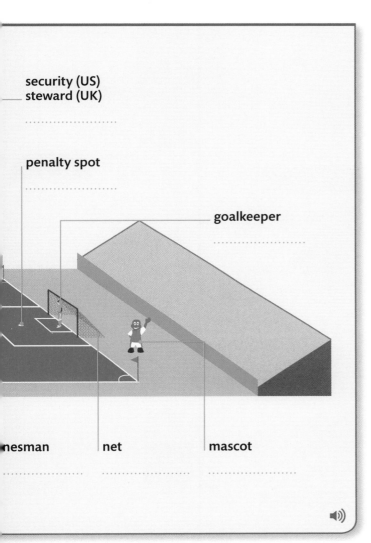

security (US)
steward (UK)

penalty spot

goalkeeper

nesman   net   mascot

61.2 VERBS

to tackle   to kick

to score a goal   to be booked

to be sent off   to win

to lose   to tie (US)
                  to draw (UK)

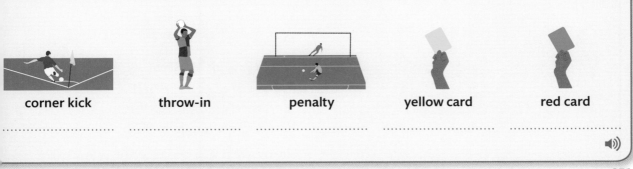

corner kick   throw-in   penalty   yellow card   red card

Aa 61.4 WRITE THE CORRECT WORD OR EXPRESSION UNDER EACH PICTURE

kickoff

 1 _____

 2 _____

 3 _____

 4 _____

 5 _____

 6 _____

 7 _____

 8 _____

 9 _____

 10 _____

 11 _____

 12 _____

 13 _____

 14 _____

Aa 61.5 MARK THE CORRECT WORD OR EXPRESSION FOR EACH PICTURE

to tackle	☐
to win	☐
throw-in	☑

 1

to be booked	☐
to lose	☐
to score a goal	☐

 2

to kick	☐
to tie	☐
goalkeeper	☐

 3

to lose	☐
to be sent off	☐
to win	☐

 4

final whistle	☐
kickoff	☐
bar	☐

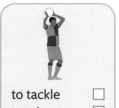 5

substitutes	☐
security	☐
fans	☐

 6

manager	☐
mascot	☐
security	☐

 7

stoppage time	☐
kickoff	☐
to tackle	☐

 8

full time	☐
stoppage time	☐
red card	☐

 9

to lose	☐
to tie	☐
to be booked	☐

252

61.6 LISTEN TO THE AUDIO, THEN NUMBER THE PICTURES IN THE ORDER YOU HEAR THEM

A ☐ B 1 C ☐ D ☐

E ☐ F ☐ G ☐ H ☐

I ☐ J ☐ K ☐ L ☐

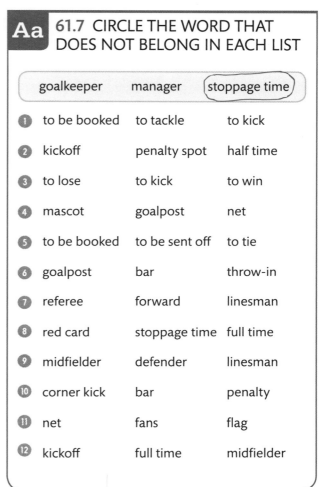

Aa 61.7 CIRCLE THE WORD THAT DOES NOT BELONG IN EACH LIST

goalkeeper   manager   (stoppage time)

1 to be booked   to tackle   to kick

2 kickoff   penalty spot   half time

3 to lose   to kick   to win

4 mascot   goalpost   net

5 to be booked   to be sent off   to tie

6 goalpost   bar   throw-in

7 referee   forward   linesman

8 red card   stoppage time   full time

9 midfielder   defender   linesman

10 corner kick   bar   penalty

11 net   fans   flag

12 kickoff   full time   midfielder

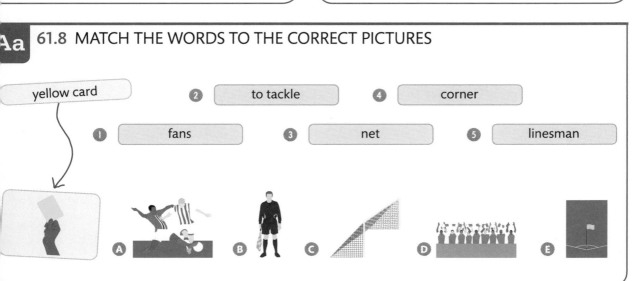

Aa 61.8 MATCH THE WORDS TO THE CORRECT PICTURES

yellow card

2 to tackle   4 corner

1 fans   3 net   5 linesman

A   B   C   D   E

62.1 EQUIPMENT

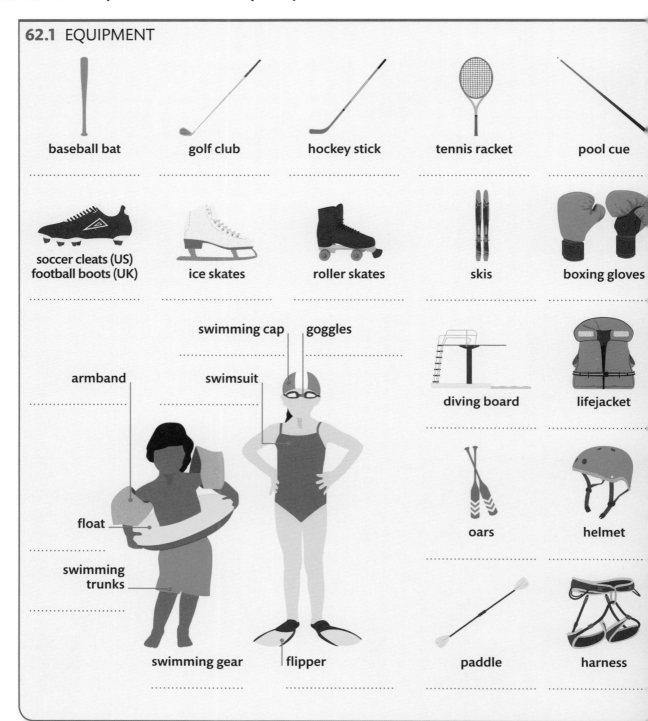

baseball bat

golf club

hockey stick

tennis racket

pool cue

soccer cleats (US)
football boots (UK)

ice skates

roller skates

skis

boxing gloves

swimming cap

goggles

armband

swimsuit

diving board

lifejacket

float

oars

helmet

swimming
trunks

swimming gear

flipper

paddle

harness

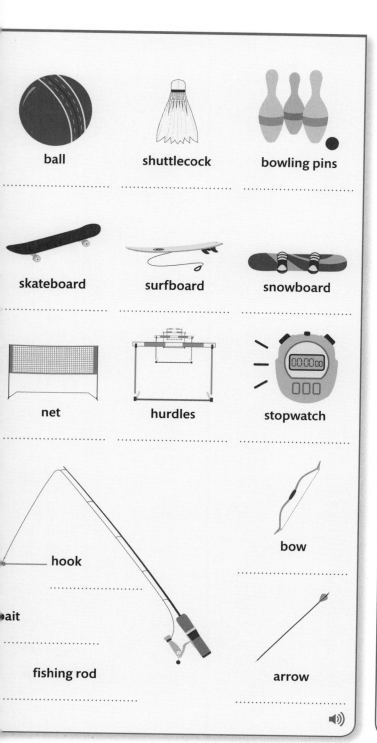

ball

shuttlecock

bowling pins

skateboard

surfboard

snowboard

net

hurdles

stopwatch

hook

bait

fishing rod

bow

arrow

62.2 VENUES

field (US) /
pitch (UK)

stadium

running track

golf course

tennis court

gym

boxing ring

swimming pool

ice rink

ski slope

Aa 62.3 MATCH THE WORDS TO THE CORRECT PICTURES

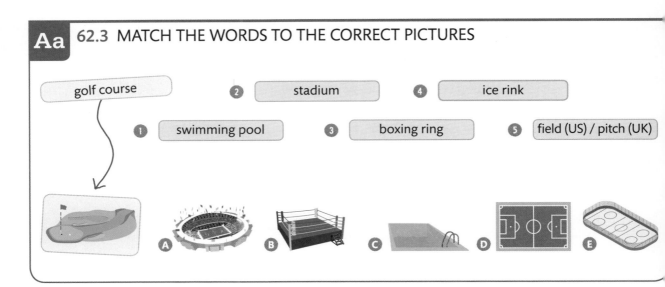

golf course

② stadium

④ ice rink

① swimming pool

③ boxing ring

⑤ field (US) / pitch (UK)

Aa 62.4 LOOK AT THE PICTURE AND WRITE THE CORRECT WORD FOR EACH LABEL

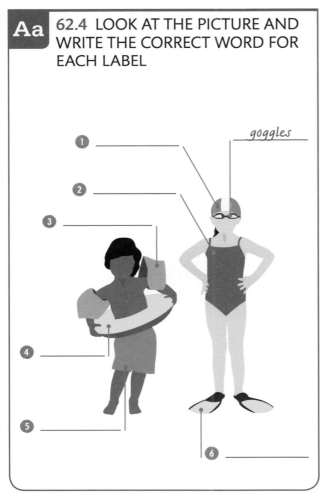

goggles

62.5 LISTEN TO THE AUDIO AND CIRCLE THE WORDS YOU HEAR

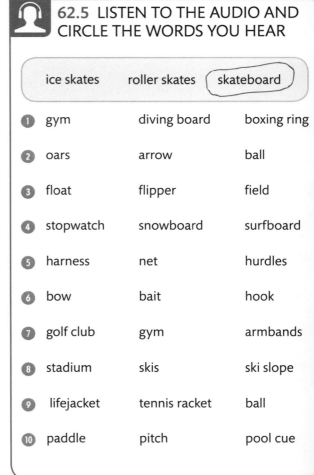

ice skates　　roller skates　　(skateboard)

① gym	diving board	boxing ring
② oars	arrow	ball
③ float	flipper	field
④ stopwatch	snowboard	surfboard
⑤ harness	net	hurdles
⑥ bow	bait	hook
⑦ golf club	gym	armbands
⑧ stadium	skis	ski slope
⑨ lifejacket	tennis racket	ball
⑩ paddle	pitch	pool cue

62.6 FILL IN THE GAPS, PUTTING THE WORDS FROM THE PANEL INTO THE CORRECT CATEGORIES

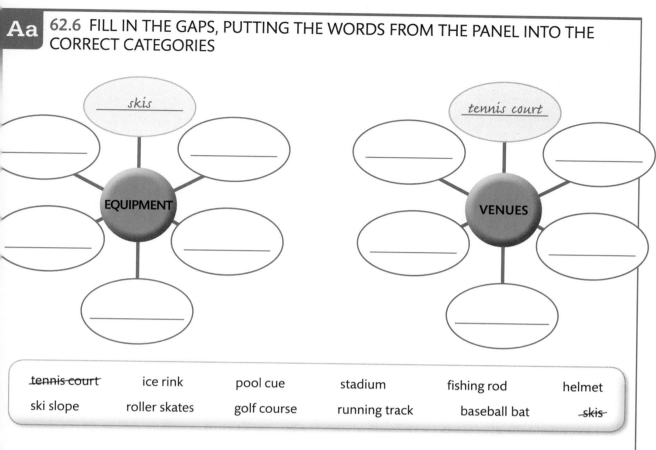

skis

tennis court

EQUIPMENT

VENUES

| ~~tennis court~~ | ice rink | pool cue | stadium | fishing rod | helmet |
| ski slope | roller skates | golf course | running track | baseball bat | ~~skis~~ |

62.7 REWRITE THE WORDS, CORRECTING THE SPELLINGS

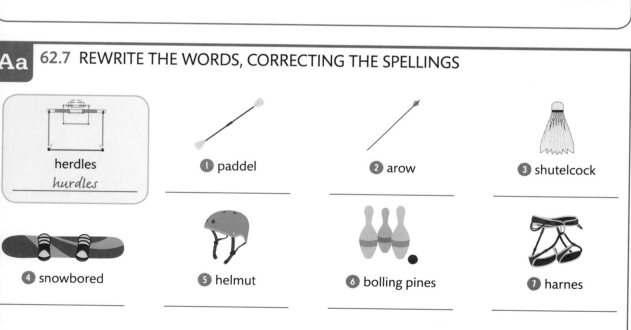

herdles
hurdles

① paddel

② arow

③ shutelcock

④ snowbored

⑤ helmut

⑥ bolling pines

⑦ harnes

63 Books and reading

63.1 BOOKS

illustration   page

cover

book   spine

author

novel

chapter

hardback

paperback

e-reader

63.2 USEFUL EXPRESSIONS

His new novel has received glowing reviews from all the critics.

glowing reviews
[highly positive reviews]

I flipped through the guidebook and decided to buy it.

to flip (US) / flick (UK) through
[to take a quick look inside a book]

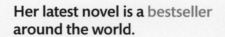

I find the plot difficult to understand in most fantasy novels.

a plot
[a series of events that make up a story]

Her latest novel is a bestseller around the world.

a bestseller
[a book that sells a large number of copies]

I'm reading a crime novel. It's a real page-turner.

a page-turner
[a novel that makes you want to read more]

The novel was too highbrow for me. I prefer popular fiction.

???

highbrow
[containing difficult or intellectual ideas]

63.3 READING AND GENRES

fiction

romance

crime fiction

science-fiction

fantasy

non-fiction

biography

autobiography

humor (US)
humour (UK)

self-help

nature writing

travel writing

guidebook

cookbook

textbook / course book

dictionary

encyclopedia

comic

gossip magazine

TV guide

headline

article

newspaper

puzzles

horoscope

coloring book (US)
colouring book (UK)

Aa 63.4 WRITE THE CORRECT WORD UNDER EACH PICTURE

fantasy

① _____

② _____

③ _____

④ _____

⑤ _____

⑥ _____

⑦ _____

⑧ _____

⑨ _____

⑩ _____

⑪ _____

⑫ _____

⑬ _____

⑭ _____

Aa 63.5 LOOK AT THE PICTURE CLUES AND WRITE THE ANSWERS IN THE CORRECT PLACES ON THE GRID

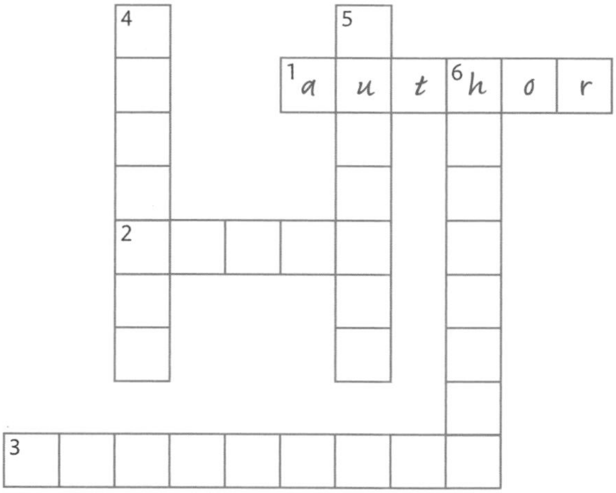

Crossword grid:
- 1 across: a u t h o r
- 4 down, 5 down, 6 down, 2 across, 3 across (empty)

①

②

③

④

⑤

⑥

Aa 63.6 MATCH THE BEGINNINGS OF THE SENTENCES TO THE CORRECT ENDINGS

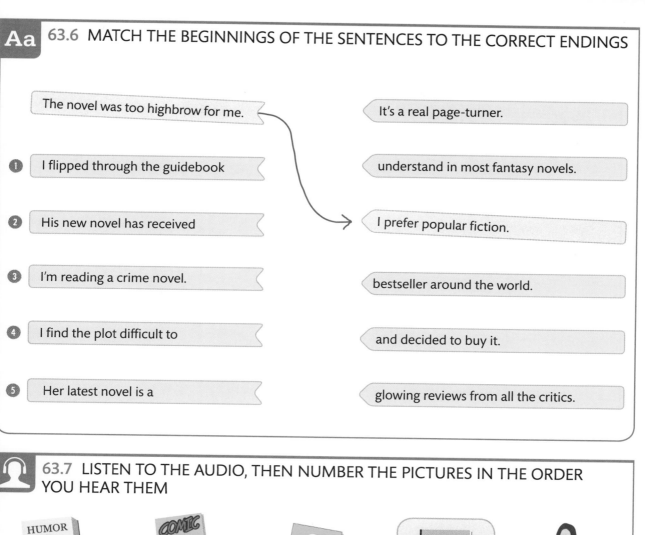

The novel was too highbrow for me. — I prefer popular fiction.

It's a real page-turner.

1. I flipped through the guidebook

understand in most fantasy novels.

2. His new novel has received

3. I'm reading a crime novel.

bestseller around the world.

4. I find the plot difficult to

and decided to buy it.

5. Her latest novel is a

glowing reviews from all the critics.

63.7 LISTEN TO THE AUDIO, THEN NUMBER THE PICTURES IN THE ORDER YOU HEAR THEM

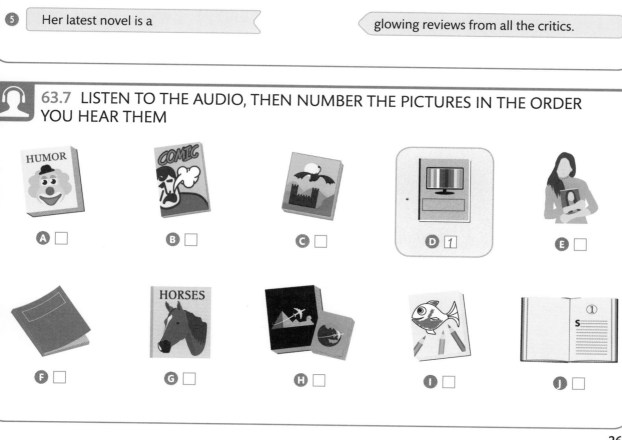

A ☐ B ☐ C ☐ D ☑ 1 E ☐

F ☐ G ☐ H ☐ I ☐ J ☐

64.1 MUSICAL INSTRUMENTS

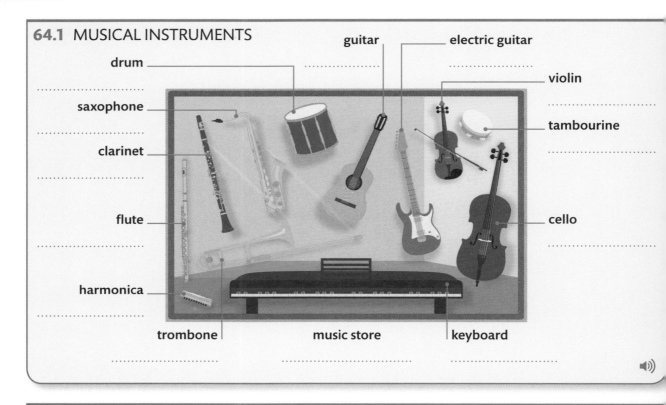

drum

saxophone

clarinet

flute

harmonica

trombone

guitar

electric guitar

violin

tambourine

cello

music store

keyboard

64.2 VERBS

to practice (US)
to practise (UK)

to rehearse

to play the
trumpet

to sing

to conduct

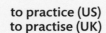

to listen

to perform

to busk

to compose

to record

64.3 MUSICAL GENRES

hip-hop | classical | jazz | country | opera

soul | rap | rock | pop | latin

64.4 PERFORMANCE

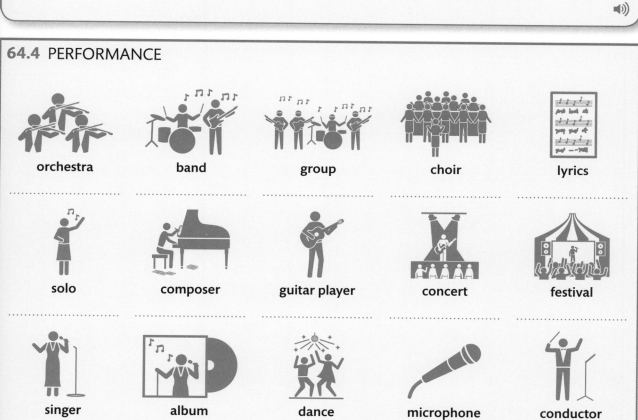

orchestra | band | group | choir | lyrics

solo | composer | guitar player | concert | festival

singer | album | dance | microphone | conductor

Aa 64.5 LOOK AT THE PICTURE AND WRITE THE CORRECT WORD FOR EACH LABEL

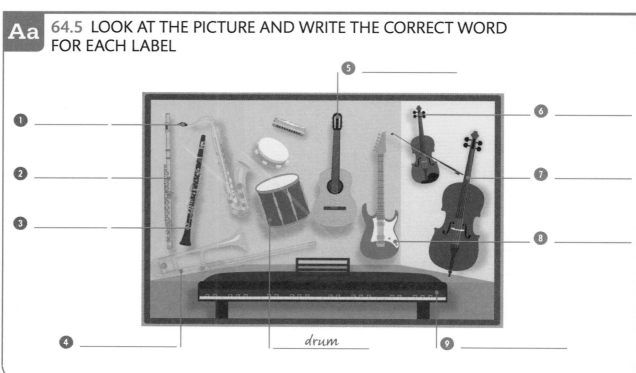

❶ _____
❷ _____
❸ _____
❹ _____
❺ _____
❻ _____
❼ _____
❽ _____
❾ _____

drum

Aa 64.6 MARK THE CORRECT WORD FOR EACH PICTURE

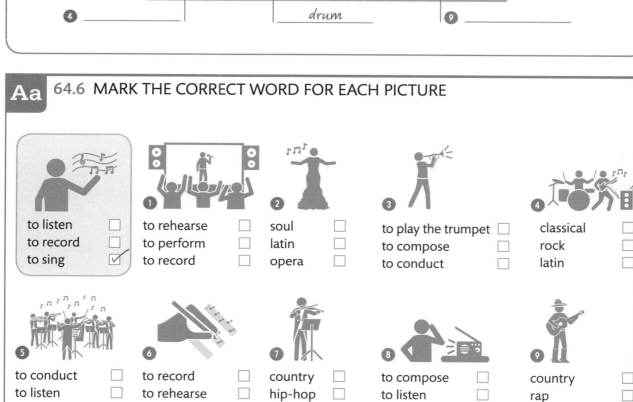

to listen ☐
to record ☐
to sing ☑

❶
to rehearse ☐
to perform ☐
to record ☐

❷
soul ☐
latin ☐
opera ☐

❸
to play the trumpet ☐
to compose ☐
to conduct ☐

❹
classical ☐
rock ☐
latin ☐

❺
to conduct ☐
to listen ☐
to busk ☐

❻
to record ☐
to rehearse ☐
to compose ☐

❼
country ☐
hip-hop ☐
classical ☐

❽
to compose ☐
to listen ☐
to perform ☐

❾
country ☐
rap ☐
jazz ☐

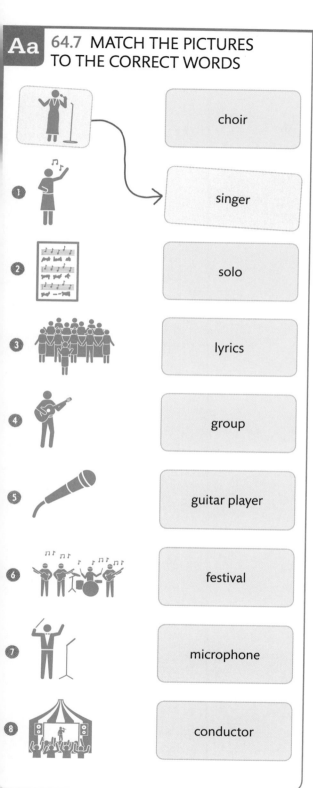

Aa 64.7 MATCH THE PICTURES TO THE CORRECT WORDS

choir

singer

solo

lyrics

group

guitar player

festival

microphone

conductor

64.8 LISTEN TO THE AUDIO AND MARK THE CORRECT PICTURE FOR EACH WORD YOU HEAR

A ☐   B ☐   C ☑

1 A ☐   B ☐   C ☐

2 A ☐   B ☐   C ☐

3 A ☐   B ☐   C ☐

4 A ☐   B ☐   C ☐

5 A ☐   B ☐   C ☐

6 A ☐   B ☐   C ☐

65 Movies and plays

65.1 MOVIES

movie theater (US)
cinema (UK)

movie (US)
film (UK)

movie star (US)
film star (UK)

main character

hero

villain

director

drama

musical

science fiction

thriller

comedy

action movie

horror

cartoon

romantic comedy

crime drama

western

special effects

stunt

audience

screen

box office

multiplex

popcorn

266

65.2 PLAYS AND SHOWS

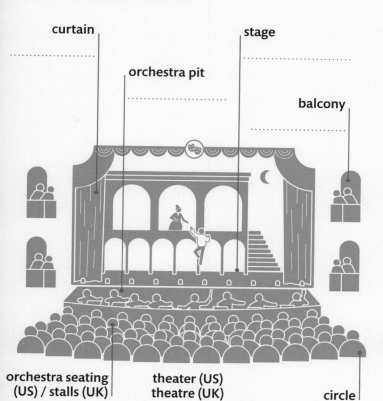

curtain

orchestra pit

stage

balcony

orchestra seating (US) / stalls (UK)

theater (US) theatre (UK)

circle

opera

opera house

ballet

tragedy

sets

props

costumes

cast

performance

script

program (US) programme (UK)

applause

dialog (US) dialogue (UK)

encore

standing ovation

usher

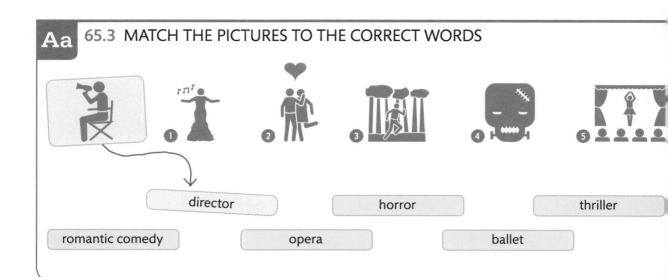

Aa 65.3 MATCH THE PICTURES TO THE CORRECT WORDS

director

horror

thriller

romantic comedy

opera

ballet

Aa 65.4 CIRCLE THE WORD THAT DOES NOT BELONG IN EACH LIST

hero	villain	stage
1 western	costumes	science fiction
2 multiplex	sets	props
3 comedy	tragedy	script
4 applause	popcorn	encore
5 multiplex	screen	villain
6 usher	opera	ballet
7 cartoon	curtain	balcony
8 audience	cast	stunt
9 thriller	director	drama

65.5 LISTEN TO THE AUDIO AND CIRCLE THE WORDS YOU HEAR

stunt	screen	science fiction
1 cast	sets	script
2 hero	horror	western
3 villain	movie	musical
4 dialog	director	drama
5 applause	multiplex	encore
6 usher	popcorn	audience
7 tragedy	ballet	box office
8 cartoon	crime drama	curtain
9 script	props	performance
10 villain	thriller	ballet

Aa 65.6 LOOK AT THE PICTURE AND WRITE THE CORRECT WORD FOR EACH LABEL

curtain

Aa 65.7 REWRITE THE WORDS, CORRECTING THE SPELLINGS

opara

opera

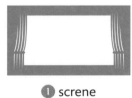

1 screne

2 custumes

3 acton movie

4 movee star

5 audeince

6 carton

7 encor

269

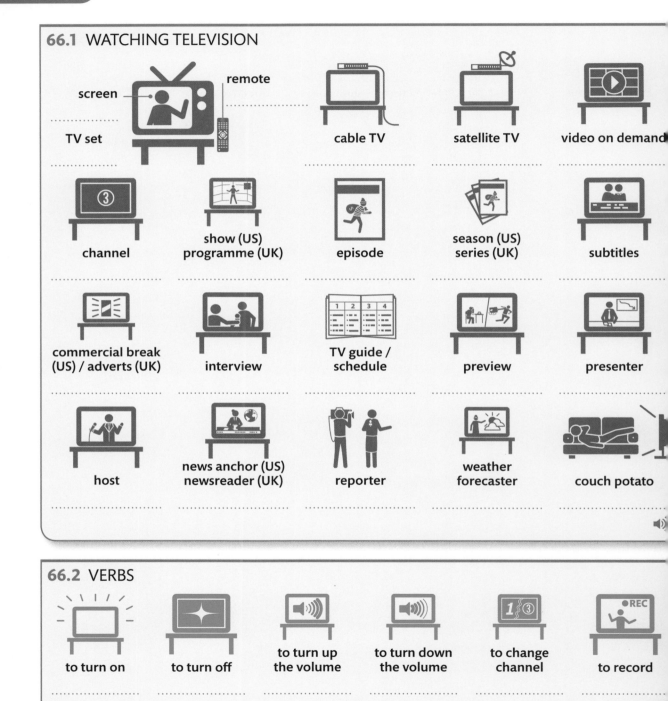

66.1 WATCHING TELEVISION

TV set — screen, remote

cable TV

satellite TV

video on demand

channel

show (US) / programme (UK)

episode

season (US) / series (UK)

subtitles

commercial break (US) / adverts (UK)

interview

TV guide / schedule

preview

presenter

host

news anchor (US) / newsreader (UK)

reporter

weather forecaster

couch potato

66.2 VERBS

to turn on

to turn off

to turn up the volume

to turn down the volume

to change channel

to record

66.3 TV SHOWS AND CHANNELS

cooking show

talk show (US) / chat show (UK)

sports show (US) / programme (UK)

documentary

nature documentary

period / costume drama

sitcom

quiz show

current affairs

news

weather

soap opera

game show

comedy

drama

cartoon

crime

thriller

satire

children's show (US) / TV (UK)

breakfast TV

reality TV

catch-up TV

shopping channel

music channel

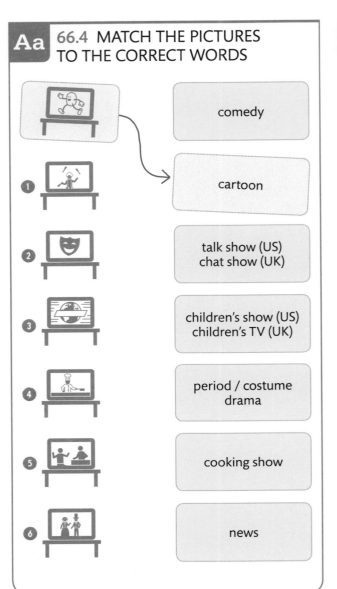

Aa 66.4 MATCH THE PICTURES TO THE CORRECT WORDS

comedy

cartoon

talk show (US)
chat show (UK)

children's show (US)
children's TV (UK)

period / costume
drama

cooking show

news

Aa 66.5 LISTEN TO THE AUDIO, THEN NUMBER THE PICTURES IN THE ORDER YOU HEAR THEM

A ☐   B ☐   C ☐

D ☐   E 1   F ☐

G ☐   H ☐   I ☐

J ☐   K ☐   L ☐

Aa 66.6 MARK THE BEGINNING AND ENDING OF EACH WORD IN THE CHAIN OF LETTERS

episode / documentarychannelremotesatirereporterweatherdramascreenpreviewsitcom

presenter

① _____

② _____

③ _____

④ _____

⑤ _____

⑥ _____

⑦ _____

⑧ _____

⑨ _____

⑩ _____

⑪ _____

66.8 FIND EIGHT MORE WORDS IN THE GRID THAT MATCH THE PICTURES

```
T H R I L L E R C S L H
R A J Q X W E A T H E R
E E D E M J D M D A N E
P C I N C A R T O O N N
O T S C X W A X B L A C
R E H C R I M E D E H I
T M O L O L A O Z R C L
E A W E I C H A N N E L
R E I N T E R V I E W L
```

①

②

③

④

⑤

⑥

⑦

⑧

67 Media and celebrity

67.1 USEFUL EXPRESSIONS

I think the newspaper has sensationalized this story.

to sensationalize
[to make something more dramatic or exciting than it is]

The politician's lies were exposed in the interview.

to expose
[to reveal something hidden]

Politicians can easily be exploited by the media.

to exploit
[to use something or someone for your own gain]

You don't always need to be talented to become a celebrity.

to become a celebrity
[to become a famous person]

This chef has been a household name for years.

a household name
[someone who is known by most people]

John would really love to have his name in lights.

to have your name in lights
[to be very famous]

PRESENTS
JOHN

The success of her latest movie has gone to her head.

to go to somebody's head
[to make somebody feel more important than they are]

Lucinda is used to being in the public eye.

in the public eye
[seen and well known by the public]

This morning's newspaper headline is shocking!

a newspaper headline
[the large text at the top of a newspaper page]

This singer's wedding was headline news last week.

headline news
[news that is widely reported]

Social media has supported the rise of **celebrity culture**.

celebrity culture
[the popular culture that surrounds famous people]

Some people go on **talent shows** to become famous.

talent show
[a competition with performances by entertainers showcasing their skills]

It's not fair when **the paparazzi** invade people's privacy.

the paparazzi
[photographers who take pictures of famous people without their consent]

My favorite actors were on **the red carpet** this evening.

the red carpet
[a carpet for important guests to walk or stand on at an event]

Read our **exclusive interview** with the stars of the movie tomorrow!

an exclusive interview
[an interview that no other source has obtained]

Lee's **claim to fame** was that he could eat five burgers in five minutes.

a claim to fame
[the thing that somebody or something is known for, often said jokingly]

I enjoy **reality shows** because I'm nosy about people's lives.

a reality show
[a show based on or around real-life events]

The opening night of the show was a great success.

the opening night
[the first night of a show or movie]

Kelly has had a truly **meteoric rise** in the music industry.

a meteoric rise
[a very rapid rise, often in a career]

Everyone was talking about her **attention-grabbing** dress.

attention-grabbing
[designed or intended to get your attention quickly]

67.2 REWRITE THE SENTENCES, CORRECTING THE ERRORS

> This chef has been a homehold name for years.
> *This chef has been a household name for years.*

❶ Lee's **call to fame** was that he could eat five burgers in five minutes.

_____

❷ **The beginning night** of the show was a great success.

_____

❸ Lucinda is used to being **in the people's eye**.

_____

❹ The success of her latest movie has **gone to her heart**.

_____

Aa **67.3 MATCH THE PICTURES TO THE CORRECT SENTENCES**

My favorite actors were on the red carpet this evening.

❶

I enjoy reality shows because I'm nosy about people's lives.

❷

This singer's wedding was headline news last week.

❸

Everyone was talking about her attention-grabbing dress.

❹

Social media has supported the rise of celebrity culture.

Aa 67.4 MATCH THE BEGINNINGS OF THE SENTENCES TO THE CORRECT ENDINGS

I think the newspaper has → sensationalized this story.

1. John would really love to have — his name in lights.

2. This morning's newspaper — headline is shocking!

3. Kelly has had a truly meteoric — rise in the music industry.

4. Some people go on talent — shows to become famous.

5. Politicians can easily — be exploited by the media.

6. The politician's lies were — exposed in the interview.

67.5 LISTEN TO THE AUDIO, THEN NUMBER THE SENTENCES IN THE ORDER YOU HEAR THEM

A. You don't always need to be talented to become a celebrity. ☐

D. This singer's wedding was headline news last week. ☐

B. The opening night of the show was a great success. 1

E. The politician's lies were exposed in the interview. ☐

C. It's not fair when the paparazzi invade people's privacy. ☐

F. PRESENTS JOHN — John would really love to have his name in lights. ☐

68 Sickness

68.1 SICKNESS AND CONDITIONS

flu

cold

hay fever / allergies

virus

infection

tonsillitis

appendicitis

food poisoning

indigestion

migraine

nosebleed

eczema

measles

mumps

chickenpox

asthma

diabetes

high blood pressure

stress

insomnia

68.2 ADJECTIVES FOR SICKNESS

sick (US) / ill (UK)

sore

itchy

swollen

painful

68.3 SYMPTOMS

symptoms

fever (US)
temperature (UK)

cough

runny nose

sore throat

headache

backache

stomachache (US)
stomach ache (UK)

pain

diarrhea (US)
diarrhoea (UK)

68.4 VERBS FOR SYMPTOMS

to vomit

to cough

to sneeze

to hurt / to ache

to bleed

68.5 ACCIDENTS AND INJURIES

accident

broken bone

sprain

wound

bruise

burn

bite

sting

splinter

cut

Aa 68.6 MARK THE CORRECT PICTURE FOR EACH WORD

to vomit

A ☐   B ☑   C ☐

3 sting

A ☐   B ☐   C ☐

1 insomnia

A ☐   B ☐   C ☐

4 headache

A ☐   B ☐   C ☐

2 hay fever / allergies

A ☐   B ☐   C ☐

5 cut

A ☐   B ☐   C ☐

68.7 LISTEN TO THE AUDIO AND WRITE THE WORD THAT IS SHOWN IN EACH PICTURE

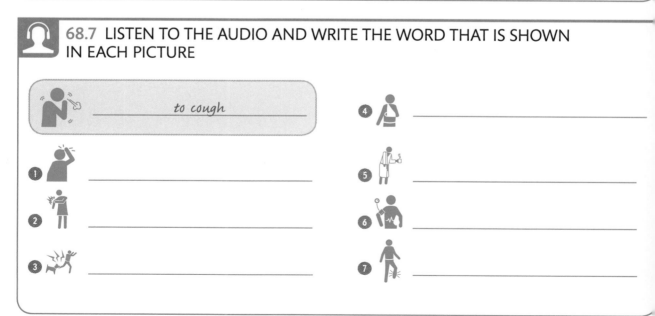

to cough

1

2

3

4

5

6

7

Aa 68.8 FILL IN THE GAPS, PUTTING THE WORDS FROM THE PANEL INTO THE CORRECT CATEGORIES

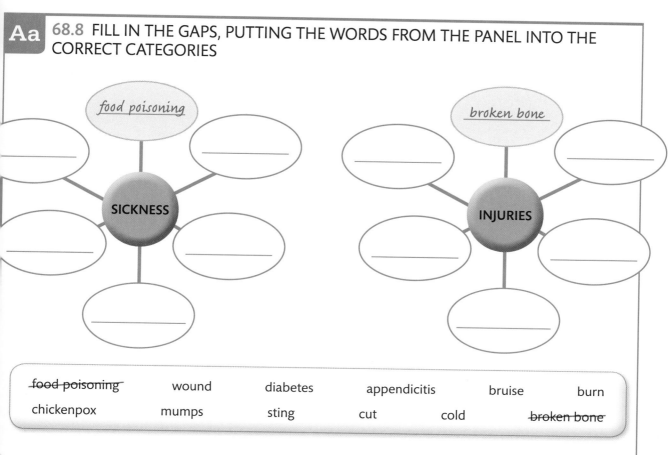

food poisoning

broken bone

SICKNESS

INJURIES

~~food poisoning~~   wound   diabetes   appendicitis   bruise   burn

chickenpox   mumps   sting   cut   cold   ~~broken bone~~

Aa 68.9 LOOK AT THE PICTURE CLUES AND WRITE THE ANSWERS IN THE CORRECT PLACES ON THE GRID

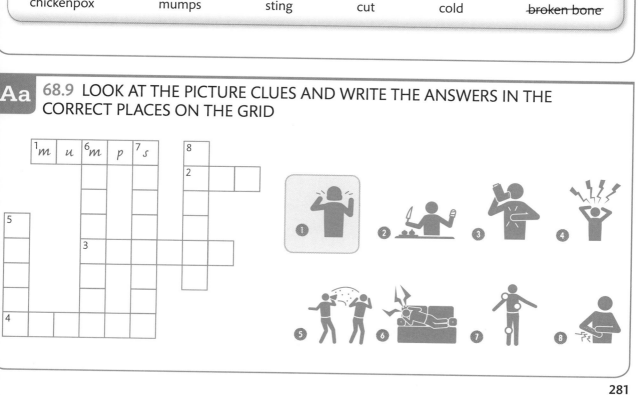

281

69.1 MEDICINE AND TREATMENT

doctor

nurse

patient

clinic (US) / doctor's surgery (UK)

hospital

waiting room

appointment

prescription

ambulance

paramedic

medicine / medication

pills / tablets

injection

blood test

test results

treatment

operation

physical therapy (US) physiotherapy (UK)

stitches

X-ray

stethoscope

inhaler

syringe

scales

thermometer

69.2 FIRST AID

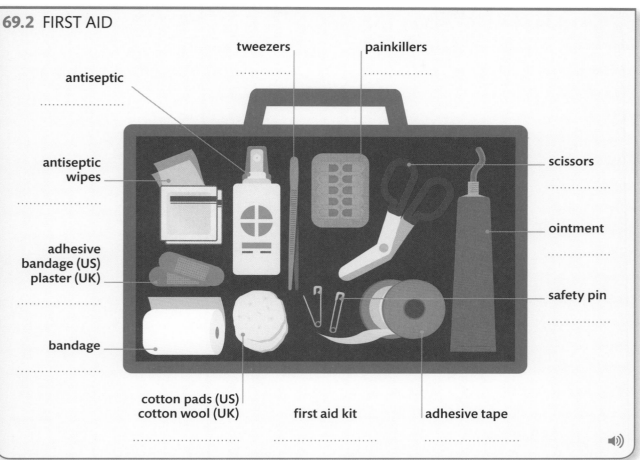

- antiseptic
- antiseptic wipes
- adhesive bandage (US) plaster (UK)
- bandage
- tweezers
- painkillers
- scissors
- ointment
- safety pin
- cotton pads (US) cotton wool (UK)
- first aid kit
- adhesive tape

69.3 VERBS

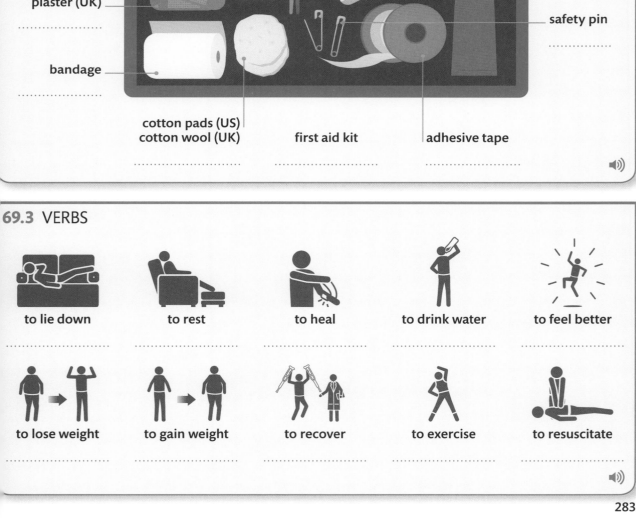

- to lie down
- to rest
- to heal
- to drink water
- to feel better
- to lose weight
- to gain weight
- to recover
- to exercise
- to resuscitate

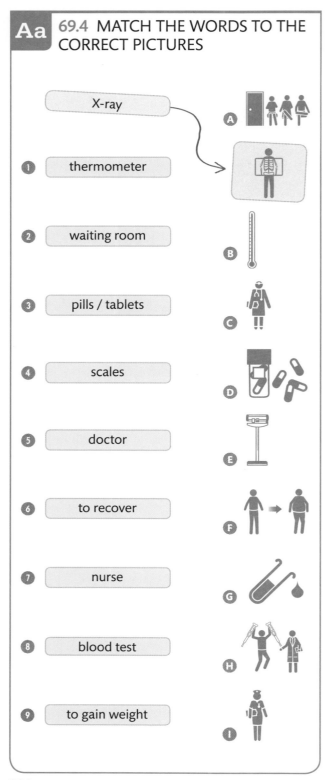

Aa 69.4 MATCH THE WORDS TO THE CORRECT PICTURES

X-ray

1. thermometer
2. waiting room
3. pills / tablets
4. scales
5. doctor
6. to recover
7. nurse
8. blood test
9. to gain weight

Aa 69.5 REWRITE THE WORDS, CORRECTING THE SPELLINGS

stiches
stitches

1. proscription
2. ambulence
3. apointment
4. siringe
5. to heel
6. to excercise
7. injecsion
8. tretment
9. to resussitate

Aa 69.6 LOOK AT THE PICTURE AND WRITE THE CORRECT WORD FOR EACH LABEL

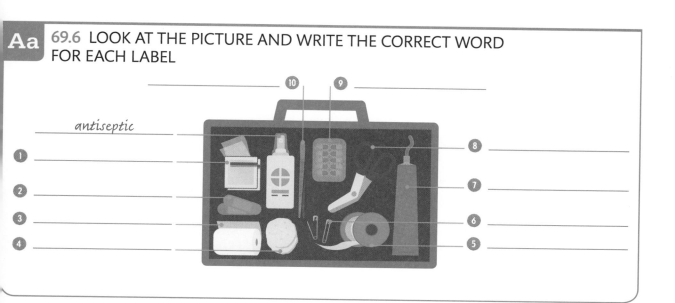

antiseptic

10

9

1

2

3

4

8

7

6

5

Aa 69.7 MARK THE BEGINNING AND ENDING OF EACH WORD IN THE CHAIN OF LETTERS

stethoscope|physicaltherapyoperationpatientdbloodtestinhalerparamedicbandageointment

69.8 LISTEN TO THE AUDIO, THEN NUMBER THE PICTURES IN THE ORDER YOU HEAR THEM

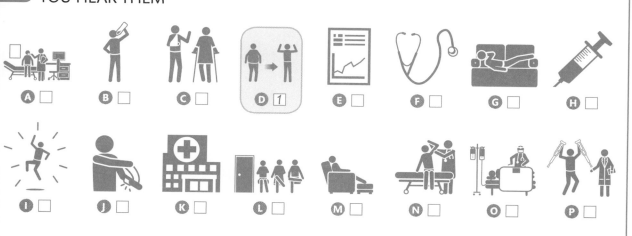

A ☐ B ☐ C ☐ D 1 E ☐ F ☐ G ☐ H ☐

I ☐ J ☐ K ☐ L ☐ M ☐ N ☐ O ☐ P ☐

70.1 NUTRITION AND DIETS

protein

carbohydrates

fiber (US)
fibre (UK)

dairy

legumes (US)
pulses (UK)

sugar

salt

saturated fat

unsaturated fat

5 kCal   300 kCal
calories / energy

vitamins

minerals

calcium

iron

cholesterol

superfoods

processed food

a balanced diet

a calorie-
controlled diet

a detox

vegetarian

vegan

pescatarian

gluten-free

dairy-free

70.2 USEFUL EXPRESSIONS

You should eat smaller portions if you want to lose weight.

a portion
[the amount of food you eat in one meal]

Fish is very good for you because it's high in protein.

high in something
[containing a large amount of something]

I'm trying to cut down on sugary drinks because I know they're bad for me.

to cut down on something
[to eat or drink less of something]

I'm trying to eat more vegetables because they're low in fat.

low in something
[containing a small amount of something]

Pedro has given up chocolate this month.

to give up something / to give something up
[to stop eating or drinking something]

Brown bread is a good source of fiber.

a good source of something
[containing a lot of something healthy]

No dessert for me, thank you. I'm watching my weight.

to watch your weight
[to try to avoid gaining weight]

It's okay to eat treats like cake in moderation.

to eat something in moderation
[to avoid eating too much of something]

Mia must not eat nuts because she's allergic to them.

allergic to something
[unable to eat or drink something without having a bad reaction]

Convenience food saves people time, but isn't always good for them.

convenience food
[food that is quick and easy to make]

Aa 70.3 MATCH THE WORDS TO THE CORRECT PICTURES

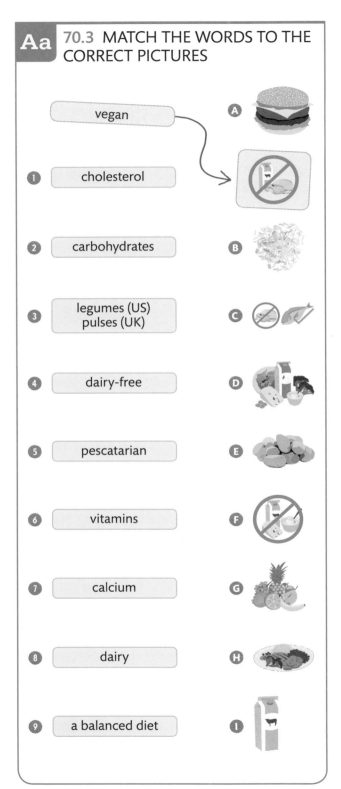

vegan — Ⓐ

1 cholesterol

2 carbohydrates — Ⓑ

3 legumes (US) pulses (UK) — Ⓒ

4 dairy-free — Ⓓ

5 pescatarian — Ⓔ

6 vitamins — Ⓕ

7 calcium — Ⓖ

8 dairy — Ⓗ

9 a balanced diet — Ⓘ

70.4 LISTEN TO THE AUDIO AND MARK THE CORRECT PICTURE FOR EACH WORD YOU HEAR

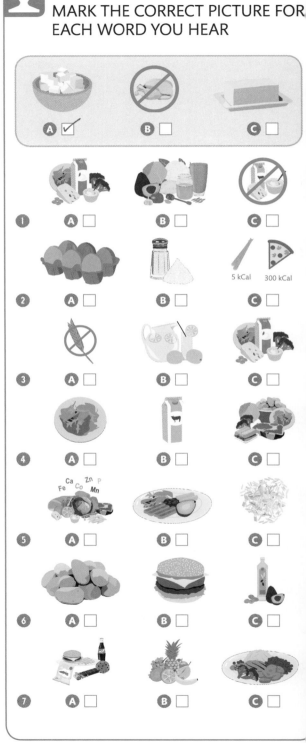

Ⓐ ✓   Ⓑ ☐   Ⓒ ☐

1 Ⓐ ☐   Ⓑ ☐   Ⓒ ☐

2 Ⓐ ☐   Ⓑ ☐   Ⓒ ☐

3 Ⓐ ☐   Ⓑ ☐   Ⓒ ☐

4 Ⓐ ☐   Ⓑ ☐   Ⓒ ☐

5 Ⓐ ☐   Ⓑ ☐   Ⓒ ☐

6 Ⓐ ☐   Ⓑ ☐   Ⓒ ☐

7 Ⓐ ☐   Ⓑ ☐   Ⓒ ☐

70.5 MARK THE SENTENCES THAT ARE CORRECT

No dessert for me, thank you. I'm watching my weight. ☑
No dessert for me, thank you. I'm seeing my weight. ☐

1. Pedro has given up chocolate this month. ☐
   Pedro has given for chocolate this month. ☐

2. I'm trying to eat more vegetables because they're low of fat. ☐
   I'm trying to eat more vegetables because they're low in fat. ☐

3. Brown bread is a good source of fiber. ☐
   Brown bread is a good cause of fiber. ☐

4. You should eat smaller portions if you want to lose weight. ☐
   You should eat smaller partions if you want to lose weight. ☐

5. Convenient food saves people time, but isn't always good for them. ☐
   Convenience food saves people time, but isn't always good for them. ☐

70.6 REWRITE THE SENTENCES, CORRECTING THE ERRORS

Fish is very good for you because it's **high of** protein.
Fish is very good for you because it's high in protein.

1. I'm trying to **reduce down on** sugary drinks because I know they're bad for me.

   _____

2. Mia must not eat nuts because she's **allergic for** them.

   _____

3. I'm trying to eat more vegetables because they're **down in** fat.

   _____

4. It's okay to **eat** treats like cake **on moderation**.

   _____

71 Fitness and well-being

71.1 AT THE GYM

rowing machine

elliptical (US)
cross-trainer (UK)

exercise bike

weights

treadmill

exercise mat   gym   personal trainer

71.2 VERBS FOR FITNESS

to warm up

to work out (US)
to keep fit (UK)

to train

to run

to jog

to skip

to exercise /
to work out

to stretch

to squat

to cool down

71.3 FITNESS

locker room (US)
changing room (UK)

lockers

jump rope (US)
skipping rope (UK)

push-up (US)
press-up (UK)

sit-up

heart rate

circuit training

boot camp

exercise class

aerobics

71.4 WELL-BEING

to relax /
to chill out

to meditate

to sleep well

deep breathing

massage

spa

sauna

steam room

hot tub

Pilates

yoga

acupuncture

reflexology

aromatherapy

counseling (US)
counselling (UK)

Aa 71.5 MARK THE CORRECT WORD FOR EACH PICTURE

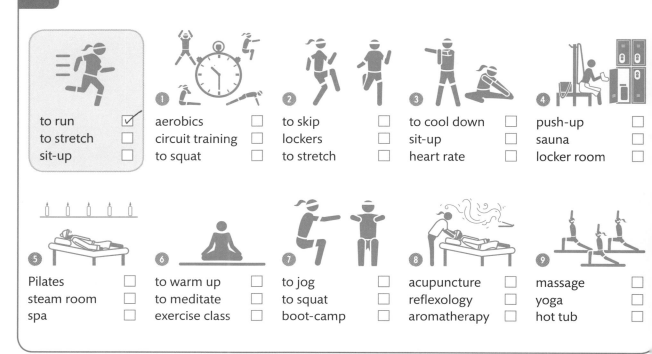

to run ✓
to stretch ☐
sit-up ☐

1. aerobics ☐
circuit training ☐
to squat ☐

2. to skip ☐
lockers ☐
to stretch ☐

3. to cool down ☐
sit-up ☐
heart rate ☐

4. push-up ☐
sauna ☐
locker room ☐

5. Pilates ☐
steam room ☐
spa ☐

6. to warm up ☐
to meditate ☐
exercise class ☐

7. to jog ☐
to squat ☐
boot-camp ☐

8. acupuncture ☐
reflexology ☐
aromatherapy ☐

9. massage ☐
yoga ☐
hot tub ☐

Aa 71.6 LOOK AT THE PICTURE AND WRITE THE CORRECT WORD FOR EACH LABEL

rowing machine

1. _____
2. _____
3. _____
4. _____
5. _____
6. _____

71.7 LISTEN TO THE AUDIO AND WRITE THE WORD THAT IS SHOWN IN EACH PICTURE

aerobics

1. _____
2. _____
3. _____
4. _____
5. _____
6. _____
7. _____
8. _____
9. _____
10. _____
11. _____
12. _____
13. _____

71.8 CIRCLE THE WORD THAT DOES NOT BELONG IN EACH LIST

circuit training	exercise class	(hot tub)
1. to stretch	to warm up	personal trainer
2. treadmill	massage	acupuncture
3. to chill out	to jog	to run
4. yoga	boot camp	to meditate
5. treadmill	spa	weights
6. lockers	Pilates	reflexology
7. sit-up	steam room	push-up

71.9 COMPLETE THE WORD FOR EACH PICTURE, FILLING IN THE MISSING LETTERS

d e e p   b r e a t h i n g

1. r _ f l _ _ _ l _ g _

2. _ x _ r c _ _ s _   c l _ _ _ s

3. s _ _ n _

4. s _ _ _ m   r _ _ m

5. t _   s l _ _ p   w _ _ l

6. t _   w _ r _   _ p

293

72.1 AROUND TOWN

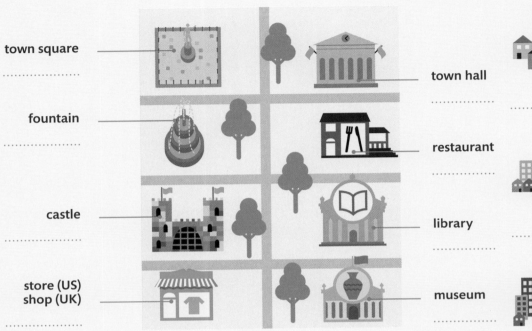

town square

fountain

castle

store (US)
shop (UK)

town hall

restaurant

library

museum

street map

village

town

city

downtown (US)
city centre (UK)

commercial
district

historic quarter

police station

bus station

train station

fire station

airport

factory

post office

 office building

 park

 bridge

 swimming pool

 café

 bar

 theater (US)
theatre (UK)

 movie theater (US)
cinema (UK)

hotel

church

 mosque

 synagogue

 temple

 hospital

 nightclub

 gas station (US)
petrol station (UK)

 government
building

 law court

 skyscraper

 shopping mall

 tourist office (US) /
information (UK)

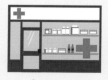 pharmacy

 cemetery

 sports / leisure
center (centre)

 concert hall

72.2 LOOK AT THE PICTURE AND WRITE THE CORRECT WORD FOR EACH LABEL

1
2
3
4
5
6
7

museum

72.3 FIND FIVE MORE WORDS IN THE GRID THAT MATCH THE PICTURES

```
H O T E L  I  R A C S A F
T E M P L E K Q H T Q A
A E D E M J S M E A M C
P H A R M A C Y D P T T
L T B C X W D X I L X O
E E N I G H T C L U B R
H O S P I T A L T R O Y
```

1
2
3
4
5

72.4 LISTEN TO THE AUDIO AND MARK THE CORRECT PICTURE FOR EACH WORD YOU HEAR

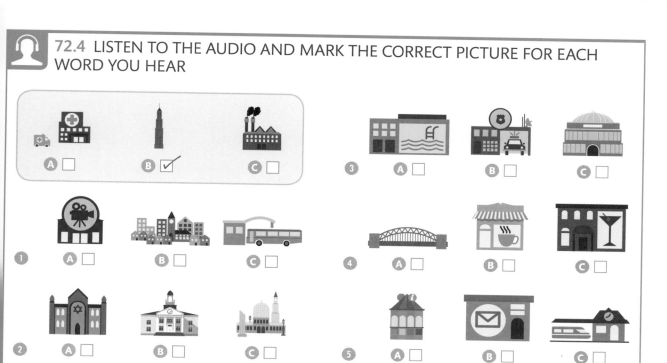

A ☐ B ☑ C ☐

1 A ☐ B ☐ C ☐

2 A ☐ B ☐ C ☐

3 A ☐ B ☐ C ☐

4 A ☐ B ☐ C ☐

5 A ☐ B ☐ C ☐

72.5 WRITE THE CORRECT WORD UNDER EACH PICTURE

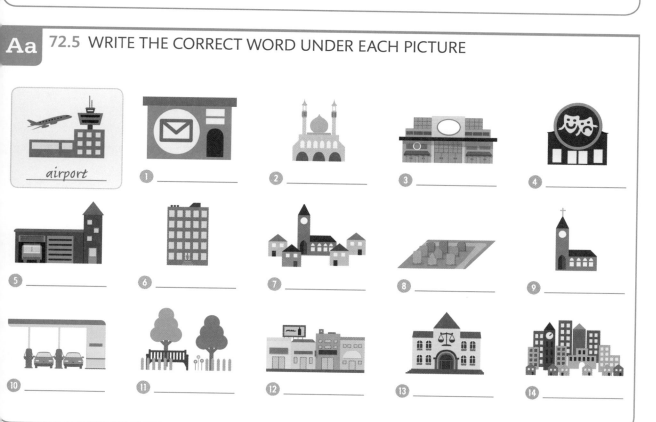

airport

1 _____
2 _____
3 _____
4 _____
5 _____
6 _____
7 _____
8 _____
9 _____
10 _____
11 _____
12 _____
13 _____
14 _____

73 Shopping

73.1 STORES (US) / SHOPS (UK)

butcher

baker

bookstore (US)
bookshop (UK)

fish dealer (US)
fishmonger (UK)

greengrocer

boutique

shoe store (US)
shoe shop (UK)

street market

delicatessen

jewelers (US)
jewellers (UK)

dry cleaners

florist

hardware store

bank

toy store (US)
toy shop (UK)

73.2 VERBS

to choose

to sell

to want

to fit

to buy

to pay

to try on

to haggle

to exchange

to refund

73.3 USEFUL EXPRESSIONS

I love going bargain-hunting at my local market.

bargain-hunting
[searching for goods that are cheaper than normal]

It's always worth shopping around when buying a new car.

to shop around
[to compare prices at various stores]

You can buy almost anything you want at the flea market in town.

a flea market
[an open-air market that sells old or used items]

My new phone was a real rip-off. It broke after only a couple of weeks.

a rip-off
[a low-quality product that costs more than it should]

I spent Saturday morning window shopping with my friends.

window shopping
[looking at goods in store windows without buying them]

There's 50 percent off all winter coats at this department store.

50 percent off
[a 50 percent reduction]

I'm on a tight budget. I can't afford to buy many Christmas presents.

on a tight budget
[having only a small amount of money to spend]

I got a good deal on my new pair of shoes. They were reduced by $20.

a good deal
[a good price]

The local hardware store has slashed its prices. You can find some real bargains.

to slash prices
[to reduce prices dramatically]

I thought the restaurant was overpriced. The food was very disappointing.

overpriced
[costing too much]

73.4 WRITE THE CORRECT WORD UNDER EACH PICTURE

dry cleaners

1 _____

2 _____

3 _____

4 _____

5 _____

6 _____

7 _____

8 _____

9 _____

73.5 MARK THE CORRECT WORD FOR EACH PICTURE

to pay ☑
to fit ☐
to try on ☐

1

to buy ☐
to try on ☐
to haggle ☐

2

bank ☐
bookstore ☐
butcher ☐

3

to refund ☐
to sell ☐
to choose ☐

4

dry cleaners ☐
boutique ☐
jewelers ☐

5

to haggle ☐
to exchange ☐
to buy ☐

6

hardware store ☐
toy store ☐
fishmonger ☐

7

to refund ☐
to fit ☐
to want ☐

8

to choose ☐
to pay ☐
to haggle ☐

9

hardware store ☐
dry cleaners ☐
delicatessen ☐

73.6 LISTEN TO THE AUDIO AND COMPLETE THE SENTENCES THAT DESCRIBE EACH PICTURE

 I spent Saturday morning _window shopping_ with my friends.

 ③ I love going _____ at my local market.

 ① You can buy almost anything you want at the _____ in town.

 ④ I thought the restaurant was _____ . The food was very disappointing.

 ② It's always worth _____ when buying a new car.

 ⑤ The local electrical store has _____ . You can find some real bargains.

Aa 73.7 MATCH THE DEFINITIONS TO THE CORRECT PHRASES

costing too much	to slash prices
① a good price	a flea market
② to reduce prices dramatically	bargain-hunting
③ having only a small amount of money to spend	overpriced
④ an open-air market that sells old or used items	a rip-off
⑤ to compare prices at various stores	a good deal
⑥ a low-quality product that costs more than it should	on a tight budget
⑦ searching for goods that are cheaper than normal	to shop around

74 At the supermarket

74.1 SUPERMARKET

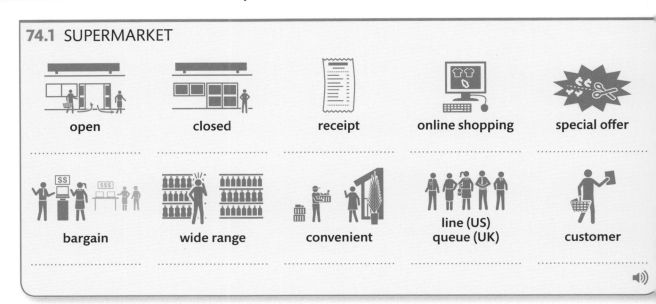

open   **closed**   **receipt**   **online shopping**   **special offer**

bargain   **wide range**   **convenient**   **line (US) queue (UK)**   **customer**

74.2 AT THE CHECKOUT

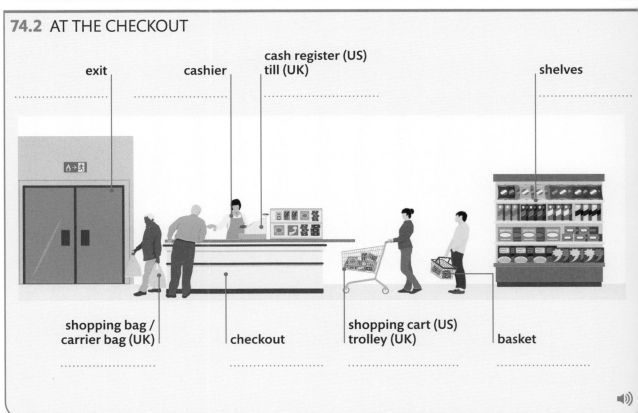

exit

cashier

cash register (US) till (UK)

shelves

shopping bag / carrier bag (UK)

checkout

shopping cart (US) trolley (UK)

basket

escalator

elevator (US)
lift (UK)

guarantee

sale

price tag

first floor (US)
ground floor (UK)

basement

loyalty card

upmarket

second floor (US)
first floor (UK)

designer labels

men's wear

women's wear

children's
department

customer service

kitchenware

home furnishings

changing rooms

baby changing
facilities

food court

lingerie

cosmetics (US)
perfumery (UK)

beauty

electrical
appliances

lighting

Aa 74.4 LOOK AT THE PICTURE AND WRITE THE CORRECT WORD FOR EACH LABEL

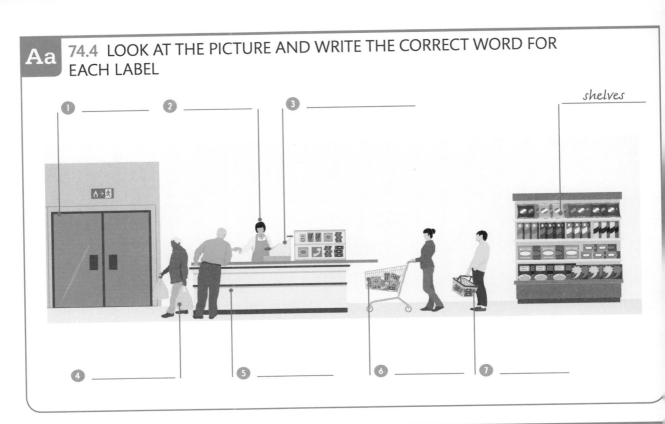

shelves

1 _____ 2 _____ 3 _____

4 _____ 5 _____ 6 _____ 7 _____

Aa 74.5 REWRITE THE WORDS, CORRECTING THE SPELLINGS

bargin
bargain

1 conveniente
_____

2 reciept
_____

3 speciel ofer
_____

4 basment
_____

5 custommer
_____

6 garantee
_____

7 escallator
_____

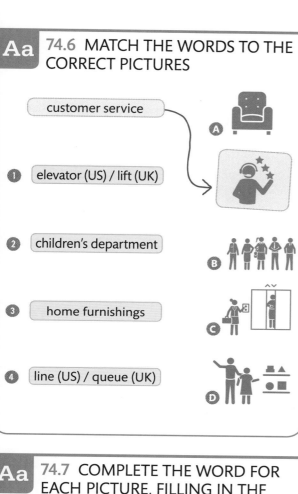

Aa 74.6 MATCH THE WORDS TO THE CORRECT PICTURES

customer service — A

1 elevator (US) / lift (UK)

2 children's department B

3 home furnishings C

4 line (US) / queue (UK) D

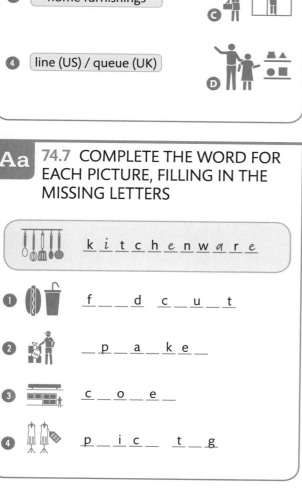

Aa 74.7 COMPLETE THE WORD FOR EACH PICTURE, FILLING IN THE MISSING LETTERS

k i t c h e n w a r e

1 f _ _ d c _ u _ t

2 _ p _ a _ k e _

3 c _ o _ e _

4 p _ _ i c _ _ t _ g

74.8 LISTEN TO THE AUDIO, THEN NUMBER THE PICTURES IN THE ORDER YOU HEAR THEM

A ☐   B 1   C ☐

D ☐   E ☐   F ☐

G ☐   H ☐   I ☐

J ☐   K ☐   L ☐

75 Urban life

75.1 USEFUL EXPRESSIONS

It's sometimes impossible to get on the bus during rush hour.

rush hour
[the period of the day when most people travel to or from work]

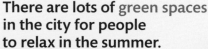

The vandalism in my area makes the buildings look very ugly.

vandalism
[illegal damage to or destruction of property]

There's a greater choice of cafés and restaurants in large cities.

a greater choice
[a larger number of shops, restaurants, and services]

There are lots of green spaces in the city for people to relax in the summer.

green spaces
[outdoor areas with grass or vegetation]

The crime rate in most cities has been dropping in recent years.

the crime rate
[the frequency of crimes in an area]

I offer guided tours of the city's historic buildings.

historic buildings
[buildings that have been important in history]

A good way to avoid traffic jams is to travel by train.

a traffic jam
[a line of traffic that is unable to move]

I live in a poor part of town with many derelict buildings.

derelict buildings
[buildings that have not been repaired for many years]

I live in a suburb, but I can walk downtown.

a suburb
[an urban area that is outside the center of a town or city]

New York is one of the world's most cosmopolitan cities.

cosmopolitan
[containing people or cultures from around the world]

Dan found life in the city too **fast-paced**, so he moved to the countryside.

fast-paced
[active and full of energy]

Good **infrastructure**, such as roads and telecommunications, is essential for a modern city.

infrastructure [the basic services that a city needs to run well]

There is a huge **carnival** in Rio de Janeiro in the spring.

a carnival
[a festival that often involves people dancing in the street]

Greater **work opportunities** are one reason why people move to the city.

work opportunities
[the chances you have of finding a job]

Overcrowding on London's trains means it's often hard to find a seat.

overcrowding
[when there are too many people in one place]

The **road work** meant that it took me two hours to arrive at the office today.

road work
[repairs that are made to roads]

Moscow has a **lively nightlife**, with bars and nightclubs that stay open until dawn.

a lively nightlife
[nighttime entertainment such as bars, cafés, and nightclubs]

The **pollution** in my city can be terrible in the summer months.

pollution
[harmful substances in air or water]

The Eiffel Tower is the best-known **tourist attraction** in Paris.

a tourist attraction
[a place that attracts large numbers of tourists]

The pace of life is much faster in the city than in the countryside.

the pace of life
[how quickly people lead their lives]

Aa 75.2 FILL IN THE GAPS USING THE WORDS IN THE PANEL

The crime _____ *rate* _____ in most cities has been dropping in recent years.

1. There are lots of green _____ in the city for people to relax in the summer.
2. There's a greater _____ of cafés and restaurants in large cities.
3. Moscow has a _____ nightlife, with bars and nightclubs that stay open until dawn.
4. The _____ work meant that it took me two hours to arrive at the office today.
5. It's sometimes impossible to get on the bus during _____ hour.
6. The _____ in my city can be terrible in the summer months.

| rush | pollution | choice | spaces | lively | road | ~~rate~~ |

Aa 75.3 MATCH THE PICTURES TO THE CORRECT SENTENCES

Overcrowding on London's trains means it's often hard to find a seat.

1.

Dan found life in the city too fast-paced, so he moved to the countryside.

2.

Good infrastructure, such as roads and telecommunications, is essential for a modern city.

3.

I offer guided tours of the city's historic buildings.

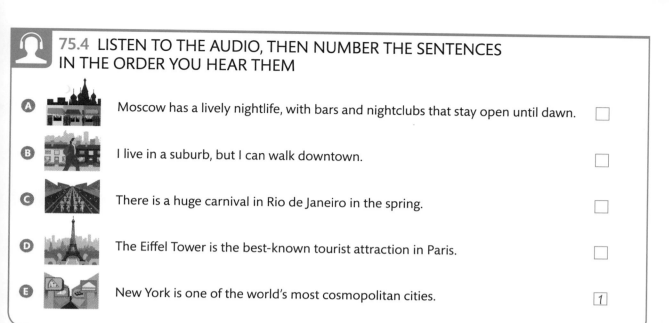

75.4 LISTEN TO THE AUDIO, THEN NUMBER THE SENTENCES IN THE ORDER YOU HEAR THEM

A Moscow has a lively nightlife, with bars and nightclubs that stay open until dawn. ☐

B I live in a suburb, but I can walk downtown. ☐

C There is a huge carnival in Rio de Janeiro in the spring. ☐

D The Eiffel Tower is the best-known tourist attraction in Paris. ☐

E New York is one of the world's most cosmopolitan cities. ☑ 1

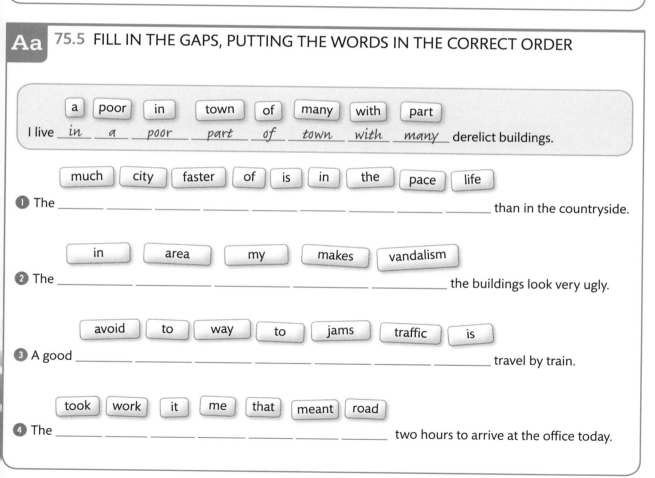

Aa 75.5 FILL IN THE GAPS, PUTTING THE WORDS IN THE CORRECT ORDER

a | poor | in | town | of | many | with | part

I live _in_ _a_ _poor_ _part_ _of_ _town_ _with_ _many_ derelict buildings.

much | city | faster | of | is | in | the | pace | life

❶ The _____ _____ _____ _____ _____ _____ _____ _____ _____ than in the countryside.

in | area | my | makes | vandalism

❷ The _____ _____ _____ _____ _____ the buildings look very ugly.

avoid | to | way | to | jams | traffic | is

❸ A good _____ _____ _____ _____ _____ _____ _____ travel by train.

took | work | it | me | that | meant | road

❹ The _____ _____ _____ _____ _____ _____ _____ two hours to arrive at the office today.

76.1 DIGITAL TECHNOLOGY

screen

router

camera

earphones

wire

tablet

laptop

mouse

desktop computer

mouse pad (US) / mat (UK)

e-reader

power cord (US)
lead (UK)

keyboard

computer desk

Wi-Fi

wireless

smartwatch

memory card

bulb

battery

USB drive

hard drive

GPS (US)
satnav (UK)

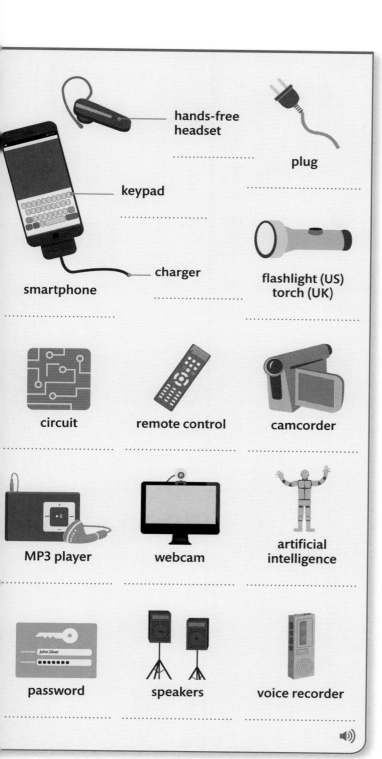

hands-free headset

plug

keypad

smartphone

charger

flashlight (US)
torch (UK)

circuit

remote control

camcorder

MP3 player

webcam

artificial
intelligence

password

speakers

voice recorder

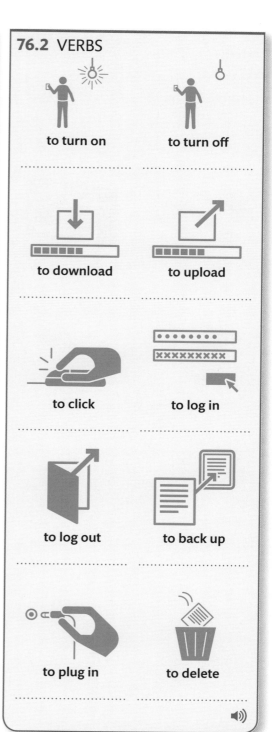

76.2 VERBS

to turn on

to turn off

to download

to upload

to click

to log in

to log out

to back up

to plug in

to delete

Aa 76.3 WRITE THE CORRECT WORD UNDER EACH PICTURE

earphones

① _____

② _____

③ _____

④ _____

⑤ _____

⑥ _____

⑦ _____

⑧ _____

⑨ _____

⑩ _____

⑪ _____

⑫ _____

⑬ _____

⑭ _____

Aa 76.4 MATCH THE WORDS TO THE CORRECT PICTURES

to plug in

② to click   ④ to turn off

① to turn on   ③ to delete   ⑤ to back up

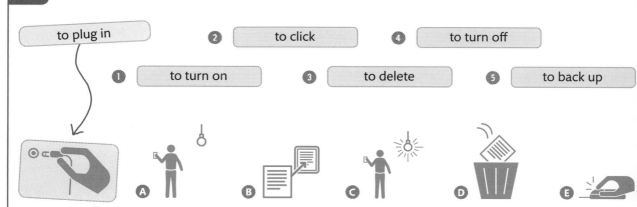

A   B   C   D   E

76.5 LISTEN TO THE AUDIO AND WRITE THE WORD THAT IS SHOWN IN EACH PICTURE

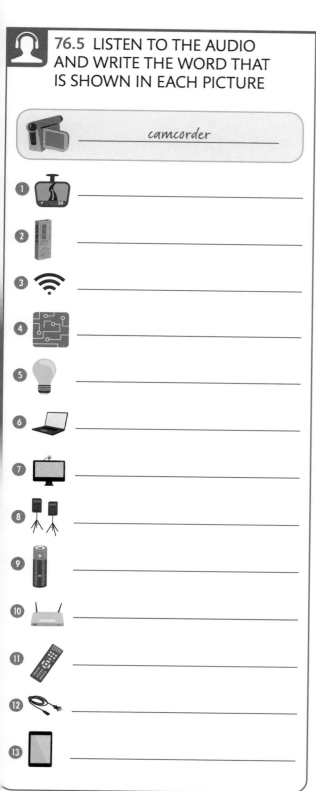

camcorder

1 _____

2 _____

3 _____

4 _____

5 _____

6 _____

7 _____

8 _____

9 _____

10 _____

11 _____

12 _____

13 _____

Aa 76.6 LOOK AT THE PICTURE AND WRITE THE CORRECT WORD FOR EACH LABEL

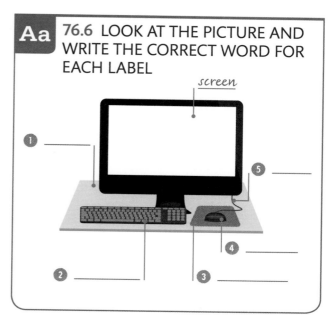

screen

1 _____
2 _____
3 _____
4 _____
5 _____

Aa 76.7 LOOK AT THE PICTURE CLUES AND WRITE THE ANSWERS IN THE CORRECT PLACES ON THE GRID

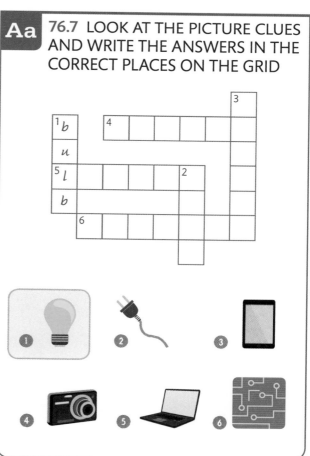

77 Technology and the future

77.1 USEFUL EXPRESSIONS

The internet has had an impact on how we communicate at work.

to have an impact on something
[to affect something powerfully]

Ruth's new product won an award for technical innovation.

innovation
[inventiveness or creation of new ideas]

Laila is making predictions about what will happen in the new year.

to make predictions
[to say what you think might happen in the future]

The internet has caused a revolution in the way we learn.

a revolution
[a huge change in ideas or methods]

None of us can know exactly what the future holds.

what the future holds
[what will happen in the future]

His cutting-edge designs have made millions of dollars.

cutting-edge
[extremely modern and innovative]

The car was expensive, but it will save us money in the long run.

in the long run
[eventually, after a long time]

Higher prices could be the shape of things to come.

the shape of things to come
[the way things are likely to develop in the future]

In this digital age, many people have a laptop and smartphone.

a digital age
[an era based on digital information, when technology is dominant]

I really want to buy the latest model of their smartphone.

the latest model
[the most recent version of a product]

The research scientists made an amazing breakthrough.

a breakthrough
[an important discovery or achievement]

You need to be computer literate to find a good job these days.

computer literate
[able to use computer technology effectively]

Our customers love our state-of-the-art kitchen equipment.

state-of-the-art
[very modern and up-to-date]

Seb's such a technophile. He has to have the latest phone.

a technophile
[a person who enjoys using new technology]

We must future-proof our designs or our sales will start to fall.

to future-proof
[to design something to work in the future, even if technology changes]

My uncle's a technophobe. He still uses a typewriter.

a technophobe
[a person who dislikes or refuses to use new technology]

It's only a matter of time before we sell one of these paintings.

only a matter of time
[sure to happen at some point in the future]

CDs and cassettes have become obsolete because of online streaming.

obsolete / out of date
[no longer needed or useful because of a new invention]

Only time will tell whether we will live on Mars one day.

only time will tell
[the results will only become clear in the future]

My new smartphone is light-years ahead of my old one.

light-years ahead
[much more advanced than its competitors]

Aa 77.2 CROSS OUT THE INCORRECT WORDS IN EACH SENTENCE

 None of us can know exactly what the future ~~carries~~ / holds / ~~bears~~.

1 The car was expensive, but it will save us money in the long walk / time / run.

2 Higher prices could be the shape / size / sound of things to come.

3 It's only a matter of age / time / future before we sell one of these paintings.

4 Laila is making / doing / taking predictions about what will happen in the new year.

Aa 77.3 MATCH THE PICTURES TO THE CORRECT SENTENCES

My uncle's a technophobe. He still uses a typewriter.

1

The research scientists made an amazing breakthrough.

2

I really want to buy the latest model of their smartphone.

3

Seb's such a technophile. He has to have the latest phone.

4

The internet has caused a revolution in the way we learn.

Aa 77.4 FILL IN THE GAPS, PUTTING THE WORDS IN THE CORRECT ORDER

| will | Only | tell | time |

Only _time_ _will_ _tell_ whether we will live on Mars one day.

| be | to | literate | to | computer |

1 You need _____ _____ _____ _____ _____ find a good job these days.

| of | light-years | ahead | is |

2 My new smartphone _____ _____ _____ _____ my old one.

| obsolete | of | become | because |

3 CDs and cassettes have _____ _____ _____ _____ online streaming.

| age, | digital | many | this |

4 In _____ _____ _____ _____ people have a laptop and smartphone.

| breakthrough | made | amazing | an |

5 The research scientists _____ _____ _____ _____ .

77.5 LISTEN TO THE AUDIO, THEN NUMBER THE SENTENCES IN THE ORDER YOU HEAR THEM

A Ruth's new product won an award for technical innovation. ☐

B We must future-proof our designs or our sales will start to fall. ☐

C The internet has had an impact on how we communicate at work. ☐

D His cutting-edge designs have made millions of dollars. ☐

E Our customers love our state-of-the-art kitchen equipment. ☐ 1

78.1 SCIENCE AND SCIENTIFIC EQUIPMENT

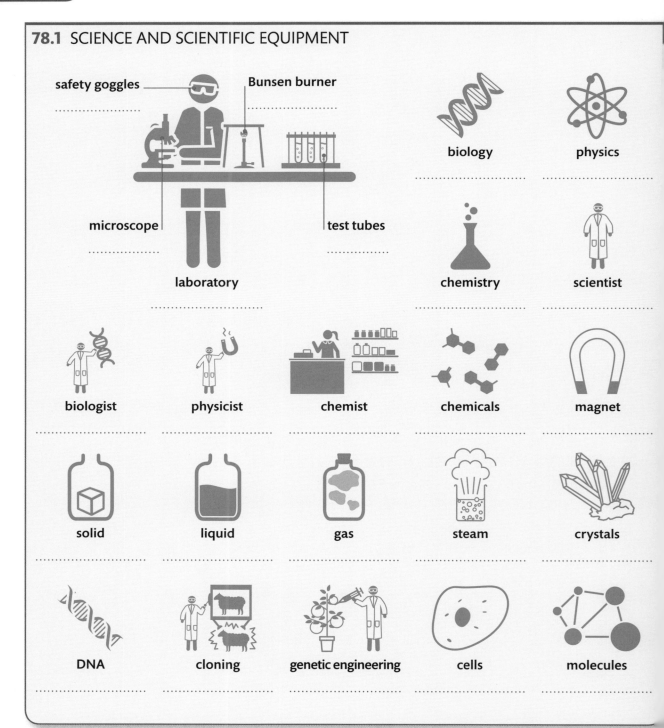

safety goggles

Bunsen burner

microscope

test tubes

laboratory

biology

physics

chemistry

scientist

biologist

physicist

chemist

chemicals

magnet

solid

liquid

gas

steam

crystals

DNA

cloning

genetic engineering

cells

molecules

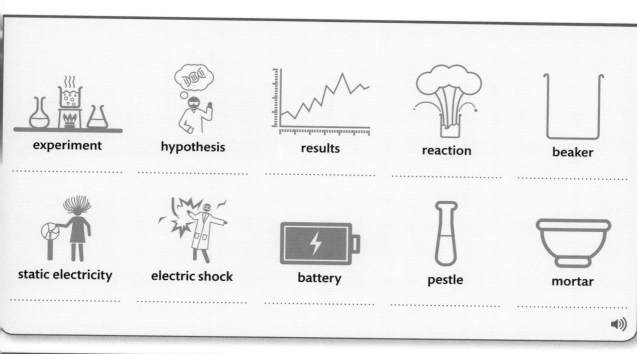

experiment

hypothesis

results

reaction

beaker

static electricity

electric shock

battery

pestle

mortar

78.2 VERBS

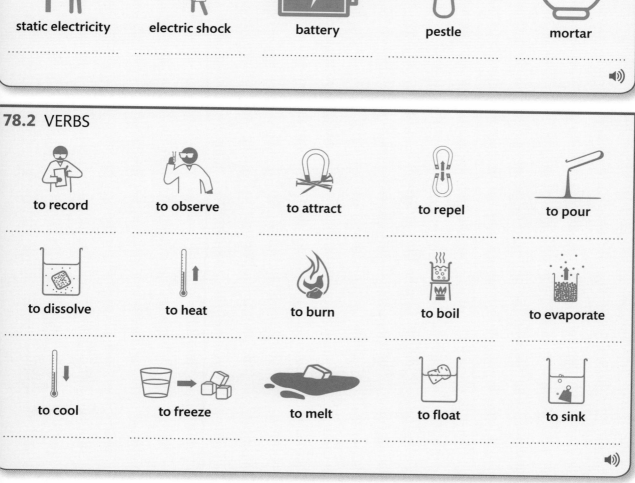

to record

to observe

to attract

to repel

to pour

to dissolve

to heat

to burn

to boil

to evaporate

to cool

to freeze

to melt

to float

to sink

Aa 78.3 CIRCLE THE WORD THAT DOES NOT BELONG IN EACH LIST

	biology	beaker	physics
1	pestle	steam	mortar
2	to attract	to record	to repel
3	to observe	to freeze	to melt
4	chemist	crystals	physicist
5	liquid	solid	cloning
6	DNA	cells	battery
7	hypothesis	microscope	Bunsen burner

Aa 78.4 LOOK AT THE PICTURE AND WRITE THE CORRECT WORD FOR EACH LABEL

1 _____

3 _____

test tubes

2 _____

Aa 78.5 REWRITE THE WORDS, CORRECTING THE SPELLINGS

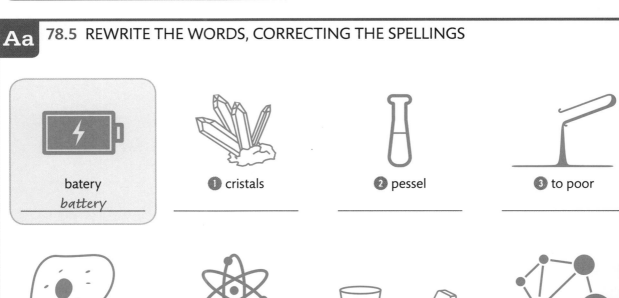

batery
battery

1 cristals
_____

2 pessel
_____

3 to poor
_____

4 sells
_____

5 phisycs
_____

6 to frieze
_____

7 mollecules
_____

Aa 78.6 MARK THE CORRECT WORD ILLUSTRATED IN EACH PICTURE

magnet ✓
steam ☐
cells ☐

1
to float ☐
to dissolve ☐
to boil ☐

2
beaker ☐
chemistry ☐
DNA ☐

3
chemicals ☐
cloning ☐
gas ☐

4
to record ☐
to observe ☐
to melt ☐

5
biology ☐
results ☐
electric shock ☐

6
to sink ☐
to burn ☐
to evaporate ☐

7
steam ☐
electric shock ☐
magnet ☐

8
scientist ☐
mortar ☐
reaction ☐

9
static electricity ☐
solid ☐
experiment ☐

78.7 LISTEN TO THE AUDIO AND MARK THE CORRECT PICTURE FOR EACH WORD YOU HEAR

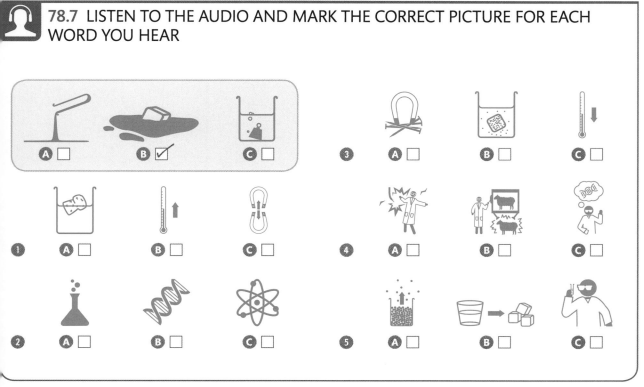

A ☐ B ✓ C ☐

3 A ☐ B ☐ C ☐

1 A ☐ B ☐ C ☐

4 A ☐ B ☐ C ☐

2 A ☐ B ☐ C ☐

5 A ☐ B ☐ C ☐

Answers

01

1.3
1. India
2. Germany
3. Mongolia
4. Egypt
5. Canada
6. Thailand
7. Slovakia
8. Russia
9. Japan

1.4
1. Indonesia
2. France
3. China
4. Pakistan
5. South Korea
6. Brazil
7. Singapore
8. Argentina

1.5
1. Indian
2. Turkish
3. Greece
4. Netherlands
5. Portuguese
6. German
7. Mongolian
8. China

1.6
COUNTRIES:
Russia, **United Kingdom / UK**, **Poland**,
Pakistan, **Japan**
NATIONALITIES:
Russian, **British**, **Polish**,
Pakistani, **Japanese**

1.7
1. Portugal
2. Greece
3. Philippines
4. Turkey
5. Spain
6. United States of America (US)
7. New Zealand
8. Republic of Ireland (ROI)
9. Poland

02

2.5
1. twelve
2. twenty
3. thirty
4. one hundred and ten
5. thirteen
6. one thousand, one hundred
7. seventeen
8. eight

2.6
1. a hundred
2. eighth
3. a thousand
4. forty
5. thirteen
6. twentieth
7. nineteen
8. ninety
9. twelfth
10. fifty

2.7
1. B 2. C 3. B 4. A 5. C 6. A

2.8
1. one thousand, two hundred
2. three hundred and forty-two
3. seven hundred and fifty
4. six point three
5. five hundred and forty-two
6. forty-five percent
7. three point nine five

2.9
1. a third 2. a half
3. a quarter 4. two thirds

03

3.3
1. Tuesday 2. decade
3. November 4. week
5. August 6. year

3.4
1. October 2. hour 3. Friday
4. millennium 5. winter 6. century
7. minute 8. hourly 9. often

3.5
1. spring
2. decade
3. day
4. Friday
5. April
6. never

3.6
1. A 2. A 3. B 4. C 5. A 6. C 7. B

3.7
1. weekly
2. September
3. afternoon
4. hourly
5. sometimes
6. every day
7. usually
8. twice a week

04

4.2
1. B 2. C 3. C 4. A 5. B

4.3
1. to wash the dishes
2. to arrive late
3. to wash your face
4. to put the children to bed
5. to do the housework

4.4
1. to check your emails
2. to iron a shirt
3. to walk the dog
4. to go to bed
5. to brush your teeth
6. to make the bed
7. to take / have a shower
8. to wake up
9. to finish work
10. to catch the train
11. to shave
12. to have / eat dinner
13. to start work
14. to dry your hair

4.5
A. 11 B. 12 C. 2 D. 7 E. 4 F. 9
G. 1 H. 8 I. 6 J. 3 K. 10 L. 5

05

5.4
1. brown
2. cream
3. orange
4. yellow
5. purple

6 blue
7 green

5.5
1 wool
2 silk
3 glass
4 fabric

5.6
1 near
2 clean
3 loose
4 high
5 light
6 short

5.7
1 C **2** A **3** A **4** B **5** B

5.8
A 5 **B** 1 **C** 3 **D** 2 **E** 8 **F** 4
G 6 **H** 7

06

6.4
POSITIVE:
**fantastic, breathtaking, incredible,
fun, amazing, exciting**
NEGATIVE:
**awful, disastrous, annoying,
nasty, disgusting, terrible**

6.5
1 magnificent
2 wonderful
3 disappointing
4 outstanding
5 respectable
6 delicious
7 special
8 pretty

6.6
1 irritating
2 thrilling
3 frightening
4 graceful
5 old-fashioned

6.7
1 tiring **2** unpleasant **3** boring
4 important **5** harmless **6** relaxing

6.8
1 ugly
2 stunning
3 useless

4 beautiful
5 respectable

07

7.5
1 title
2 middle name
3 last name
4 street address
5 cell phone number (US) /
phone number (UK)
6 email address
7 city

7.6
1 name **2** job title
3 company name **4** business card

7.7
1 to send
2 to print
3 to forward
4 to reply
5 inbox
6 to reply all
7 signature
8 attachment
9 subject

7.8
1 trash
2 spam
3 memo
4 mail
5 state
6 contact
7 outbox
8 website
9 draft
10 phone call
11 title

7.9
1 text message **2** phone call **3** note
4 letter **5** email **6** online chat

08

8.2
1 Tamsin got cold feet about giving a
presentation to the sales team.
2 I'm so tired today! I'm really not on the ball.
3 Susan is feeling under the weather today.
I think she should go home.

4 I have to face the music and tell Julia that
I broke her new vase.

8.3
1 I didn't mean to offend Luisa, but I think
her reaction was over the top.
2 Hamid is working against the clock to
finish his report this week.
3 Leo has a heart of gold. He always helps his
grandma with her shopping.
4 I don't know who to vote for yet. I'm still on
the fence.
5 You two really let your hair down at Sunita's
party last night.

8.4
1 You're so right about Jim. He's really lazy!
You've hit the nail on the head.
2 I'm planning a surprise party for Joe. Don't
let the cat out of the bag.
3 You can't believe all her stories. **Take them
with a pinch of** salt.
4 If **you cut corners to** finish a project on
time, the quality will suffer.

8.5
A 2 **B** 1 **C** 4 **D** 3 **E** 5

09

9.2
1 bedroom
2 light
3 table
4 rug
5 shower
6 dresser (US) / chest of drawers (UK)
7 trash can (US) / bin (UK)
8 window

9.3
1 cabinet
2 bed
3 table
4 roof
5 kitchen
6 sink
7 lamp
8 living room

9.4
1 upstairs **2** downstairs
3 basement **4** stairs
5 yard (US) / garden (UK)

9.5
A 6 **B** 1 **C** 5 **D** 7 **E** 4
F 3 **G** 9 **H** 2 **I** 10 **J** 8

9.6

KITCHEN:
**dishwasher, refrigerator / fridge,
stove (US) / cooker (UK),
cabinet (US) / cupboard (UK)**
BATHROOM:
**bathtub (US) / bath (UK), toilet,
sink, shower**
LIVING ROOM:
**armchair, cushion,
couch (US) / sofa (UK),
television / TV**
BEDROOM:
**bed, bedside table,
lamp, wardrobe**

10

10.3

KITCHEN:
**whisk, knife, frying pan,
bowl, plate, cup**
BATHROOM:
**mouthwash, conditioner, sponge,
shampoo, soap, toothbrush**

10.4
1 shaving foam 2 spatula
3 microwave 4 toothpaste
5 peeler 6 moisturizer
7 dental floss 8 colander

10.5
1 toaster 2 scissors
3 corkscrew 4 blender
5 spatula 6 grater
7 wok 8 mug
9 can opener (US) / tin opener (UK)

10.6
1 C 2 A 3 C 4 A 5 B 6 A 7 C

11

11.3
1 cloth
2 bucket
3 dustpan
4 mop
5 brush
6 duster
7 scouring pad
8 polish

11.4
1 laundry detergent
2 sponge

3 recycling bin
4 to scrub the floor
5 to clear the table
6 bleach
7 to load the dishwasher

11.5
1 C 2 A 3 D 4 B
5 G 6 H 7 F 8 E

11.6
1 washing machine
2 to fold clothes
3 tumble dryer
4 to set the table
5 to mop the floor

11.7
1 clothes line 2 rubber gloves
3 bucket 4 iron

12

12.5
1 to plant bulbs
2 to put up shelves
3 to mow the lawn
4 to water the flowers
5 to paint a room
6 to plaster the walls
7 to trim a hedge

12.6
1 wrench (US) / spanner (UK)
2 shears 3 nail 4 vise (US) / vice (UK)
5 fork 6 tool box 7 saw

12.7
TOOLS:
**paintbrush, hammer, hacksaw,
plane, file, jigsaw**
GARDENING EQUIPMENT:
**hoe, rake, sprinkler,
hose, wheelbarrow, trowel**

12.8
1 C 2 B 3 B

13

13.3
1 keys 2 boxes 3 landlord
4 cottage 5 storage 6 rent

13.4
A 12 B 11 C 1 D 9 E 4 F 3
G 6 H 2 I 5 J 8 K 10 L 7

13.5
1 unfurnished
2 landlord
3 tenant
4 apartments
5 storage

13.6
1 real estate (US) / property (UK)
2 a residential area
3 local
4 a deposit
5 including utilities

13.7
1 We had a **house-warming** party to celebrate buying our new apartment.
2 We have a **roomer** who lives in our spare bedroom.
3 My **roommate** never does the dishes.
4 We **gave** notice to our landlord two months before moving out.
5 We live in an attractive **residential** area with lots of parks.

14

14.3
1 head 2 chin 3 chest 4 finger
5 shin 6 toe 7 neck 8 shoulder
9 waist 10 hip 11 thigh 12 knee 13 foot

14.4
eyelashes, teeth, nose, mouth, eyebrow,
nostrils, ear, ankle, lips, forehead, thigh,
finger, stomach, chin, hip

14.5
1 to wave
2 to shiver
3 to shrug
4 to cry
5 to breathe
6 to lick
7 to yawn
8 to sigh
9 to nod

14.6
1 B 2 C 3 B 4 A 5 A

15

15.4
1 jacket
2 sweater (US) / jumper (UK)
3 blouse

4 pants (US) / trousers (UK)
5 skirt
6 t-shirt
7 boxer shorts
8 dress
9 uniform

15.5
1 cuff **2** sleeve **3** button

15.6
1 bathrobe **2** coat **3** raincoat
4 shorts **5** socks **6** tie
7 denim **8** suit **9** leather
10 bra **11** t-shirt

15.7
A 10 **B** 8 **C** 9 **D** 1 **E** 5
F 7 **G** 2 **H** 4 **I** 6 **J** 3

15.8
1 striped **2** plain
3 polka dot **4** leather
5 denim **6** cotton
7 silk **8** woolen

16

16.4
1 handkerchief
2 sandals
3 backpack
4 scarf
5 wallet

16.5
1 shoes
2 belt
3 hair band
4 eyeliner
5 handkerchief
6 scarf
7 umbrella

16.6
A 3 **B** 6 **C** 2 **D** 1 **E** 4
F 5 **G** 8 **H** 10 **I** 9 **J** 7

16.7
1 nail polish **2** bow tie
3 high heels **4** lipstick
5 flip-flops **6** ring
7 purse (US) / handbag (UK) **8** hat

16.8
1 brooch **2** earrings
3 umbrella **4** comb
5 perfume **6** sunglasses
7 necklace

17

17.5
1 D **2** A **3** F **4** H **5** B
6 I **7** C **8** G **9** E

17.6
1 brown hair
2 to style your hair
3 middle-aged
4 facial hair
5 to shave
6 curly hair
7 blond hair
8 sideburns
9 to have / get your hair cut

17.7
1 short hair
2 fair skin
3 beard
4 frizzy hair
5 red hair
6 to grow your hair
7 bald
8 to style your hair
9 glamorous
10 straight hair
11 black hair

17.8
1 C **2** B **3** B **4** A **5** B

18

18.2
1 assertive **2** rude
3 impatient **4** unreliable
5 lazy **6** considerate
7 talented **8** approachable
9 insensitive

18.3
1 optimistic **2** brave
3 arrogant **4** laid-back
5 assertive **6** insensitive

18.4
1 caring
2 mean
3 eccentric
4 assertive
5 talented
6 passionate
7 calm
8 unapproachable
9 generous

18.5
1 B **2** A **3** B
4 A **5** B **6** C

18.6
1 secretive
2 passionate
3 calm
4 mean
5 shy
6 critical
7 silly
8 impatient
9 reliable

19

19.2
1 jealous
2 calm
3 disgusted
4 surprised
5 frightened
6 serious
7 delighted
8 exhausted
9 amused
10 irritated
11 cheerful
12 nervous
13 grateful
14 angry / mad (US)
15 unenthusiastic
16 curious
17 proud
18 worried
19 disappointed

19.3
delighted, annoyed, grateful, embarrassed, ecstatic, worried, curious, unenthusiastic, jealous, confused

19.4
1 disgusted **2** grateful
3 amazed **4** scared
5 interested **6** disappointed
7 depressed **8** annoyed
9 bored **10** proud
11 relaxed **12** miserable

19.5
1 happy
2 interested
3 nervous
4 calm
5 miserable
6 proud
7 amused

19.6

Ⓐ 11 Ⓑ 1 Ⓒ 7 Ⓓ 5 Ⓔ 14
Ⓕ 2 Ⓖ 12 Ⓗ 16 Ⓘ 8 Ⓙ 4
Ⓚ 15 Ⓛ 6 Ⓜ 9 Ⓝ 3 Ⓞ 10 Ⓟ 13

20

20.8
1. grandfather
2. grandparents
3. mother / mom (US) / mum (UK)
4. aunt
5. sister-in-law
6. wife
7. cousin
8. son
9. children
10. granddaughter
11. grandson
12. grandchildren

20.9
1. adults
2. girl
3. triplets
4. baby
5. male

20.10
1. widower 2. grandmother
3. boyfriend and girlfriend
4. twins 5. grandfather

20.11
1. father / dad
2. stepsister
3. stepbrother

20.12
1. female
2. partner
3. nephew
4. daughter
5. husband
6. widow
7. girlfriend

21

21.2
1. I love playing with my grandson. I think the world of him.
2. My siblings are always falling out with each other.
3. We often bump into Mary at the local store.
4. We see eye to eye about most important issues.

21.3
1. Caroline **looks** up to her eldest brother.
2. Sadie takes **after** her mother. They are both very kind.
3. My cousin **gave** birth to a baby boy last year.
4. I stick **up** for my friends if people are mean to them.
5. I **made** friends with Miguel after he moved to my town.

21.4
Ⓐ 6 Ⓑ 3 Ⓒ 2 Ⓓ 5 Ⓔ 1 Ⓕ 4

21.5
1. Jo **gets along with** her boss.
2. We've been **close friends** since we shared an apartment.
3. I love playing with my grandson. I **think the world of** him.
4. We **broke up** because I didn't love him any more.
5. My siblings are always **falling out with** each other.

22

22.3
1. B 2. A 3. D
4. E 5. F 6. C

22.4
Ⓐ 14 Ⓑ 7 Ⓒ 6 Ⓓ 1 Ⓔ 8 Ⓕ 13
Ⓖ 2 Ⓗ 5 Ⓘ 3 Ⓙ 15 Ⓚ 4 Ⓛ 9
Ⓜ 10 Ⓝ 16 Ⓞ 12 Ⓟ 11

22.5
booties, nursery, toy, sandbox, swings, train set, doll, marbles, bottle, kite, puppet, changing table, rattle

22.6
EQUIPMENT:
baby monitor, **bottle**, **bib**,
potty, **high chair**, **wet wipe**
TOYS:
spinning top, **puppet**,
building blocks, **playing cards**
kite, **slide**

22.7
1. snowsuit
2. rattle
3. doll
4. diaper
5. marbles
6. toy
7. mobile
8. high chair

23

23.4
1. C 2. A 3. A 4. B 5. C

23.5
1. to fail
2. classroom
3. law
4. medicine
5. degree

23.6
1. art
2. business studies
3. professor
4. exercise book
5. physics
6. history
7. school
8. drama
9. biology
10. laboratory
11. to study a subject
12. lecture
13. exam

23.7
1. math (US) / maths (UK)
2. college (US) / university (UK)
3. architecture
4. essay
5. teacher
6. student
7. music
8. psychology
9. geography

24

24.2
1. Rowena is taking a year off before she starts college.
2. Practicing for her class presentation made a world of difference.
3. I expect my students to attend classes every week.
4. Their views on teaching a class are polar opposites.
5. Chris passed his final college exams with flying colors.

24.3
1. When Gavin was a **freshman**, he was very nervous about starting college.
2. There is a **clear distinction** between these two experiments.

3 Emma **took her driving test** last week, and she passed.
4 It's important to give students **regular feedback** on their work.
5 Amira is studying for a **graduate degree** in chemistry.
6 Boris almost **missed the deadline** for his research project.

24.4
1 an undergraduate
2 a first draft
3 a freshman (US) / fresher (UK)
4 continuous assessment
5 to pass with flying colors

24.5
1 I like **continuous assessment** more than just taking final exams.
2 I've finished the **first draft** of my essay, but I'm sure that I'll have to make lots of changes to it.
3 Matt **enrolled in** a computer science course last month.
4 I'd like you to **compare and contrast** these two pictures.
5 Many **undergraduates** live in a dormitory in their first year of college.

25.2
1 After only a few weeks living in Italy, I was able to **make** myself understood.
2 I have a good **ear** for languages. I learned Swahili in six months.
3 The language **barrier** stopped me from talking to Wen.
4 My uncle is fluent **in** five different languages.
5 I speak **conversational** German, but my grammar is awful.
6 Juan finds the **pronunciation** of the word "squirrel" impossible.

25.3
1 an accent
2 bilingual
3 a native speaker
4 speaking
5 to speak accurately
6 vocabulary
7 fluent in

25.4
1 I was taught French **by a native speaker from** Marseilles.
2 English **acts as a lingua franca for** the people at the conference.

3 I understand some Hebrew, **but find the writing** impossible.
4 Although Pedro has **a strong accent, he does speak** accurately.

25.5
A 2 **B** 6 **C** 3 **D** 5 **E** 1 **F** 4

26.2
1 Do you **really believe in ghosts**?
2 I really enjoy **reading fairy tales to my** grandchildren.
3 We **have a sneaking suspicion that** Tim won't come to the party with us.
4 Farah **started a rumor** that Kerry stole a car.

26.3
1 Tara is **dropping** a hint that she would like new shoes for her birthday.
2 Jenna told a **white** lie and said she liked Barry's new suit.
3 I've never played this game, so I'm hoping for **beginner's** luck.
4 He has a very old-fashioned **set** of beliefs.

26.4
1 to make a wish
2 pure luck
3 an urban myth
4 folklore
5 to gossip

26.5
1 I often find out about new products **by word of mouth**.
2 Anyone can win this game. It's a game of **pure luck**.
3 You shouldn't be a **tattletale** at school.
4 To some people, a black cat is a **good omen**; to others, a **bad omen**.
5 Martin loves **to gossip** about other people's relationships.

27.4
1 shoplifting
2 hacking
3 burglary
4 fine
5 smuggling

27.5
1 law court **2** judge **3** trial

27.6
1 B **2** C **3** A **4** A **5** B

27.7
1 The recent crime wave in my home town is very worrying.
2 The jury found Colin guilty of car theft.
3 The burglar wouldn't admit he had committed a crime.
4 After discussing all the evidence, the jury reached a verdict.
5 It's a police officer's job to enforce the law.

27.8
1 The police officer **arrested** Tina for shoplifting.
2 It's a police officer's job to **enforce** the law.
3 **Street crime**, such as mugging, can be a problem in our cities.
4 Paul was **sentenced** to 100 hours of community service.
5 André is trained to deal with **white-collar crime**, such as fraud.

28.5
MEAT:
sausages, chicken, lamb, ham
SEAFOOD:
sardines, salmon, lobster, sushi
DAIRY:
milk, fried egg, butter, cheese
FAST FOOD:
hot dog, fries (US) / chips (UK), pizza, kebab

28.6
1 cream **2** soup **3** bacon
4 beef **5** mackerel

28.7
1 soup
2 scrambled eggs
3 salad
4 wrap
5 chips (US) / crisps (UK)
6 scallops
7 cottage cheese
8 burger

28.8
A 5 **B** 8 **C** 1 **D** 4
E 9 **F** 7 **G** 10
H 2 **I** 3 **J** 6

29.3
1. apricot
2. kiwi fruit
3. banana
4. cherries
5. grapes
6. coconut
7. papaya
8. lemon
9. pear
10. pomegranate
11. blackberries
12. gooseberries
13. starfruit
14. watermelon

29.4
1. peanut
2. pistachio
3. walnut
4. hazelnut
5. raisin
6. golden raisin (US) / sultana (UK)
7. currant
8. fig
9. date

29.5
1. fries
2. quince
3. salmon
4. pistachio
5. yolk
6. soup
7. lamb
8. pizza

29.6
A) 7 B) 2 C) 3 D) 8 E) 1
F) 5 G) 9 H) 6 I) 4

29.7
1. watermelon
2. mango
3. walnut
4. papaya
5. pear
6. passion fruit

30.2
1. butternut squash
2. lettuce
3. cauliflower
4. garlic
5. beans
6. sweetcorn / corn
7. avocados
8. eggplants (US) / aubergines (UK)
9. carrots
10. onions
11. zucchini (US) / courgettes (UK)
12. peppers
13. asparagus
14. broccoli

30.3
1. artichokes
2. spinach
3. mushrooms
4. cauliflower
5. cucumbers
6. eggplants
7. asparagus
8. sweetcorn

30.4
1. B 2. A 3. B 4. C 5. A

30.5
1. cabbage
2. tomatoes
3. leeks
4. cucumbers
5. butternut squash
6. mushrooms
7. spinach
8. artichokes
9. sweet potatoes

31.3
1. C 2. C 3. A 4. B 5. B

31.4
1. flour
2. noodles
3. dumplings
4. pancakes
5. chocolate

31.5
1. oil
2. mint
3. soy sauce
4. ketchup
5. pepper
6. jam
7. peanut butter
8. basil
9. spices
10. chutney
11. honey
12. toast
13. pancakes
14. mustard
15. parsley
16. noodles
17. salt

31.6
1. marmalade
2. spaghetti
3. roll
4. mayonnaise
5. cupcake
6. chili flakes (US) / chilli flakes (UK)
7. meringue

32.5
1. C 2. E 3. A 4. B 5. G
6. D 7. F 8. I 9. H

32.6
1. strong
2. gone off
3. sour
4. fresh
5. iced
6. sweet
7. tasty
8. delicious
9. savory
10. bitter
11. disgusting
12. spicy

32.7
1. B 2. A 3. C 4. A 5. C
6. A 7. B

32.8
1. to gulp
2. to drink
3. to taste
4. to bite
5. to eat
6. to dine
7. to chew
8. to nibble
9. to swallow

33.5
1. to whisk
2. to roast

3 to simmer
4 to mash
5 to grate
6 to bake
7 to fry
8 to peel
9 to cut

33.6
1 tip
2 lunch
3 menu
4 breakfast
5 dinner
6 buffet

33.7
1 napkin
2 dessert / pudding (UK)
3 appetizer (US) / starter (UK)
4 check (US) / bill (UK)
5 restaurant
6 waitress
7 snack
8 café
9 chef
10 to slice
11 fixed menu (US) / set menu (UK)
12 to stir
13 food stall
14 buffet

33.8
A 7 **B** 12 **C** 1 **D** 14 **E** 6
F 4 **G** 11 **H** 8 **I** 2 **J** 13
K 10 **L** 9 **M** 3 **N** 15 **O** 5

34

34.2
1 writer
2 mechanic
3 librarian
4 pilot
5 dentist
6 actor
7 plumber
8 scientist
9 tour guide
10 lawyer
11 sales assistant
12 waitress
13 fashion designer
14 gardener

34.3
psychologist, judge, driver, photographer,
paramedic, businessman, journalist,
engineer, scientist

34.4
1 B **2** D **3** A **4** E **5** C

34.5
1 lawyer
2 teacher
3 scientist
4 artist
5 train driver
6 butcher
7 librarian
8 mechanic
9 chef
10 psychologist
11 designer
12 architect

34.6
1 judge
2 businessman
3 dentist
4 scientist
5 waiter
6 nurse
7 teacher
8 actor
9 plumber
10 farmer
11 train driver

35

35.4
1 assistant
2 manager
3 employee
4 intern
5 staff
6 client
7 apprentice

35.5
1 to call in sick
2 to work from home
3 to work full-time
4 to earn
5 to have a day off
6 to work shifts
7 to get fired
8 to go on maternity leave
9 to work part-time

35.6
1 The store pays its staff an **hourly rate** of $15.
2 We will pay **overtime** to all staff who are willing to work weekends.
3 I'm looking for a job with a **salary** of at least $25,000.
4 **Benefits** include gym membership and health insurance.
5 My **bonus** this year was $1,000, so I'm going to go on vacation.
6 I had to find a new job last year because I **was laid off**.
7 I got a **promotion** after working for the company for only six months.

35.7
1 benefits
2 wages
3 a pay cut
4 a raise
5 an hourly rate

36

36.3
1 C **2** A **3** B **4** G **5** H **6** E
7 D **8** I **9** F

36.4
1 healthcare
2 agriculture
3 finance
4 shipping
5 energy
6 advertising
7 journalism
8 tourism
9 aerospace

36.5
A 3 **B** 2 **C** 9 **D** 8
E 4 **F** 1 **G** 6 **H** 10
I 7 **J** 11 **K** 12 **L** 5

36.6
1 Human Resources (HR)
2 Accounts / Finance
3 Legal
4 Administration
5 Public Relations (PR)
6 Sales
7 Marketing

37

37.4
1 trays
2 desk
3 bulletin board (US) / notice board (UK)
4 water cooler
5 trash can (US) / bin (UK)
6 filing cabinet
7 chair

37.5
1 laptop
2 envelope
3 stapler
4 paper
5 printer
6 pencil

37.6
1 B 2 A 3 C
4 A 5 B 6 A

37.7
1 calendar
2 scissors
3 photocopier
4 rubber bands
5 clipboard
6 laptop
7 shredder
8 paper clips
9 scanner
10 highlighter
11 envelope
12 hole punch

38

38.3
1 currency
2 cash machine
3 bank loan
4 check
5 stock exchange
6 bank statement
7 interest rate
8 mobile banking
9 PIN
10 credit card
11 wallet
12 mortgage
13 cash register
14 coins

38.4
mortgage
cash machine
invoice
wallet
coins
bank
receipt
check
mobile banking
stock exchange

38.5
1 The store has gone out of business because most people download movies now.

2 The bank charges $10 per month for overdrafts.
3 The exchange rate has made trips to some countries more expensive.
4 If we can't sell more products, we will get into debt.
5 Our income fell after we lost an important client.

38.6
1 B 2 A 3 A
4 B 5 A

39

39.2
1 to get ahead
2 to take off
3 to take someone on
4 give and take
5 to step down

39.3
1 All our employees are fully trained and have **hands-on experience**.
2 Gavin **was fired** because he was caught stealing from the warehouse.
3 Bruno's career **took off** after he won an important new client.
4 People who work in childcare **have their hands full** all day.
5 We've **set our sights on** winning more industry awards.
6 I need to **tackle this problem head-on** or it will get worse.
7 Working well with clients involves a lot of **give and take**.

39.4
1 My boss started working here **at the bottom of the career** ladder.
2 Lucas has been **stuck in a dead-end job** for two years.
3 I don't work **a nine-to-five job** because I have two young children.
4 I'm **stepping down from this job** because I need more training.

39.5
1 Elena's chosen career **path** involves a lot of travel.
2 Can I call you back later? I'm **snowed** under right now.
3 Clive always goes the extra **mile** to deliver our products on time.
4 Some of the factory workers were laid **off** after our profits fell.

40

40.2
1 We easily reached a consensus on the best poster design.
2 Stefan is on vacation and will be absent from this meeting.
3 I'm sorry to interrupt, but your client is waiting in reception.
4 Our poor sales figures will be on the agenda today.

40.3
A 3 B 4 C 1 D 5 E 2

40.4
1 on the agenda
2 to sum up
3 to attend a meeting
4 the main objective
5 to reach a consensus
6 absent
7 to run out of time
8 to give a presentation
9 action points

40.5
1 To sum up, sales of our older products have fallen this year.
2 Stefan is on vacation and will be absent from this meeting.
3 I'll talk through the report and then I'll take questions.
4 Our poor sales figures will be on the agenda today.
5 Let's wrap up this meeting. It's almost one o'clock.

41

41.3
1 This is a difficult job. Make sure you **do everything by the book**.
2 Great! We're all **on the same page** about this marketing campaign.
3 This client will never be satisfied because he keeps **moving the goalposts**.
4 Health and safety in the warehouse involves a lot of **red tape**.

41.4
1 Could I touch base with you for a quick update on this project?
2 Rohit clinched the deal after offering the clients a discount.
3 We're losing money, so we need a game plan for increasing sales.

4 We don't know the exact costs, but here's a ballpark figure.

41.5
1 We expected a change of pace **after we received several large orders**.
2 This product will never sell. We're **throwing money down the drain**.
3 This client will never be satisfied because **he keeps moving the goalposts**.
4 They've cornered the **market with their new range of shoes**.
5 This is a difficult job. Make **sure you do everything by the book**.

41.6
A 2 **B** 6
C 1 **D** 7
E 4 **F** 5
G 3 **H** 8

42

42.4
1 Professional achievements
2 Career summary
3 Education
4 Key skills
5 Interests
6 References

42.5
1 recruitment agency
2 job ad (US) / advert (UK)
3 cover letter (US) / covering letter (UK)
4 portfolio

42.6
1 to manage
2 to have an interview
3 to negotiate
4 to organize
5 to supervise
6 to apply for a job
7 to collaborate
8 to fill out a form
9 to coordinate

42.7
1 I am **responsible for** six other staff members.
2 I have an **in-depth knowledge** of hair-coloring techniques.
3 I have a **proven track record** in the catering industry.
4 As an ex-car salesman, I have a **service-oriented** background.
5 I am **proficient in** all major types of accounting software.

43

43.3
1 determined
2 organization
3 public speaking
4 numeracy
5 flexible
6 competitive
7 practical
8 responsible
9 teamwork
10 research
11 punctual
12 initiative
13 fast learner
14 negotiating

43.4
professional, reliable, hardworking, responsible, administration, motivated, research, organized, calm

43.5
1 fluent in languages
2 attention to detail
3 time management
4 customer-focused
5 problem-solving

43.6
1 confident
2 patient
3 honest
4 research
5 innovative
6 ambitious
7 efficient
8 fast learner
9 organization
10 competitive
11 decision-making

43.7
1 ambitious **2** team player **3** energetic
4 interpersonal skills **5** efficient

44

44.4
1 B **2** C **3** D
4 A **5** F **6** H
7 E **8** I **9** G

44.5
1 passengers
2 platform

3 bicycle
4 pedestrian
5 commuters
6 coach
7 yacht
8 moped
9 van

44.6
1 train
2 helicopter
3 boat
4 ferry
5 camel
6 yacht
7 horse
8 taxi
9 van

44.7
A 4 **B** 10 **C** 1 **D** 11 **E** 6
F 9 **G** 3 **H** 15 **I** 2 **J** 14
K 8 **L** 13 **M** 5 **N** 12 **O** 7

45

45.3
1 seatbelt
2 car wash
3 fuel
4 to check the tires (US) / tyres (UK)
5 to brake
6 speed camera
7 wipers
8 to slow down
9 pedestrian crossing
10 steering wheel
11 to check the oil
12 traffic jam
13 parking ticket
14 to signal (US) / to indicate (UK)

45.4
1 trunk
2 diesel
3 mechanic
4 gasoline
5 traffic jam
6 headlight
7 steering wheel
8 parking attendant

45.5
1 hood (US) / bonnet (UK)
2 trunk (US) / boot (UK)
3 tire (US) / tyre (UK)
4 wheel

45.6

1. parking lot
2. flat tire
3. car wash
4. wipers
5. to slow down
6. insurance
7. speed limit
8. oil

45.7

1. traffic lights
2. parking lot
3. to pass
4. wheel clamp
5. road sign
6. to set off
7. speed limit

46

46.4

1. north
2. northeast
3. east
4. southeast
5. south
6. southwest
7. west

46.5

1. turn
2. block
3. mile
4. distance
5. footpath

46.6

1. street
2. roadmap (US) / streetmap (UK)
3. key
4. shoulder (US) / hard shoulder (UK)
5. yard
6. intersection (US) / crossroads (UK)
7. sidewalk (US) / pavement (UK)
8. one-way street
9. avenue

46.7

1. to go / turn left
2. to go / turn right
3. to take the second right
4. to take the first left
5. to stop at (the hotel)
6. to go straight ahead (US) / on (UK)
7. to ask directions

46.8

1. A 2. B 3. A 4. C 5. B

47

47.5

1. to make a reservation
2. to check in
3. to check out
4. to stay in a hotel

47.6

1. room service
2. passport
3. apartment
4. luggage
5. boarding pass
6. laundry service
7. passport control
8. en-suite bathroom (UK)
9. cabin
10. window seat
11. to go abroad
12. all-inclusive
13. double room
14. hostel

47.7

A. 4 B. 1 C. 5 D. 2 E. 9 F. 3
G. 6 H. 8 I. 7 J. 11 K. 10 L. 12

47.8

1. direct flight
2. to book a vacation
3. dorm
4. walking vacation
5. safe
6. one-way ticket
7. single room

48

48.2

1. We like to stay in places that are off **the beaten path**.
2. Zoe is really looking forward **to visiting the pyramids**.
3. We got hopelessly **lost when we tried to drive into Tokyo**.
4. The palace is such a tourist **trap in the summer**.
5. We're checking out **the zoo that you recommended**.
6. I love to get away **from it all when I'm on vacation**.
7. I'm taking Clara to look **around the park today**.
8. I save lots of money on train tickets **by booking in advance**.

48.3

1. I don't like going abroad because I **feel homesick**.
2. I save lots of money on train tickets by **booking in advance**.
3. We got **hopelessly lost** when we tried to drive into Tokyo.
4. We like to stay in places that are **off the beaten path**.

48.4

1. Brendan loves sports and has a real thirst for adventure.
2. I like to travel out of season, when it's nice and quiet.
3. This place is so different from home. It's such a culture shock.
4. Let's stop off at the gallery before we check into our hotel.
5. Dan's parents came to the airport to see him off.

48.5

1. This hotel looks very **run-down**. Let's stay somewhere else.
2. I don't like going abroad because I feel **homesick**.
3. I save lots of money on train tickets by **booking in advance**.
4. I love to **get away** from it all when I'm on vacation.
5. We don't need another suitcase. It's just a weekend **getaway**.

49

49.3

1. saddle
2. handlebar
3. pedal
4. frame

49.4

1. cycle pump
2. reflector
3. basket
4. bicycle lane

49.5

1. gear
2. hot drink container (US) / flask (UK)
3. campsite
4. tent
5. walking boots
6. pothole
7. camping stove
8. backpack / rucksack (UK)
9. lock

49.6

1. shower block
2. racing bike
3. unicycle
4. waterproofs
5. bike rack
6. tandem
7. campfire
8. caravan
9. tent
10. bicycle lane
11. barbecue
12. brakes

49.7

A 3 B 6 C 1 D 18 E 2
F 10 G 7 H 4 I 5 J 11
K 16 L 8 M 13 N 9 O 17
P 12 Q 15 R 14

50

50.2

1. surfing
2. picnic basket
3. beach ball
4. wet suit
5. wave
6. sunscreen (US) / sun cream (UK)
7. snorkel and mask
8. life preserver (US) / life ring (UK)
9. kite
10. towel
11. flip-flops
12. jet ski
13. shell
14. sunbathing

50.3

1. wet suit
2. swimsuit
3. swimming trunks
4. sandcastle
5. kite
6. bodyboarding
7. life preserver
8. jet ski

50.4

1. bodyboarding 2. windbreak
3. windsurfing 4. sea 5. crab
6. deck chair 7. flippers
8. picnic blanket 9. sandcastle

50.5

1. B 2. A
3. C 4. A
5. B 6. A

51

51.4

1. cool
2. stifling
3. freezing
4. downpour
5. Fahrenheit
6. overcast
7. chilly
8. thunder
9. raindrop
10. humidity
11. flood

51.5

1. thundery 2. rainy
3. cloudy 4. icy
5. windy

51.6

1. drought
2. blizzard
3. lightning
4. snowflake
5. snowstorm
6. heatwave
7. puddle
8. gale

51.7

A 7 B 1 C 3 D 8
E 6 F 2 G 5 H 10
I 4 J 9 K 12 L 11

52

52.2

1. wood
2. canyon
3. ocean
4. high tide
5. sand dune
6. grassland
7. wave
8. low tide
9. glacier
10. rocks
11. cave
12. mountain range
13. swamp
14. farmland

52.3

1. countryside
2. canyon
3. plateau
4. volcano
5. meadow
6. rain forest (US) / rainforest (UK)
7. mountain range
8. polar region

52.4

1. hill
2. forest
3. peak
4. stream
5. river

52.5

1. C 2. B 3. A 4. C
5. A 6. B 7. A

53

53.2

1. Fossil fuels such as coal and oil produce carbon dioxide.
2. Carbon dioxide is one of the best-known greenhouse gases.
3. Solar panels on your house can help you save electricity.
4. Factory emissions are a cause of global warming.
5. It can be much cheaper to use renewable energy.

53.3

1. endangered
2. global warming
3. wind power
4. solar power
5. alternative energy

53.4

1. We need to **tackle pollution** in our rivers.
2. Dinosaurs became **extinct** millions of years ago.
3. The traffic in our cities is **harmful to the environment**.
4. We can reduce pollution by using more types of **alternative energy**.
5. **Climate change** is a huge threat to many animals.

53.5

1. This **wind farm** has been running for several years.
2. We must work together to stop the **destruction** of our forests.
3. **Climate change** is a huge threat to many animals.
4. If we don't reduce pollution, Earth will undergo **irreversible change**.

54

54.4
1. hamster
2. to quack
3. doghouse (US) / kennel (UK)
4. fish
5. to squeak
6. rabbit hutch
7. parrot
8. basket

54.5
1. horse
2. turkey
3. sheep
4. to purr
5. to meow
6. mouse
7. to croak
8. donkey
9. collar

54.6
1. whiskers
2. tail
3. paws
4. claws

54.7
1. to scratch
2. goose
3. tortoise
4. aquarium
5. bird seed

54.8
A 10 B 6 C 3 D 1 E 2
F 5 G 7 H 4 I 9 J 8

55

55.3
1. B
2. A
3. B
4. C
5. C

55.4
1. koala
2. frog
3. giraffe
4. chipmunk
5. snake
6. bison
7. polar bear

55.5
1. bat
2. buffalo
3. hippopotamus
4. tiger
5. wolf
6. elephant
7. mongoose
8. jaguar

55.6
1. gazelle
2. lion
3. moose
4. zebra
5. to roar
6. panda
7. to burrow
8. yak
9. tapir
10. to swing
11. tiger
12. raccoon
13. to hunt
14. meerkat

56

56.4
BUGS:
moth, spider, wasp, caterpillar, ant, snail
BIRDS:
hawk, vulture, penguin, duck, swan, dove

56.5
1. to hatch
2. to hoot
3. to sing
4. to peck
5. to swoop

56.6
1. beak
2. wing
3. claw

56.7
1. claw
2. to flap
3. toucan
4. dove
5. pelican
6. seagull
7. beak
8. caterpillar

56.8
1. woodpecker
2. worm
3. eagle
4. butterfly
5. beetle
6. chicken
7. parrot
8. cockroach
9. pelican

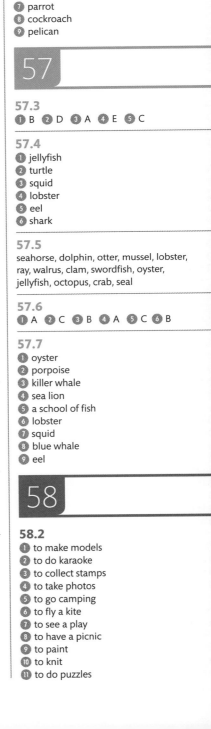

57

57.3
1 B 2 D 3 A 4 E 5 C

57.4
1. jellyfish
2. turtle
3. squid
4. lobster
5. eel
6. shark

57.5
seahorse, dolphin, otter, mussel, lobster, ray, walrus, clam, swordfish, oyster, jellyfish, octopus, crab, seal

57.6
1 A 2 C 3 B 4 A 5 C 6 B

57.7
1. oyster
2. porpoise
3. killer whale
4. sea lion
5. a school of fish
6. lobster
7. squid
8. blue whale
9. eel

58

58.2
1. to make models
2. to do karaoke
3. to collect stamps
4. to take photos
5. to go camping
6. to fly a kite
7. to see a play
8. to have a picnic
9. to paint
10. to knit
11. to do puzzles

58.3
① C ② B ③ D ④ A

58.4
① to collect stamps
② to draw
③ to sew
④ to visit a museum
⑤ to stay home
⑥ to ride a horse
⑦ to bake
⑧ to do yoga
⑨ to go to a book club

58.5
① to go jogging
② to write
③ to go to a party
④ to do the gardening
⑤ to play video games
⑥ to play board games
⑦ to play a musical instrument
⑧ to go foraging
⑨ to go to the gym
⑩ to walk / to hike
⑪ to watch television
⑫ to listen to music
⑬ to do exercise
⑭ to arrange flowers

59

59.2
① to run
② to spell
③ to carry
④ to pull
⑤ to point
⑥ to taste
⑦ to sing
⑧ to think
⑨ to repair
⑩ to whisper
⑪ to work
⑫ to smell
⑬ to blow
⑭ to decide

59.3
Ⓐ 2 Ⓑ 3 Ⓒ 1 Ⓓ 6 Ⓔ 4
Ⓕ 5 Ⓖ 7 Ⓗ 10 Ⓘ 8 Ⓙ 14
Ⓚ 13 Ⓛ 9 Ⓜ 12 Ⓝ 11

59.4
① B ② A ③ D ④ E ⑤ C

59.5
① C ② A ③ A
④ B ⑤ C

60

60.3
① skating
② fishing
③ basketball
④ cricket
⑤ hockey
⑥ rugby
⑦ tennis
⑧ golf
⑨ archery

60.4
① rock climbing
② surfing
③ judo
④ motor racing
⑤ volleyball
⑥ paragliding
⑦ skydiving
⑧ skateboarding

60.5
① B ② C ③ B ④ A ⑤ B ⑥ C

60.6
① badminton
② baseball
③ gymnastics
④ cycling
⑤ squash
⑥ skateboarding
⑦ scuba diving
⑧ table tennis
⑨ skydiving
⑩ volleyball
⑪ abseiling
⑫ swimming

61

61.4
① penalty
② to be booked
③ half time
④ flag
⑤ red card
⑥ goalkeeper
⑦ corner kick
⑧ stoppage time (US) / injury time (UK)
⑨ field (US) / pitch (UK)
⑩ manager
⑪ substitutes
⑫ to be sent off
⑬ final whistle
⑭ linesman

61.5
① to score a goal
② to kick
③ to lose
④ final whistle
⑤ fans
⑥ mascot
⑦ to tackle
⑧ full time
⑨ to tie

61.6
Ⓐ 4 Ⓑ 1 Ⓒ 5 Ⓓ 2 Ⓔ 3
Ⓕ 7 Ⓖ 6 Ⓗ 9 Ⓘ 8 Ⓙ 10
Ⓚ 12 Ⓛ 11

61.7
① to be booked
② penalty spot
③ to kick
④ mascot
⑤ to tie
⑥ throw-in
⑦ forward
⑧ red card
⑨ linesman
⑩ bar
⑪ fans
⑫ midfielder

61.8
① D ② A ③ C
④ E ⑤ B

62

62.3
① C ② A ③ B
④ E ⑤ D

62.4
① swimming cap
② swimsuit
③ armband
④ float
⑤ swimming trunks
⑥ flipper

62.5
① boxing ring
② arrow
③ flipper
④ stopwatch
⑤ hurdles
⑥ bow
⑦ gym
⑧ skis
⑨ lifejacket
⑩ pool cue

62.6
EQUIPMENT:
skis, pool cue, fishing rod, helmet, roller skates, baseball bat
VENUES:
tennis court, ice rink, stadium, ski slope, golf course, running track

62.7
1. paddle
2. arrow
3. shuttlecock
4. snowboard
5. helmet
6. bowling pins
7. harness

63

63.4
1. science-fiction
2. autobiography
3. travel writing
4. crime fiction
5. e-reader
6. nature writing
7. biography
8. cookbook
9. novel
10. dictionary
11. textbook / course book
12. encyclopedia
13. gossip magazine
14. horoscope

63.5
1. author
2. novel
3. guidebook
4. romance
5. puzzles
6. hardback

63.6
1. I flipped through the guidebook **and decided to buy it**.
2. His new novel has received **glowing reviews from all the critics**.
3. I'm reading a crime novel. **It's a real page-turner**.
4. I find the plot difficult to **understand in most fantasy novels**.
5. Her latest novel is a **bestseller around the world**.

63.7
A 4 B 2 C 6 D 1 E 3
F 5 G 10 H 9 I 7 J 8

64

64.5
1. saxophone
2. flute
3. clarinet
4. trombone
5. guitar
6. violin
7. cello
8. electric guitar
9. keyboard

64.6
1. to perform
2. opera
3. to play the trumpet
4. rock
5. to conduct
6. to compose
7. classical
8. to listen
9. country

64.7
1. solo
2. lyrics
3. choir
4. guitar player
5. microphone
6. group
7. conductor
8. festival

64.8
1 C 2 C 3 A
4 B 5 B 6 A

65

65.3
1. opera
2. romantic comedy
3. thriller
4. horror
5. ballet

65.4
1. costumes
2. multiplex
3. script
4. popcorn
5. villain
6. usher
7. cartoon
8. stunt
9. director

65.5
1. script
2. hero
3. movie
4. dialog
5. encore
6. audience
7. box office
8. crime drama
9. props
10. villain

65.6
1. orchestra seating (US) / stalls (UK)
2. orchestra pit
3. stage
4. balcony
5. circle

65.7
1. screen
2. costumes
3. action movie
4. movie star
5. audience
6. cartoon
7. encore

66

66.4
1. children's show (US) / children's TV (UK)
2. comedy
3. news
4. cooking show
5. talk show (US) / chat show (UK)
6. period / costume drama

66.5
A 5 B 7
C 2 D 4
E 1 F 3
G 6 H 9
I 11 J 8
K 12 L 10

66.6
episode
documentary
channel
remote
satire
reporter
weather
drama
screen
preview
sitcom

66.7

1. to change channel
2. thriller
3. to record
4. season (US) / series (UK)
5. weather
6. to turn down the volume
7. talk show (US) / chat show (UK)
8. video on demand
9. shopping channel
10. couch potato
11. to turn off

66.8

1. weather
2. show
3. reporter
4. drama
5. interview
6. channel
7. crime
8. cartoon

67

67.2

1. Lee's **claim to fame** was that he could eat five burgers in five minutes.
2. **The opening night** of the show was a great success.
3. Lucinda is used to being **in the public eye**.
4. The success of her latest movie has **gone to her head**.

67.3

1. My favorite actors were on the red carpet this evening.
2. Social media has supported the rise of celebrity culture.
3. This singer's wedding was headline news last week.
4. Everyone was talking about her attention-grabbing dress.

67.4

1. John would really love to have **his name in lights**.
2. This morning's newspaper **headline is shocking**!
3. Kelly has had a truly meteoric **rise in the music industry**.
4. Some people go on talent **shows to become famous**.
5. Politicians can easily **be exploited by the media**.
6. The politician's lies were **exposed in the interview**.

67.5

A. 6
B. 1
C. 4
D. 3
E. 2
F. 5

68

68.6

1. C
2. B
3. A
4. B
5. C

68.7

1. sore
2. pain
3. bite
4. sprain
5. flu
6. high blood pressure
7. swollen

68.8

SICKNESS:
food poisoning, diabetes, appendicitis, chickenpox, mumps, cold
INJURIES:
broken bone, wound, bruise, burn, sting, cut

68.9

1. mumps
2. cut
3. asthma
4. stress
5. virus
6. migraine
7. symptoms
8. eczema

69

69.4

1. B
2. A
3. D
4. E
5. C
6. H
7. I
8. G
9. F

69.5

1. prescription
2. ambulance
3. appointment
4. syringe
5. to heal
6. to exercise
7. injection
8. treatment
9. to resuscitate

69.6

1. antiseptic wipes
2. adhesive bandage (US) / plaster (UK)
3. bandage
4. cotton pads (US) / cotton wool (UK)
5. adhesive tape
6. safety pin
7. ointment
8. scissors
9. painkillers
10. tweezers

69.7

stethoscope, physical therapy, operation, patient, blood test, inhaler, paramedic, bandage, ointment

69.8

A. 13
B. 4
C. 14
D. 1
E. 15
F. 5
G. 2
H. 6
I. 8
J. 3
K. 7
L. 9
M. 11
N. 16
O. 10
P. 12

70

70.3

1. A
2. E
3. B
4. F
5. C
6. G
7. D
8. I
9. H

70.4

1. B
2. B
3. A
4. A
5. A
6. C
7. A

70.5

1. Pedro has given up chocolate this month.
2. I'm trying to eat more vegetables because they're low in fat.
3. Brown bread is a good source of fiber.
4. You should eat smaller portions if you want to lose weight.
5. Convenience food saves people time, but isn't always good for them.

70.6

1. I'm trying to **cut down on** sugary drinks because I know they're bad for me.
2. Mia must not eat nuts because she's **allergic to** them.
3. I'm trying to eat more vegetables because they're **low in** fat.
4. It's okay to **eat** treats like cake **in moderation**.

71

71.5

1. circuit training
2. to skip
3. to cool down
4. locker room
5. spa
6. to meditate
7. to squat
8. aromatherapy
9. yoga

71.6
1. elliptical (US) / cross-trainer (UK)
2. weights
3. exercise mat
4. personal trainer
5. treadmill
6. exercise bike

71.7
1. to work out (US) / to keep fit (UK)
2. to sleep well
3. to stretch
4. to relax / to chill out
5. lockers
6. acupuncture
7. heart rate
8. push-up (US) / press-up (UK)
9. counseling (US) / counselling (UK)
10. massage
11. sit-up
12. jump rope (US) / skipping rope (UK)
13. boot camp

71.8
1. personal trainer
2. treadmill
3. to chill out
4. boot camp
5. spa
6. Pilates
7. steam room

71.9
1. reflexology
2. exercise class
3. sauna
4. steam room
5. to sleep well
6. to warm up

72

72.2
1. town square
2. fountain
3. castle
4. store (US) / shop (UK)
5. town hall
6. restaurant
7. library

72.3
1. hospital 2. pharmacy
3. temple 4. factory
5. nightclub

72.4
1. B
2. A

3. C
4. A
5. C

72.5
1. post office
2. mosque
3. shopping mall
4. theater (US) / theatre (UK)
5. fire station
6. office building
7. village
8. cemetery
9. church
10. gas station (US) / petrol station (UK)
11. park
12. commercial district
13. law court
14. city

73

73.4
1. greengrocer
2. baker
3. fish dealer (US) / fishmonger (UK)
4. bookstore (US) / bookshop (UK)
5. boutique
6. toy store (US) / toy shop (UK)
7. butcher
8. street market
9. florist

73.5
1. to try on
2. bank
3. to sell
4. jewelers
5. to exchange
6. hardware store
7. to fit
8. to choose
9. delicatessen

73.6
1. You can buy almost anything you want at the **flea market** in town.
2. It's always worth **shopping around** when buying a new car.
3. I love going **bargain-hunting** at my local market.
4. I thought the restaurant was **overpriced**. The food was very disappointing.
5. The local hardware store has **slashed its prices**. You can find some real bargains.

73.7
1. a good deal
2. to slash prices

3. on a tight budget
4. a flea market
5. to shop around
6. a rip-off
7. bargain-hunting

74

74.4
1. exit
2. cashier
3. cash register (US) / till (UK)
4. shopping bag / carrier bag (UK)
5. checkout
6. shopping cart (US) / trolley (UK)
7. basket

74.5
1. convenient
2. receipt
3. special offer
4. basement
5. customer
6. guarantee
7. escalator

74.6
1. C 2. D
3. A 4. B

74.7
1. food court
2. upmarket
3. closed
4. price tag

74.8
A. 3 B. 1 C. 6
D. 2 E. 4 F. 9
G. 12 H. 5 I. 7
J. 10 K. 8 L. 11

75

75.2
1. There are lots of green **spaces** in the city for people to relax in the summer.
2. There's a greater **choice** of cafés and restaurants in large cities.
3. Moscow has a **lively** nightlife, with bars and nightclubs that stay open until dawn.
4. The **road** work meant that it took me two hours to arrive at the office today.
5. It's sometimes impossible to get on the bus during **rush** hour.
6. The **pollution** in my city can be terrible in the summer months.

75.3

1 Overcrowding on London's trains means it's often hard to find a seat.
2 I offer guided tours of the city's historic buildings.
3 Good infrastructure, such as roads and telecommunications, is essential for a modern city.

75.4

(A) 5
(B) 3
(C) 2
(D) 4
(E) 1

75.5

1 The **pace of life is much faster in the city** than in the countryside.
2 The **vandalism in my area makes** the buildings look very ugly.
3 A good **way to avoid traffic jams is to** travel by train.
4 The **road work meant that it took me** two hours to arrive at the office today.

76

76.3

1 password
2 artificial intelligence
3 e-reader
4 smartwatch
5 USB drive
6 camera
7 plug
8 wireless
9 MP3 player
10 smartphone
11 remote control
12 memory card
13 flashlight (US) / torch (UK)
14 hands-free headset

76.4

1 C
2 E
3 D
4 A
5 B

76.5

1 GPS
2 voice recorder
3 Wi-Fi
4 circuit
5 bulb
6 laptop
7 webcam

8 speakers
9 battery
10 router
11 remote control
12 power cord
13 tablet

76.6

1 computer desk
2 keyboard
3 mouse pad (US) / mat (UK)
4 mouse
5 wire

76.7

1 bulb
2 plug
3 tablet
4 camera
5 laptop
6 circuit

77

77.2

1 The car was expensive, but it will save us money in the long **run**.
2 Higher prices could be the **shape** of things to come.
3 It's only a matter of **time** before we sell one of these paintings.
4 Laila is **making** predictions about what will happen in the new year.

77.3

1 I really want to buy the latest model of their smartphone.
2 My uncle's a technophobe. He still uses a typewriter.
3 The internet has caused a revolution in the way we learn.
4 Seb's such a technophile. He has to have the latest phone.

77.4

1 You need **to be computer literate to** find a good job these days.
2 My new smartphone **is light-years ahead of** my old one.
3 CDs and cassettes have **become obsolete because of** online streaming.
4 In **this digital age, many** people have a laptop and smartphone.
5 The research scientists **made an amazing breakthrough**.

77.5

(A) 5
(B) 2

(C) 4
(D) 3
(E) 1

78

78.3

1 steam
2 to record
3 to observe
4 crystals
5 cloning
6 battery
7 hypothesis

78.4

1 safety goggles
2 microscope
3 Bunsen burner

78.5

1 crystals
2 pestle
3 to pour
4 cells
5 physics
6 to freeze
7 molecules

78.6

1 to boil
2 beaker
3 gas
4 to record
5 results
6 to burn
7 steam
8 reaction
9 static electricity

78.7

1 A
2 A
3 B
4 A
5 C

Word list

Numbers refer to the unit number. Words separated by a forward slash usually indicate the differences between US and UK spelling.

A

abilities 59
able to drive 43
abseiling 60
absent 40
accent 25
accessories 16
accident 68
accommodation 13, 47
Accounts (department) 36
accurate 43
ache 68
across from 46
act 59
action movie 65
action points 40
actions 59
actor 34
acupuncture 71
adaptable 43
add 33, 59
adhesive bandage 69
adhesive tape 37, 69
administration 43
Administration (department) 36
adults 20
advertising industry 36
adverts 66
aerobics 71
aeroplane 44
aerospace industry 36
afternoon 3
aftershave 16
against the clock 8
agriculture 36
ahead 46
ahead of the game 41
air bed 49
air mattress 49
airplane 44
airport 44, 72
alarm goes off 4
album 64
Alice band 16
Allen keys 12
allergic to something 70

allergies 68, 70
all-inclusive 47
alternative energy 53
always 3
amazed 19
amazing 6
ambitious 43
ambulance 69
American 1
American football 60
amused 19
anemone 57
angry 19
ankle 14
annoyed 19
annoying 6
annual leave 35
annual vacation 35
ant 56
antelope 55
antiseptic 69
antiseptic wipes 69
anxious 19
any other business 40
AOB 40
apartment block 9
apartments 13, 47
appearance 17
appendicitis 68
appetizer 33
applause 65
apple 29
application form 42
apply for a job 42
appointment 69
apprentice 35
approachable 18
apricot 29
April 3
aquarium 54
archery 60
architecture 23, 34
Argentina 1
Argentinian 1
arm 14
armadillo 55
armband 62
armchair 9
aromatherapy 71
arrange flowers 58
arrest somebody 27
arrive late 4
arrogant 18
arrow 62
art 23
artichokes 30

article 63
artist 34
ask directions 46
asparagus 30
assertive 18
assistant 35
asthma 68
ATM 38
attachment 7
attend a meeting 40
attend classes 24
attention to detail 43
attention-grabbing 67
attic 9
attract 78
aubergines 30
audience 65
August 3
aunt 20
Australia 1
author 63
auto repair ship 45
autobiography 63
autumn 3
avenue 46
avocados 30
awful 6
ax / axe 12

B

baby 20
baby carriage 22
baby changing facilities 74
baby equipment 22
baby monitor 22
babygro 22
back up 76
backache 68
backpack 16, 49
bacon 28
bad 6
bad omen 26
badge 16
badminton 60
bagel 31, 32
bait 62
bake 33, 58
baker 73
balanced diet 70
balcony (building) 9
balcony (theater / theatre) 65
bald 17
ball 22, 61, 62
ball is in your court 41
ballet 65

F

X

Y

Z

Acknowledgments

The publisher would like to thank:
Sarah Edwards, Carrie Lewis, Daniel Mills, Aisvarya Misra, and Christine Stroyan for editorial assistance; Rabia Ahmad, Debjyoti Mukherjee, and Sonakshi Singh for design assistance; Simon Mumford for national flags; Viola Wang for additional illustration; Steph Lewis for proofreading; Elizabeth Wise for indexing; Christine Stroyan for audio recording management; and ID Audio for audio recording and production.